THE CECIL KING DIARY
1965-1970

also by Cecil King

WITH MALICE TOWARD NONE

STRICTLY PERSONAL

WITHOUT FEAR OR FAVOUR

THE
CECIL KING
DIARY

1965-1970

JONATHAN CAPE
THIRTY BEDFORD SQUARE LONDON

FIRST PUBLISHED 1972
REPRINTED 1972
© 1972 BY CECIL KING

JONATHAN CAPE LTD
30 BEDFORD SQUARE, LONDON WCI

ISBN 0 224 00854 4

PRINTED AND BOUND IN GREAT BRITAIN
BY W. & J. MACKAY LIMITED, CHATHAM

CONTENTS

ACKNOWLEDGMENTS

I am indebted to Mr and Mrs William Armstrong for their valuable help in cutting and editing the manuscript. I should also like to thank the publisher's researcher for providing the background notes to each year and the footnotes.

C.K.

INTRODUCTION

It was an amusing interview between Hugh Cudlipp and Hore-Belisha on the subject of the latter's resignation from the War Office that gave me the necessary nudge to start writing a diary in January 1940. The war was on; I was not medically fit enough for military service; had time on my hands; and, as director of the *Daily Mirror* and editorial director of the *Sunday Pictorial*, was in close touch with what was happening in Whitehall, in Westminster and in Fleet Street. When the Abdication took place in 1936 I had found that at the *Daily Mirror* we had no reliable contacts to tell us what was going on behind the scenes. From that time on it was my aim to acquire a wide circle of acquaintances in all aspects of public life so as to be well-informed. So even in 1940 I knew a lot of people, from Churchill downwards – I had even met Colonel House, the *éminence grise* of Woodrow Wilson, as far back as 1919.

I kept the diary up until after the end of the war but found the politics of the Attlee Government uninteresting and gradually stopped writing, finally ending in 1947.

At first when Mr Wilson took office in 1964 I did not think of resuming my diary. But as months went by I found my seat in the front row of the political stalls increasingly interesting and in July 1965 I restarted it. It was written out of interest and with no thought of publication. It might interest my family – who knows? In any case it could not have been published until after my retirement. My method of diary-writing is to jot down what strikes me as interesting on the day it happens – or at latest the following day. I never look back at what I have written for fear that I might adjust subsequent entries to make my judgment seem better than it really was.

The justification for a diary of this sort is the picture it presents of contemporary politics as they appeared to the writer – a privileged and experienced observer with no axe to grind. As the diary begins after Wilson had been in office nine months, I add a few pages

9

of political comment to bring the story up to the date when the diary begins.

When harking back to 1963 one has to remember that Harold Macmillan had been in office for seven years. Even his colleagues would now admit that his last two years did him no credit. Then there was his dramatic resignation at the party conference and the emergence of Sir Alec Douglas-Home as the new Prime Minister. Whatever the virtues of Sir Alec may be, he showed himself quite unable to get over to the British people. So in 1964 you had a Conservative Party that had been in office for thirteen years, the last three of which were notably undistinguished. The Conservatives had in fact run out of steam, as well as of ideas. In any case our Parliamentary system only works if there is a fairly frequent change of the party in office. So apart from the fact that Labour's turn for office was overdue, the Conservatives needed a period in opposition to recharge their batteries. When in office promotion is too much in the hands of the reigning Prime Minister, while in Opposition the patronage of the Leader is far less decisive, and the younger men of ability have a better chance of coming forward.

At the elections of 1951, 1956 and 1959 the result was a foregone conclusion long before polling day. At one time it looked as if Labour might win in 1959 but an ill-timed bus strike certainly did not help and may have had a decisive influence. Then, the *Daily Mirror* which had been friendly to Labour since 1934 could only try and minimize the Tory victory. 'Keep the Tories tame' was our slogan on one occasion – i.e. keep the Tory majority as low as possible.

However, in 1964 it really looked as if Labour might have a chance. An unglamorous Tory Prime Minister had run Parliament out to the bitter end; Labour had a new young leader who had put on a wonderful performance as Leader of the Opposition. If, after thirteen years in opposition, Labour could not win, the Party might degenerate into a mere faction. I think the mood of the country was that it wanted a change but was distrustful of the Labour Party's fitness for government. There was still a strong feeling among the working class that the toffs are better at ruling the country – they have more experience. It was obviously going to be a close-run affair.

Though the *Daily Mirror* and its companion papers were pro-Labour, we could be aggressively or passively so – or without being actually Tory we could be helpful to the Tory Party. It seemed to me at the time that we could certainly secure the return of Douglas-Home, but that only if we pulled out every stop might we just swing the balance to Labour. A newspaper has limited political influence, but in a finely balanced election a newspaper read by half the adult population of the country can influence enough voters to affect the result. Anyway we decided to go flat out for Labour. Most newspapers start their election propaganda too soon and by election day their readers – particularly their women readers – are sick of the whole subject. The better policy is to hold your fire until you see the whites of their eyes, so to speak. We did everything for Wilson and the Labour Party we could think of. I even drove about London in my office Rolls with a red flag on the bonnet saying 'Vote Labour'. As we all know, Labour did just scrape home. The result seemed to me at the time – and to Mr Wilson (as he told me) – to reflect no enthusiasm for the Labour Party, but the feeling that it was time for a change.

After what has happened in the intervening years, it is difficult to cast one's mind back eight years and recapture the mood of October 1964. After thirteen years of the Tories we had a change of party and a relatively unknown Prime Minister. Not only had he been in Attlee's Cabinet at the early age of thirty-one but he was the youngest occupant of 10 Downing Street for many years. He enjoyed a degree of goodwill that no Prime Minister had experienced for a very long time. The Conservative newspapers gave him a better press than they ever gave Macmillan. Even the City of London was all set to help. He had not come to the Premiership as a result of any compromise or bargain – there were no strings.

But what the world did not fully realize is that the requirements of government and opposition are quite different. Skill in opposition demands good debating ability, well-timed speeches, clever Parliamentary tactics. No action is called for nor is any action possible. However, on attaining office, a speech is only important in so far as it leads to action: Parliamentary debates take place to explain to the voter what the government is doing and why. In opposition the City and big business are of no help to a Labour leader. In office their co-operation is essential. In opposition you cannot expect much help from the government party's press, but in government you need all the help you can get to put over your policy. Administrative ability which is at a discount in opposition becomes important for the survival of the administration.

The weakness of the Labour Shadow Cabinet had been that it did not contain one single member who had ever run anything. So it seemed to me that Wilson would have to bring in someone with experience of administration and of the business world. The most obvious appointment at that time was Jock Campbell, now Lord Campbell of Eskan, then Chairman of Booker Bros. However, no such appointment was made. The outsiders brought in were Frank Cousins, Lord Bowden and C. P. Snow – as if there weren't enough trades union officials and academics already on the Labour front bench. Douglas Jay, of all people, was made President of the Board of Trade. In fact administrative ability was ignored in the composition of Harold Wilson's Cabinet; instead exaggerated regard was paid to those members of his party who had promoted his candidature for the leadership of the Party against Hugh Gaitskell. This bid had been so ill-timed and so unsuccessful that it had been almost forgotten by the outside world; but the loyalties it engendered did much to explain the emergence of Barbara Castle and other even less successful ministers.

On settling into 10 Downing Street Mr Wilson asked me to lunch and told me I was his first luncheon guest. He thanked me for winning the election – as George Brown did later – and offered me a peerage. Hugh Gaitskell had offered me a peerage if I would join the Labour Party. This one was offered without strings. I didn't want a title, had no leisure to take part in the proceedings of the House of Lords, and thought the political independence of the newspapers would be better served if we declined any honour.

From the time Harold Wilson became Leader of the Labour Party until the end of 1967 I saw a good deal of him. After the 1964 elections, having the entrée to No. 10, I early paid him two visits to offer suggestions. The first visit was about Rhodesia. A couple of ycars previously I had been lunching with Mr Macmillan and he asked what I would do about Rhodesia. I said the Rhodesians should not be given their independence, but there was no way of preventing them taking it. So when it came to Mr Wilson's turn to tackle the problem, I thought I would pass on the impressions gained by Hugh Cudlipp on a trip around that part of the world which he had just completed. The advice I offered was that on no account must armed force be used against the Rhodesians. Fighting would result in casualties to British ex-servicemen fighting on the Rhodesian side which would cause bitter dissension here in England. To my way of thinking the unity of this country was far more important than the regime in Salisbury. I afterwards learnt that the military appreciation was that an invasion of Rhodesia that met with armed resistance would require two divisions. We had neither the divisions nor the means of getting them to Rhodesia. So that idea, which still crops up from time to time, was a dead duck anyway.

The other idea concerned Ireland. There had been trouble around 1959–60, but in 1964 Ireland was entirely quiet. Forty years had passed since the 'troubles' and it might be possible to negotiate a permanent settlement of the Irish question. I pointed out to Mr Wilson that it was much easier for a Labour Government than for a Conservative one to negotiate a final settlement in Ireland and this might well be an opportunity for him to figure prominently in the history books. The final answer must be a united Ireland enjoying closer links with this country than the Republic does at present. It might not have been possible to achieve anything permanent in 1964 but it would have been easier in 1964 than it will be in 1972 or 1973. It was well worth a good try. It was perhaps over this that I learnt that Mr Wilson is no statesman. His life is the House of Commons. He had been a brilliant Leader of the Opposition: he had an instinct for the right issue to raise, was an excellent and witty debater, and had a good sense of timing. To leave the chamber with the cheers of his supporters ringing in his ears is what he is in politics for. Difficult negotiations with the stubborn Irish offer no immediate kudos and would be beyond his negotiating capacity anyway. What he did was to invite Mr Lemass from Dublin and Mr O'Neill from Stormont to lunch (on different occasions). This may have pleased the Irish voters of Huyton, and it did no harm. He could then turn to the more tractable problem of Anguilla, or whatnot.

It has been said that a statesman requires foresight, administrative ability and sensitive political antennae – the ability to explain his policy to the voter and obtain acceptance for it or, on the other hand, to pick up from the public any feeling of serious dissatisfaction in time to allay it. By the middle of July 1965, when my diary begins, it was becoming clear that Mr Wilson had no gift of foresight, little or no administrative ability, and that any political antennae he might have are quite rudimentary. Those who say Mr Wilson is a wizard politician seem to mean that he is clever at playing off one man against another.

Wilson the brilliant Leader of the Opposition was becoming Wilson the disastrous Prime Minister.

1965

In October 1964, after thirteen years of Conservative government in Britain, the Labour Party gained a marginal victory at the General Election and was returned to power with a majority of five, which was reduced to three by November 1965. In practice, however, the Government's majority often proved more substantial, as the ten Liberal members usually supported a Government programme that largely accorded with Liberal policies for modernization and reform.

As far as domestic affairs were concerned, the Government's main preoccupations during 1964 and 1965 were with two related topics – the state of the economy, including the perennial balance of payments problem and the possibility of forced devaluation of the pound, and the requirement for a so-called Prices and Incomes policy, a policy to control inflation by a curb on both prices and wages. Emergency economic measures were necessary during 1965 to reduce pressure on the economy, and the effects of a serious run on sterling were only contained by complex and hasty arrangements with world and national banks. The Government publicly reiterated its determination not to devalue. However, success in stabilizing the economy was largely dependent on breaking out of the inflationary wages and prices spiral, and the Government made a number of unpopular (and largely ineffective) suggestions for and moves towards policies which would in some measure control prices, wage claims and dividends. In July there was a change in the leadership of the Conservative Party, and Edward Heath succeeded Sir Alec Douglas-Home as Leader of the Opposition.

Internationally, 1965 had few major events (except perhaps that for the first time Americans and Russians walked in space), but was rather a year in which continuing situations posed unsolved, and often apparently insoluble, problems. The war in Vietnam continued, in spite of President Johnson's peace missions, and the United States commitment increased. The European Economic Community faced a state of crisis in July, largely because of General de Gaulle's impatience towards such supranational

17

organizations, and insistence on French national independence. In the Middle East, two years before the six-day war, border incidents continued between Israel and her Arab neighbours, and in October Israel mounted its first reprisal raid against the Lebanon. The civil war in the Yemen between the royalists, backed by King Faisal of Saudi Arabia, and the republicans, supported by President Nasser of Egypt, ceased, but there was no certainty of any lasting peace in the area.

For Britain, the major problem was Rhodesia where in November the Government of Mr Ian Smith unilaterally declared its independence of Britain; the repercussions of this action were extreme, not only at home, but in Britain's relations with other Commonwealth and non-Commonwealth African states. The main defence issue facing Britain was concerned with its future posture 'east of Suez', as pressures for withdrawal from the Far East and the Persian Gulf grew.

In 1965, Cecil Harmsworth King was the chairman of the International Publishing Corporation, which, at that time, amongst many other newspapers, periodicals and interests, owned two major London daily papers, the Daily Mirror *and the* Sun, *two London Sunday papers, the* Sunday Mirror *and the* People, *and two Scottish papers, the* Daily Record *and the* Sunday Mail. *Although all these papers generally supported the Labour Party, on occasions some – and especially the* Daily Mirror – *showed themselves opposed to Labour policies and personalities. Cecil King's interests were wide; amongst other appointments, he was chairman of the Reed Paper Group and a part-time director of the Bank of England. His wife, Dame Ruth Railton, had founded, and was in 1965 the Musical Director of, the National Youth Orchestra of Great Britain and the National Junior Music School.*

Monday, July 12th, 1965

At 4.30 to see Wilson, in his room in the House of Commons. This was at his request; I had not seen him for some weeks. He was, as usual, very friendly, relaxed and confident. We talked about George Brown and the warning I had given him about a fortnight ago, that he should get out of politics on medical advice now rather than be dismissed later. Wilson knew about my talk with George, including one of the phrases I had used. George has been consulting his friends, who have offered the same advice as I have.

We talked about Vietnam: nothing new. Cabinet changes: Griffiths will go any time; Soskice is ill and slowly seizing up; Frank Longford quite useless – mental age of twelve; Fraser doubtful. Men he wished to bring forward were Roy Jenkins (in a class by himself), Prentice, Marsh, George Thomson (of the F.O.*), and Cledwyn Hughes of the C.R.O.† He recognized that the Corporation Tax‡ was a mistake, and now was going to try and soothe the City. There were to be three dinners at the Bank of England, three at 10 Downing St, and a big show at the Mansion House, with perhaps a thousand bankers dining. His view of the financial state of the country was far more optimistic than anything I hear at the Bank [of England]: balance of payments down £800 million last year, £350 million this year, and a break-even next year. The cost in foreign currency of defence has got to be cut, and in time Aden, Bahrain and Singapore will be evacuated (and, presumably, Cyprus). He spoke warmly in favour of Michael Stewart, whom I think honest, intelligent, and (on his feet) articulate, but a man so dim as almost to be invisible. He said he had been in two minds whether to appoint him or Jenkins to the F.O., and had decided on Stewart.

In the evening, the opening night of the Bolshoi in the Royal

* The Foreign Office.
† Commonwealth Relations Office.
‡ In the Budget introduced on April 6th, 1965, the Labour Government had substituted a 'Corporation Tax', somewhat similar to the United States tax of the same name, for the profits tax to which British business enterprises had previously been subject.

Festival Hall. Very unsatisfactory these great artists being used for gymnastics to amuse a very naive tourist audience. The second act of *Gisèle* quite meaningless without the first. Had some talk with Soldatov, the Russian Ambassador, who embarked on the subject of Vietnam. I said we were using what influence we had to modify American policy. After all, the Americans wanted to get out of South-East Asia: why wouldn't the Russians help them to get out without too great a loss of face? He said they had got themselves into this mess. Why should the Russians help? I said the Russians were one of the two world powers, and were necessarily concerned in keeping the peace. We got nowhere.

Tuesday, July 13th, 1965

Letter from Cecil King to Harold Wilson:

CONFIDENTIAL

Dear Harold,

I much enjoyed our talk yesterday and was glad to find you in such good heart.

There was one point I forgot to mention, and I don't know if Hugh Cudlipp did when he saw you on Friday.

Our attack on Prince Philip was not really caused by his pretty innocuous remarks about Rhodesia. But a few days earlier he had been the guest at lunch of Denis Hamilton (of the *Sunday Times*) at which various newspaper men were present, including our Edward Pickering. At this lunch Prince Philip's main theme – following the Queen's visit to Germany – was the urgent importance of the re-unification of Germany. Hugh Cudlipp thought that we cannot have Prince Philip saying in public anything like what he had said in private at this lunch. Hence the decision to seize on his remarks about Rhodesia as an opportunity to fire a shot across his bows. We are informed from the Palace that the point has been taken.

With every good wish,

Yours sincerely,
Cecil King

The Rt. Hon. Harold Wilson, O.B.E., M.P.,
10, Downing Street,
Whitehall, S.W.1.

Wednesday, July 14th, 1965

Lunch with Wolfson, a long-standing appointment, but opportune for discussing Wilfred Harvey and all that.* Wolfson had announced his general support of Harvey, but I convinced him that Harvey's behaviour was not the sort that could be condoned. So Wolfson was to get hold of Harvey, and I was to get hold of Geoffrey Crowther and Roy Thomson, to see what could be done.

Then Haikal at 3.30, editor of *Al Ahram*, the principal Egyptian newspaper. An entertaining man. He reiterated an invitation to me to visit Nasser in September. No mention of the Yemen, which the Egyptians are anxious to get out of. A lot about the necessity to get back to the U.N. resolution on Israel, which is now quite out of date. I asked about their hostility to the U.K., when we are clearly withdrawing from all our imperial commitments. No doubt I shall hear more in September.

At 6.15 to a party at *The Times* – everyone shocked at the sudden death of Adlai Stevenson. Some brief words with Alec Douglas-Home. Each time I meet him I seek some sign of anything but a general niceness and social ease. It just isn't there.

Dinner with Shawcross at the Garrick – a brilliant man and a most charming one, but hard to say why his career hasn't really been worthy of him. After a lifetime of hard work at the Bar, is now said to be lazy. We talked about a possible libel Bill to be introduced, and about his own future. Should he return to the Bar (at sixty-three) or should he supplement his Shell non-executive directorship with

---

* Mr Harvey had been the managing director of the Purnell Group, a firm of printers and binders which in 1964 had merged with Hazell Sun Ltd to form the £20 million British Printing Corporation (B.P.C.) of which he became chairman. Early in July 1965, Sir Geoffrey Crowther, Mr Max Rayne and other directors identified with Hazell Sun had written to the shareholders of B.P.C. seeking the removal of Mr Harvey and two of his colleagues (his solicitor and son-in-law), on the grounds of difficulties in reorganization and the very large sums which it was alleged Mr Harvey and his associates had claimed as remuneration and expenses. A major business struggle entertained the British public throughout the summer. Mr Harvey accepted retirement at the end of July, but in December the auditors reported that they were unsatisfied with the accounts of the Purnell Group. At B.P.C.'s annual meeting in December it was announced that a civil writ claiming repayment of nearly £300,000 had been issued against Mr Harvey, that profits for 1965 might well be several hundreds of thousands of pounds down and that four directors (including Mr Harvey's son and son-in-law) were resigning.

others. I said the British Printing Corporation would need a chairman, and I should at least be able to suggest his name. This would be very acceptable.

Thursday, July 15th, 1965

A conference in the afternoon about Harvey and B.P.C. Present: Max Rayne (a big shareholder), Grierson from Warburg's, Sir Geoffrey Crowther and Roy Thomson, in my office. Crowther emotional, vain, and speaking rather as if he were the country's conscience. There are all sorts of stories circulating about Harvey, but the problem is to get rid of him and clean up the company with the minimum loss to the shareholders and to the printing industry generally. Eventually the terms emerged which would be accepted by Crowther for the disappearance of Harvey. Wolfson was asked to the meeting, but didn't come – he was at the Royal Garden Party.

Friday, July 16th, 1965

9.30 a.m., by arrangement, Harvey, Roy Thomson and I foregathered in Wolfson's office – to find Hart and another from Ansbacher, the bankers, already installed by Wolfson's invitation. Though the Harvey story had been published, and not denied, it appeared that Wolfson, Hart, Roy and the Westminster Bank* were all still pro-Harvey. In the course of the conference, lasting two hours, it was clear to all that Harvey had no wish to face the music, and they were prepared to listen when I said there had indeed been irregularities. The problem then switched from Harvey's future to the problem of the future management of B.P.C., and from that to the financial stability of the company. From the figures we were given, it appeared that they were desperately short of cash. They have bank and other short-term loans of £14½ million, and the balance-sheet position generally is by no means happy.

At 4.30 went to the Ministry of Defence to talk politics to Denis Healey. He is said by his officials to be the best Minister of Defence

* B.P.C.'s principal bankers.

22

for a long time. He is highly intelligent. I said I was sorry Michael Stewart, and not he, got the F.O. He said he was better where he was. He had been told what money was available (£2,000 million at 1964 prices for 1970); this narrowed down the forces that would be available, and from that the foreign policy that could be pursued was more or less clearly indicated. I gathered from other sources that this means pulling out of Singapore, Bahrain, Aden and Cyprus, but building a naval base in Australia at Darwin, which could be reached via Canada or the U.S. with no over-flying difficulties.

On politics, I said I didn't think his Government was doing very well – too many gimmicks; too much very short-term thinking; too many poor appointments that, with such a small majority, could not be rectified. The Government's greatest asset at the moment was the ineptitude of Alec Home, but a government could not flourish on the poor quality of the Leader of the Opposition. Healey said he was not happy himself, but too busy and too interested in his job to worry much. Roy Jenkins (whom Wilson told me he nearly made Foreign Secretary) was more worried. I told Healey how well he was doing and, last time I saw him when I dined at his house, said I hoped to see him in 10 Downing St.

Sunday, July 25th, 1965

On Thursday afternoon rumours were rife around Fleet St (but not apparently equally rife around the H. of C.) that Home was resigning. And this he duly did in the evening. Home has always filled me with amazement. I suppose I met him first as Lord Dunglass in the 'thirties. I have never been able to detect anything in him at all. He is a pleasant country gentleman of a very familiar type. I agreed with those who greeted his appointment to the Foreign Office with derision, and his nomination to 10 Downing St with stupefaction. When he became P.M. he asked me to lunch alone and I had one and a half hours with him. Neither then, nor earlier, nor since, have I been able to catch a glimpse of anything. The legend that he is an expert on foreign affairs, but a bit out on the domestic side, has always seemed to me without foundation. He has only an elementary grasp of foreign affairs, but not even that on economics or finance. As Prime

23

Minister he was a failure; as Leader of the Opposition, a catastrophe. He has of recent months been under a blizzard of denigration from the Tory press, but proudly proclaims that he pays no attention to the press. Why this should be a point of pride, I cannot think. The newspapers are directed by such a motley crew of people that you must indeed be a failure if you unite them against you. I asked Macleod one day why the Tories had picked on Home. He said they were in confusion and in that state they return to the womb – the landed aristocracy!

When Home was Foreign Secretary, Heath asked me what I made of him. I said he would make a good vice-chairman of a sub-committee of the Berwickshire County Council. What I meant was that he was only really fit for local politics, and that not in any spectacular way. When Home became P.M., Heath said he recalled what I said before and had I seen any reason to change my mind? I said I had not.

Now the fight is on again – this time between Heath and Maudling. I know them both and like them both. Time was when Maudling had the leadership in his hand – and let it slip. This time he has another chance – mainly because Heath has enemies, though for the right reason. Heath really is a positive force – a leader – while dear Reggie, though very intelligent, does like a good lunch and parties that go on late into the night. There is no doubt in my mind that Heath is certainly the best available man to be Tory P.M., and probably the best potential P.M. in the House. The London newspapers are all supposed to be pro-Heath – or so their proprietors tell me – but there is not much sign of this today. They all seem to be hedging their bets – in case the other man wins. But surely this is the time to stand up and be counted.

Mike [King] saw Heath on Friday morning. Heath told him that he had the support of the younger men, but was not popular with the Knights of the Shires. Tufton Beamish was doing his best with the latter, and Macleod, a Maudling man before, has swung round behind Heath. Later in the day Tufton Beamish told Mike he thought Heath was in. But later today it was announced that Enoch Powell was a candidate. This is presumably a move to get his rather Goldwaterish ideas better known, though it may be an attempt to weaken

Heath. No one supposes he will score an appreciable number of votes.

Cromer rang me up from the Bank on Friday to say that the foreign bankers regard Maudling as the architect of our present financial misfortunes and that, therefore, if he is chosen as Leader the effect on the pound will be bad.

Monday, July 26th, 1965

De Courcel, the French Ambassador, to lunch. Generally regarded, I think rightly, as a nice man but a lightweight. I had asked him because he had been rather pressing in his invitations to me and I thought he might have something to say. He hadn't really, but I took the opportunity of hearing the French point of view on current topics. On Vietnam, the French were confident Johnson's policy would not work, and had said so privately several times before they said so publicly. They had wanted us to join with them in a protest; this would prove we were European and not just an American satellite. He was full of enthusiasm for joint projects like Concorde, the Channel Tunnel, etc. I asked when he thought we should qualify for joining the Common Market. He was a bit vague, but said we must show we were good Europeans: they already had the Germans and Italians who were more American than European. He said de Gaulle considered England and France to be the natural foundations of the new Europe; he had said so as far back as 1947.

He spoke about the present impasse in Brussels,* which he attributed to a plot, or plots. He said agreement had been arrived at before the meeting on all salient points and the French negotiators did not expect the meeting to last more than a day – or at most two. He seemed to think the whole thing was due to Hallstein and the Germans trying to force on the French a degree of supranationality they knew General de Gaulle would never agree to. I said but surely an economic union of Europe could only lead to a political union in

---

* At this time France was boycotting all meetings of the Common Market Commission (except those concerned with the implementation of established policies) because of her objections to the Commission's proposals for the financing of the common farm policy. French objections were mainly due to President de Gaulle's view that the Commission should not venture into 'political' areas where national interests and independence might be involved.

time. He said yes, but not in our lifetime. Both in this matter and on the question of Great Britain joining the Common Market, he was difficult to pin down. He seems to see de Gaulle fairly frequently, but really had little to say that has not already often been said in our newspapers.

Sunday, August 1st, 1965

Quite a stirring week. On Monday our papers,* the *Mail* and *The Times* came out solidly for Heath; the others more or less sat on the fence. The *Express* apparently for Maudling, though Max [Aitken] has twice told me he is for Heath. The *Financial Times* faintly for Heath, though they must know the danger to the pound from the election of Maudling. Too many papers were actuated by the fear of being wrong.

On Tuesday the result was announced: Heath 150; Maudling 133, Powell 15. Maudling immediately conceded the victory to Heath. Maudling was surprised and upset by the result; and is said only to have conceded under pressure.

The change is of real importance as we now have an alternative government, as we had not before. I have been telling Heath for at least two years that he is the Tories' best bet, and more recently have conveyed both to Whitelaw (the Conservative Chief Whip) and to Bob Renwick the view that Alec Home just will not do, and that their most marketable personality was Ted Heath.

The Harvey matter has at least got over the first hurdle. He and Dingwall Bateson are to resign; a new chairman and a new managing director are to be found; Harvey abandons his contract of 1964, and Cooper Bros, the accountants, are to conduct an inquiry. In six months' time, Crowther will retire if asked to do so by the independent chairman. So far so good, but the inquiry is bound to dig up a good deal of dirt, and the management problem is so far without a hint of solution. The agreement was finally concluded under pressure from Chesterfield, Chief General Manager of the Westminster Bank. They presumably speak for the other clearing banks. It may have helped that Wolfson, Roy Thomson and myself had all insisted that Harvey must go.

* The International Publishing Corporation (I.P.C.) papers.

26

Thursday, August 5th, 1965

A gloomy session at the Bank. There has been a run on gold and a run on sterling, and the reserves are in sight of exhaustion. It is not thought that any further deflationary gestures would produce any effect. The Governor thinks the only card left to play is a wage and price freeze. This might impress foreign opinion; nothing else would.

Lunch at No. 10. Harold Wilson more cordial than usual: perhaps a bit tired; going on holiday to the Scillies this evening. Does not take the financial crisis too seriously, particularly as the trade figures for next week will be spectacularly good. —— [a senior civil servant] was in Washington last week and has had the most definite assurances of support from the U.S. Government. Though things are going badly, Wilson is as buoyant as usual. Wants a showdown on restrictive practices; was baulked of one on liner trains by the capitulation of the union; was prepared for one with ASLEF* on the railway go-slow, but this was called off. But what about the docks? He is immensely impressed by Devlin's report and is going to adopt its recommendations, which may well involve a showdown with the dockers.† Thinks he will decide on nationalizing the docks, which would give him a chance of shelving steel nationalization.

He talked of a Government shuffle in September: Soskice to go and Roy Jenkins to join; Frank Cousins to have another department; perhaps a replacement for Frank Longford. Would I accept a peerage and a post as Minister of State in the Board of Trade in charge of our export drive? Nothing doing, know nothing of exports; however will ponder the matter and let him know later. He was in a more cordial mood than ever before: I was one of only two or three people he could open his mind to, and more flattering stuff of that kind. It is easy to argue that he feels his position slipping and is rounding up some support, but it didn't sound like that.

* Associated Society of Locomotive Engineers and Firemen.

† Lord Devlin was a former Lord of Appeal, who had headed a committee of inquiry into the port transport industry. The final report of the committee – the 'Devlin Report' – suggested that unrest in the docks was partly due to the prevalence of casual labour arrangements. Regular employment ('decasualization') and a reduction in the number of employers were considered the most urgent requirements if industrial relations in the docks were to be reformed. The report formed the basis of the present dock labour scheme.

Later

Had a word with Cromer on the telephone. C. had had lunch with Callaghan; the figures of exchange dealing yesterday were appalling. He says —— did not get a categorical promise of support from Johnson who, anyway, is constitutionally unable to give it. In fact, Cromer's and Wilson's pictures of the situation are so different as to be irreconcilable.

Friday, August 6th, 1965

Another shocking day on the exchanges, so felt I should see Ted Heath, who looked in on me for a half-hour on his way to the City. He is going abroad on Sunday, but is to leave his telephone number. He listened to what I had to say and only added that he also had been told of Johnson's underwriting of the pound. An emissary from the U.S. had assured him this was untrue, but he would check in Washington. He did this and reported back to Ted that the guarantee story was quite untrue. Ted also wanted to know if I thought he should retire from Brown, Shipley, the merchant bank, now that he was Leader of the Opposition. I said regretfully that I thought he should.

I have been telling Ted for three years that he should be leading the Tory Party. To my mind as a political leader he is head and shoulders over the other candidates. Anyway, with support in the paper and behind the scenes he has every reason to be friendly, and this may stand him in good stead later.

Saturday, August 7th, 1965
Letter from Cecil King to Harold Wilson

CONFIDENTIAL

Dear Harold,

I am writing to say that I have given thought to your offer of a post in the Government in connection with the Export drive. While flattered that you should have thought of me in this connection, I do not feel that this is a sphere in which I could deploy my talents to best advantage.

With regret,

Yours very sincerely,
Cecil King

The Rt. Hon. Harold Wilson, P.C., O.B.E., M.P.
10, Downing Street,
London, S.W.I.

Monday, August 9th, 1965

All political activity has died down: Wilson and Michael Stewart in the Scilly Islands; Callaghan in the Isle of Wight. The financial situation remains the big query. Markets have been quieter this morning, and tomorrow the trade figures will be out showing a big rise in exports. Imports are still too high, but the balance will be better than for a long time. The papers yesterday and today are mostly very optimistic, some absurdly so. This is the result of a briefing from No. 10 on Saturday. *The Times* has a short paragraph from Washington on its financial page saying that it is not true that the American Government has underwritten the pound. This is the most important news in the paper. It should have been on the main news page and not buried down-column on the City page.

Bob Renwick rang up Hugh Cudlipp this morning to say that he had had a word with du Cann (Chairman of the Tory Party) about the departure of Alec Home and his replacement by Ted Heath. They agreed that a memorandum drawn up by Hugh Cudlipp for Bob Renwick had had its effect. This memo originated in a conversation with Renwick at an A.T.V.* lunch. Cudlipp was holding forth on the impossibility of selling Home to the British public and saying that their best bet was Heath. Renwick asked Hugh to put this in writing as he said he was himself too inarticulate – anyway on paper. At my instigation Hugh drew up a memorandum and handed it to Renwick. I showed my copy to Heath and subsequently expressed similar views to Whitelaw when he came to lunch. Renwick eventually showed his copy to Home!

* Associated Television Corporation.

On August 9th Harold Wilson wrote to Cecil King from Scilly. Mr Wilson said that he was sorry Mr King could not accept his offer of a ministerial post, but understood and respected Mr King's decision. He added: '. . . this does not mean I might not approach you when your help is needed in a different, i.e. non Ministerial capacity.' He concluded his letter with some complimentary remarks about the Mirror: '*I have now seen Tuesday's and Wednesday's issues. Terrific.*'

Friday, August 13th, 1965

No further news at the Bank yesterday. Markets much quieter, but even so needing support on Tuesday and Wednesday, though not yesterday. Wilson has ostentatiously submitted to the journalists and is shown happy and relaxed – even enjoying a beer with Michael Stewart, who is staying at a nearby hotel. All this may beguile the British public, but does nothing to help the situation or to impress foreign bankers. Wage-claims proliferate, the trades unions behave worse and worse. While this continues, devaluation becomes more and more inevitable. I gather at the moment the bankers are bothered about the inability to control the wage-claims far more than by the gradual exhaustion of the reserves.

Sunday, August 15th, 1965

No particular news but have been thinking of Wilson, whose days look to be numbered.

I hardly knew Wilson when he became Leader of the Labour Party, but since then have seen a good deal of him. My first impression was that at least we had a politician leading one of the two big parties. Gaitskell was a bigger personality but no politician: he once asked me if I thought 'smoke abatement' would be a good popular vote-getter at election time! Moreover, Wilson was disposed to listen to advice as Gaitskell was not. But of course when Wilson reached 10 Downing St he was a mainly unknown quantity. He had told me before the election that I should be disheartened by his first Government, but that after twelve months there would be a big purge and I would then see the real Wilson Government.

In the event of a majority of sixty and no great financial crisis, this made sense. But with a majority of four and a very grave financial crisis, it did not. Both in this matter and otherwise, I think it is clear that Wilson did not realize that his plans had to be reconsidered in view of the smallness of his majority. He should probably have formed a very small administration with room to add younger men as opportunity offered. Instead of this we have an abnormally large administration that includes every hack in the business. There can be no serious purge because of the size of the majority and the Government will eventually have to go to the country with this lacklustre lot.

Another fact that has emerged since October is that Wilson is a very short-term tactician, obsessed with the House of Commons. I thought that when in office he would concentrate on re-election. This has not been so. He has shown no interest in re-election, because an election is far off and there is a debate in the House tomorrow.

He has also shown no interest in administration. For thirteen years the Labour Party has been in opposition, where the only possible contribution is a speech. He still thinks that a good speech in the House gets us somewhere. The implementation of the policy indicated in the speech is to him of slight concern. The Labour front bench has no one with administrative experience of any kind other than running a trade union. Therefore one would have thought the Labour Cabinet would need re-enforcement with some John Anderson or Dick Stokes element.* But not only did Wilson not provide this; it is clear that this whole train of thought never occurred to him. Instead, numbers of academic economists have been recruited – there are said to be twenty in Barbara Castle's Ministry of Overseas Development. The Labour Party has always been too doctrinaire, and this emphasizes the fact. The only ministers in the outcome who seem to show administrative ability are Denis Healey and Roy Jenkins.

Wilson himself speaks of administrative changes, but they don't take place. Before the election I said (as I had to Gaitskell) that I

---

* John Anderson (later Lord Waverley) was the best administrator in the civil service of the day, and was used by Churchill in World War II to keep the administration of the Government under control. He was successively Home Secretary, Lord President of the Council and Chancellor of the Exchequer. Richard Stokes was a highly successful businessman, who was taken into the Attlee Labour Government. Like Anderson, though in a different sphere, he had an understanding of the way things were done.

thought there should be someone at No. 10 to do such prime ministerial chores as the P.M. himself did not want to perform – e.g. patronage, honours list, etc. Wilson said he felt No. 10 was quite inadequately staffed – he wanted it to be a power-house. There was talk of a Minister of State for the P.M.'s department. In fact the staff at No. 10 is weaker than ever – a dim little secretary, Wigg, and an inadequate press man called Trevor Lloyd-Hughes.

But apart from administrative deficiencies, policy doesn't seem too good. I take it that British policy today should be, on the home front, control of inflation, and on the foreign front, into Europe. All measures should be with a view to these two objectives. In fact, we have a number of contradictory statements about Europe that amount to no action now or in the near future. On the home front the Prices and Incomes policy is regarded as George Brown's hobby, and no sorrow is expressed by Wilson when it gets into difficulties. It has been so slow getting going that it is now doubtful if George can pull it off. It will have to be effectively implemented some day by someone, but it is getting nowhere fast at the moment.

Instead we have wild talk about Britain's frontiers being on the Himalayas (at the Nehru Memorial gathering) and an apparent inability to get out of Singapore in spite of the fact that the Malaysian Federation is breaking up.

Thursday, August 19th, 1965

Yesterday Reggie Maudling to lunch – very friendly in spite of the fact that we had publicly supported Heath for the leadership. Very sore because Rothermere had come out against him in the *Daily Mail*, alleging that his election would be unfavourably viewed in international banking circles. I asked him if Cromer had had a hand in this (knowing he did), but Reggie said he was certain this was not so. I have always been on very friendly terms with Reggie. I offered him the chairmanship of Reed's some few years ago, but after long hesitation he turned the offer down. I thought maybe he had used this offer to get a promise of the Exchequer from Macmillan. Reggie is nice and very intelligent, but seems to me soft, and certainly yesterday he was both soft and defeatist. I am sure Heath will make the better P.M., but I am getting sadly disillusioned. Over the years one

32

new P.M. after another has proved inadequate or useless, even when great things were not expected of them.

Monday, August 30th, 1965

Dick Marsh came to lunch on Thursday. He is M.P. for Greenwich and Parliamentary Under-Secretary for the Ministry of Labour. He strikes me as the best of the younger Labour M.P.s – anyway the best of those I have met, and I have met all those with any reputation. I spoke warmly of his Minister, Ray Gunter, but my warmth was not matched by his. This may have been unintended, but if it was he is not the only minister to feel that way. Brown is said not to be on speaking terms with Gunter, and Wilson, in speaking to me, showed no enthusiasm. Yet Gunter has shown great courage and clarity in condemning unofficial strikes, though he is himself a former General Secretary.*

Marsh, though uneducated, to me shows intelligence and judgment. So much so that when he applied for a job outside politics I arranged for him to have £500 per annum from the *Mirror* to keep him in. Wilson knows this and says he will soon be in the Cabinet.

Wilson is now back in London, the T.U.C. Conference and the Labour Party Conference both ahead of him in September. Opinion in his party is increasingly critical. I should judge that his tactical ingenuity will get him over these two big hurdles, but he will finally be brought down by his inability to produce results. Government by gimmick is bound to fail even in the medium run.

Monday, September 20th, 1965

Returned on Wednesday from three days in Portugal with the National Youth Orchestra. B. of E. Thursday; lunch American Ambassador, David Bruce; lunch Friday, Tony Crosland.

Bruce, as usual, very friendly. Not happy about Vietnam, but what else can they do? I told him that over two years ago, in conversation with George Ball over dinner at the State Department, I had argued that the U.S. was committed too far forward in Asia and should be planning to draw back. Ball pointed out how difficult this

* Of the Transport Salaried Staffs Association (T.S.S.A.).

33

was in view of American public opinion. I said a withdrawal might be impossible at the moment, but surely an escape route could be organized. Now they want to get out but have got further in. Bruce expressed contempt for Gordon Walker, and said he could not make out what Gore-Booth did.

Tony Crosland is a curious character: good-looking, charming, very intelligent, but immature and quite silly at times. He asked how the Government was doing and I said badly. He more or less agreed. Crosland's main interest was in a Lib-Lab pact. He said the Government cannot go on as it is and an agreement with the Liberals is the only hope. I asked how this could be done as, in Parliamentary terms, a deal meant losing thirty votes on the Left for ten on the Right. He said the terms of an agreement would be support for the Government and, in return, dropping of the steel nationalization Bill* and bringing in the Alternative Vote.† I said surely this would mean no party would normally have an absolute majority? He said he believed this would not be so; that the Alternative Vote, on the basis of the last election, would give the Liberals about twenty to twenty-five more seats, while Labour would lose only two and the Tories the rest. This would avoid all the difficulties of a coalition, which would mean finding places for Liberal ministers and asking numbers of Labour candidates to stand down. I believe other calculations on this issue produce quite different results, making the Labour Party the principal losers. It is not as simple as Crosland makes out. The Liberal Party in the House are a heterogeneous lot and their consent cannot be assumed for any arrangement Grimond may want. In any case, Grimond is by no means keen on a deal except on his own

* The re-nationalization of the steel industry (originally nationalized by the Labour Government in 1951 and promptly de-nationalized by the following Conservative administration) had been in Labour's election manifesto. In spite of a White Paper published in April 1965, the compromises made necessary by the minute Labour majority prevented the introduction of the Bill until the following Labour Government had been returned in 1966.

† One of the many electoral systems under which a legislature reflects more accurately in its composition the strength of the parties amongst the electorate at large. Voters state a second preference and these second preferences are counted if no candidate receives an absolute majority on the basis of first choices. The system was recommended for use in British elections by a 1911 Royal Commission on electoral reform but has never been adopted. The effect of any such system would be to give much greater Parliamentary representation to the Liberal Party in Britain.

very stiff terms. Crosland admitted that the Alternative Vote might often leave the Liberals with the balance of power.

Saturday, September 25th, 1965

A fairly idle morning, so I will bring this diary up to date with the events of the week. Some time ago I called on Gavin Astor, now sole proprietor of *The Times*, to say that in my opinion *The Times* was on the danger list and would remain so unless its sale was at least 500,000, roughly twice what it is now. He asked what should be done and I recommended a merger with the *Sunday Times* in a new company with himself as chairman but with [Roy] Thomson in control. This nearly came off, but was bungled by Thomson. Following on a talk with Stanley Morison, I had another crack at Gavin and suggested we might come in as junior partners. The ironical outcome of my efforts has been the appointment of Haley as chief executive as well as editor, while George Pope is manager and a director. Both these men are sixty-four and have been at *The Times* for years and years and have nothing further to contribute.

Anyway, on Wednesday Haley came to pay his respects on his new appointment. He stayed half an hour and was very friendly, but I can see no progress there.

Later the same afternoon I had a visit from David Astor, to talk about a Lib-Lab pact. He is very close to Grimond and is very keen on such a pact. How did I think this should be approached? He may have just been seeking my views, but it may have been a serious approach by Grimond to Wilson through third parties. The Liberal view is that Wilson should have approached them immediately after the election and, anyway, they cannot leave a deal until Wilson is in a jam. Grimond wants a deal on law reform, civil service reform, Parliamentary reform, trades union reform – a generally radical policy. The Liberal Party would support Labour on the basis of dropping steel nationalization and bringing in the Alternative Vote. I said this sounded sensible, but had no relation to Wilson's way of operating. (1) Grimond was far too glamorous a character for Wilson to want him in the Government. (2) Wilson would certainly have to postpone steel nationalization, but is very unlikely to agree to the Alternative Vote. (3) A meeting of minds on a general radical policy

35

is something very foreign to Wilson. This is administration, in which Wilson is not interested; nor has he shown any sign of the massive administrative ability required. He might agree on the desirability of these reforms, but would almost certainly do nothing about them. It was interesting to see, in the course of nearly an hour's conversation, that neither Astor – nor, presumably, Grimond – had any idea of the sort of P.M. they have to deal with.

Hugh [Cudlipp] saw Denis Healey on Tuesday and was once more impressed, as I have been, with his clarity of thought and general ability.

On the political side it is agreed that Soskice really must go. Roy Jenkins would be a good choice for the job, but Healey thinks Wilson will keep him on ice for a bit – perhaps as a stand-in for George Brown if *he* has to go. It had been in Wilson's mind to keep Robens for this, but Alf has just been given a further stretch at the Coal Board.

The future of Frank Cousins is not clear. He is unhappy where he is; has thought of resigning; cannot establish a new department and would be a hopeless Home Secretary. So where does he go from here?

Healey wishes to stay where he is for a year or two and then move to the Exchequer rather than the F.O. Does not see himself as future P.M. and has an admiration for Wilson's dexterity without having any illusions about his character or administrative abilities.

Tuesday, October 5th, 1965

—— [a senior civil servant] to lunch today. He likes Brown but says he has no idea of organization, keeps on changing his mind and neither obtains, nor apparently seeks, the help of his colleagues on the Prices and Incomes policy. He says Wilson makes no attempt to run his Government as a team but rather by creating unrest tries to bend them all to his policy. He thinks Soskice remains as Home Secretary because he won't go quietly and Wilson cannot remove him. He knew I had been offered the post in charge of overseas trade. This surprised me, as the idea is so silly that I thought Wilson must have acted off the cuff. I said I thought Wilson rather rashly assumed our support. He said, 'He thinks your readership prevents you doing otherwise.' He is likely to have some rude shocks!

Heath to lunch last Wednesday. Somewhat cooler than usual. Arrived late and left early. No particular news. Is bringing out his policy paper on Thursday and thinks it will cause a big uproar. The two main planks are (1) into Europe and (2) trades union legislation. The general opinion in the Tory Party is that he has got off to a poor start. His first speech as Leader in the House was not good, and far inferior to Reggie's. He expressed a poor opinion of the Government's plan before he had read it, and his trip around the north of Scotland seems to have been a bit of a flop – his principal speech being a feeble one.

Tuesday, October 12th, 1965

Whitelaw to lunch. He thinks Heath is exceedingly hard-working and competent; may try too hard; is a competent speaker, but no orator, and is an excellent administrator.

Dinner last night with Luce at the Time-Life building – present: Max Aitken, Michael Berry, Haley, Denis Hamilton and Kenneth Adam of the B.B.C. Luce is getting old and deaf but is still a formidable, though unattractive, personality. He thinks the Americans are winning in Vietnam and that by next year the fighting will be over. Asked 'What then?', he said he had no idea. He said Johnson is determined to go down in history as a great president. I said this was a poor formula for greatness, but he seemed to think it would serve. He was full of praise for the progress made in Formosa and full of contempt for Red China: their steel production is only ten million tons a year – America uses that tonnage for its ash-cans! It is alarming that anyone so prejudiced and ignorant should be so powerful. Of the guests Kenneth Adam was basically talking sense but was so offensive to our host as to be embarrassing. Max Aitken talked complete nonsense. It is hard to see what can be done with such a man. He had two themes: one was how right Ian Smith was and how wrong H.M. Government was over Rhodesia, and the second was Booming Britain. I know these are the themes of the *Express* just now, but it never occurred to me that he actually believes this nonsense. He was sure the Rhodesian Government would move as fast as was appropriate towards sharing power with the Africans. All the evidence is the other way, but that doesn't bother him. On the other

37

theme, Booming Britain: this is Britain's finest hour; we have never been so inventive, so prosperous, so happy. Someone mentioned balance of payments. This was brushed aside – 'The Victorians never worried about balance of payments'!

Thursday, October 14th, 1965

George Brown to lunch yesterday. In good form. He doesn't like Wilson and makes no attempt to hide his feelings. He says Wilson has no idea how to conduct Cabinet business. Rhodesia was referred to a Cabinet committee of six. Its report was submitted to Cabinet supposedly for adoption – but not at all; the whole thing was debated afresh – Dick Crossman, Frank Cousins and Barbara Castle very much to the fore. After hours of discussion – I understood George to say four hours – the whole matter was referred to a fresh committee! Another serious fault is that Wilson cannot say no to a man's face. So, recently, Soskice got the impression from Fleet St (who got it from Wilson) that he was out. He went to see Wilson, who reassured him that his work was excellent. Meanwhile Wilson had offered the job to Roy Jenkins, who had told his friends and had even done a little celebrating. The matter is now in abeyance until perhaps Christmas. Meanwhile Soskice remains a disastrous Home Secretary. It appears that in spite of Cousins's disloyalty, he is very close to Wilson, who promised him that engineering should be detached from the Board of Trade and added to Technology. This was published in the *Sun*, whereupon George Brown rushed round to point out that this could not possibly work – what would happen to all the little Neddies, etc. etc.?* So this plan, too, is postponed.

In spite of Wilson's categorical statement at the Labour Party Conference that there had been no deal with the U.S. – trading financial support for the pound against military support in S.E. Asia – this was exactly what was done. To honour this arrangement, it is now planned that we should cut down our forces in Germany. This will have a deplorable effect on Continental opinion, and con-

* The National Economic Development Council (N.E.D.C. or 'Neddy') was established in 1961 to 'tackle the obstacles to sound growth, to consider the availability and use, or misuse, of resources, the availability of technical skills and matters of that sort'. It included representatives of Government, industry and labour, and it spawned a series of similar councils for individual industries, known as 'little Neddies'.

38

firm Europeans in their suspicions that we are not really European.

In spite of all the criticisms of Wilson, George was pleased the way things are going, and at least professed to be satisfied with the achievements of the previous twelve months.

Mike [King], just back from Washington, says Stewart was not a success in the U.S. He has too little personality to stand up to the Yanks. Dean, our Ambassador, is making no impression. He finds Britain regarded more and more as a foreign country and less and less taken seriously.

Friday, October 15th, 1965

Denis Healey to lunch. I told him that I told everyone that he is the success of this Government. He is the only one with real administrative ability.

He denies that there is any agreement to exchange support for the pound against military support in S.E. Asia. He says the Americans will try very hard to do this but that the negotiation stage has not been reached on Malaysia.

In domestic politics he thinks highly of George's drive and energy and says Dick Crossman makes a good minister. This is unexpected, as Dick changes his mind so often. Denis says the change is due to the fact that he now has a ministry, and what with the inertia of an established ministry and the limitations imposed by his previous decisions, he has to be fairly consistent! He speaks highly of Wilson's brains and tactical ingenuity. He says that having no convictions is a great help to him as he can make a purely pragmatic approach to any problem. They would like to have an election now when their stock is high, but don't feel that any plausible excuse is apparent and to have an election purely to increase their majority might be badly received.

Wednesday, October 20th, 1965

Have been in Washington since Saturday talking to all and sundry – mostly politicians and newspaper people, but also to Fowler, Secretary of the Treasury, and Balderston, Deputy Chairman of the Federal Reserve Bank. Business is booming – perhaps a little too much so. Johnson has had an operation which has pulled him down more than was expected, but really the only subject of general interest in the circles where I have been was foreign policy in general and Vietnam in particular. I think I can say, after talking to George Ball, Dean Rusk, our Ambassador Dean, and so many lesser figures, that there is really no American foreign policy.

Johnson has completed his domestic programme and may now devote more time to foreign affairs. If so, we may see a change, as he completely dominates the affairs of the country. He relies much on McNamara, whom I have not seen this time, and praises him to the skies to everyone. He also relies on McGeorge Bundy – a most brilliant man. He has the best and quickest brain I have ever met and this time I thought him nicer than he seemed to me before. He was at dinner with Mrs Philip Graham of the *Washington Post*, with his wife (nice, quiet, little woman) and his mother, a lively old girl of seventy-five with several great-grandchildren. Perhaps the family surroundings made him seem a warmer character.

Rusk seemed livelier than usual. I dare say he is a worthy soul and he is certainly no fool, but I find Ball much easier to make contact with. The idea I gather from all these people is that the war in Vietnam will go on until the Viet Cong pack up or agree to negotiations. Rusk said there were frequent contacts between them and Hanoi, but nothing at all came of them. When the fighting is over, there will be some sort of viable government in Saigon, and the Americans will keep a couple of divisions there for an indefinite period into the future. They already have forces in South Korea, and similar wars to that in Vietnam may break out in Thailand, Malaya, Burma, or anywhere else. Are the Americans prepared to keep troops in all such places if necessary? They don't see it in those terms. They are keeping back the forces of evil, and in due course non-Communist governments will take root in all these areas. I said I thought American policy was misconceived. Their vital interest is Central and South America, to a lesser extent Europe, and Asia third. They cannot control the whole world, so why not put first things first? Their reply to me for two and a half years now has been that they don't know how to get out. I said to them all that I thought the Chinese were doing splendidly. Every bomb dropped by a man with a white face on a man with a coloured face operated to the advantage of the Chinese, the champions of the coloured peoples. This point of view was not only not accepted, but seemed unfamiliar to them. They pointed out that Chinese were doing badly in Africa and even in Ceylon; and they thought Chinese influence was waning notably recently in Indonesia.

Thursday, October 21st, 1965

Have moved on to New York after two more interesting talks in Washington yesterday – with Walter Lippman, the columnist, and with Senator Fulbright, the latter the most intelligent of all the men to whom I talked foreign policy. They both told me that they are out of favour with the President, who does not like criticism. Lippman said he had had interviews with Johnson lasting three and four hours, and one lasting seven hours, in which Johnson tried to persuade him of the error of his ways! Lippman also told us that the American forces in Vietnam are the cream of the American armed forces – 200,000 picked men.

Fulbright does not see, any more than I do, how the result of the bombing in Vietnam can operate to the advantage of the U.S. Most of it has been on South Vietnam and seems designed to show the villagers that the consequences of supporting the Viet Cong are even more terrible than the consequences of defying them. This is no way to make America or the West more popular and, anyway, has created a vast refugee problem, already 700,000 and growing fast.

I was interested to meet Dean – a nice, intelligent type of civil servant. It was said that he should have succeeded Caccia as head of the F.O., and I think this was true. He would surely be much better than Gore-Booth, and at the same time it would be possible to find someone who would make a far greater impact on Washington than will Dean.

Sunday, October 24th, 1965

Had lunch with Caradon (until recently, Hugh Foot). I have known him since I stayed with him for ten days in Lagos seventeen years ago. He is a very nice man and a very able man, but never seems quite to have come off. He is now our man at the U.N. Yesterday he was to speak on Aden without, apparently, much briefing from home. He regards the Rhodesian situation as quite appalling. It is hard to see how Smith can draw back and, at the same time, U.D.I.,* or so Caradon thinks, might well lead to racial war throughout Africa. He thinks the only hope is to play for time, though this is no long-term solution as it would not allow for the inevitable eventual trouble over South Africa.

Thursday, November 11th, 1965

My first Bank meeting for some time. I arrive to find Rhodesia has just declared its independence. I asked if Rhodesian funds are to be frozen. This has been under discussion, but no decision made yet! U.D.I. for Rhodesia has been on the cards for four *years*, so surely the appropriate moves could have been decided before this.

I am surprised, returning after three weeks away, to find Wilson's stock much higher. His hitherings and thitherings over Rhodesia have kept the limelight on him – probably all they were intended to do. His handling of Rhodesia, his playing for time, has built up Smith into an international figure and has increased the magnitude of the crisis – to no advantage that I can see. It is said in Whitehall that his efforts have been so frantic because (1) he did not think he would have the nation behind him in his policy of sanctions, and (2) he was aghast at the possible economic consequences to ourselves. I do not think these fears are justified, and they don't sound like Wilson, any-way.

Monday, November 15th, 1965

To a concert at the Festival Hall last night with Ted Heath. Other guests: Lady Adeane, the Swedish Ambassador, Aidan Crawley and his wife (Virginia Cowles). Was interested to see Heath's flat in the Albany: two pictures by Churchill, good prints, excellent hi-fi equipment; signed photographs by Winston, Eden and Macmillan (none visible of Home!). Ruth [King] saw much more of him than I did: says jokes about deep-frozen smile quite unjustified; that he is warm, nervous, and shy. Clearly has difficulties with his party over Rhodesia where, as he admitted, he is walking a knife-edge between

* Unilateral declaration of independence

the actions of the Conservatives in office and the views of the Salisbury wing of the party. I had little talk with him, but he agreed that present sanctions will not bring Smith to his knees. He does not think the Russians will intervene, even if given an opening by the United Nations.

Wednesday, December 8th, 1965

On Friday we published a piece on the front page of the *Mirror* warning Wilson against military operations in Rhodesia, suggesting he pay more attention to the economic state of this country and less to the wide world outside. The front page produced an immediate reaction. Cudlipp was summoned to No. 10 for 4.30 that afternoon. Here is his report of the proceedings:

Notes of my hour-long meeting with Harold Wilson at 4.30 today:
The meeting was frank but friendly. He made many snide references to the *Mirror* piece but was anxious to explain his position.

Wilson said that it was not true that he was solely engaged with the Rhodesian crisis: on Monday, Tuesday and part of Wednesday – yes. But he is closely in touch with economic affairs and constantly sees Brown and Callaghan.

It was because of the economic aspects that he was so concerned about Rhodesia. Forty per cent of our copper comes from Zambia, and if the supply ceased we could have one million unemployed, even two million. With the aid of the Americans he believed we could fly in enough coal to keep the copper mine pumps working (to avoid flooding) but could not maintain production.

The possibility of military aid to Zambia is real and urgent, though he thought that what would happen at the meeting of the O.A.U.* Foreign Ministers in Addis Ababa would be 'masturbation'. The danger, however, was a force consisting of Egyptian MiGs and Ethiopian and Congolese troops. The additional danger was the assassination of whites in Kenya and elsewhere by Chinese-trained terrorists.

Kenyatta has been sensible throughout and is in close touch with

* Organization of African Unity.

Wilson. Kenyatta was demanding British troops to cross the Zambezi to occupy the Kariba Dam installations, but became more reasonable during the week.

Where Heath was 'naughty' in the House was in his repeated demands to Wilson to define and confine the possible role of British troops in Zambia. Wilson had not the slightest intention of crossing the border in the sense of an armed occupation of Rhodesia unless (1) Smith or his successors invited us, (2) the Governor* under certain circumstances (meaning the successful formation of a new government) invited us, or (3) in the event of a total breakdown in which the heads of the Rhodesian services might invite us.

He emphasized again and again that it was not his intention to 'invade' Rhodesia. But his difficulty in replying to Heath in the Commons was that he could not say that nobody would cross the border under *any* circumstances. He meant that if Smith deprived Zambia of power supply he reserved the right to cut off Rhodesia's supply by simple sabotage of the Special Services type – 'two electricians with a pair of pliers'.

He could not say that he would do nothing whatever the circumstances, but he was certainly not thinking in terms of military advance or occupation *without a previous guarantee of no opposition*.

He was still in touch with Smith, and still – he thought – trusted him, but not the thugs around him: Lardner-Burke, Dupont, Harper.

The nightmare he was most anxious to avoid was a situation in which Egyptian–Ethiopian–Congolese forces would promote a racial war from Zambian soil, manœuvring the British into going to the aid of a semi-Fascist Rhodesia against the blacks. 'If Smith invited us we might have to defend him.'

'Rhodesia is land-locked. It's about as difficult as invading Switzerland. If there was a sea coast there are many things that could be done if necessity required.'

Kenneth Kaunda told Wilson that his own police would prevent the ZAPU† crossing the Rhodesian border.

One of Wilson's big problems was getting the Javelins to Zambia

* Sir Humphrey Gibbs.
† Zimbabwe African People's Union.

44

from Cyprus. Egypt refused over-flying permission, so radar equipment had to be pre-positioned at Aden. The routes had to be through Turkey and Iran, all of which involved delay. The idea was, first, to fill up the Zambian airfields so that Egyptian MiGs could not land. The *Eagle* (stationed off Tanzania) came into the picture so that Sea Vixens could blow up the airfields if that eventuality arose.

About the Bay of Pigs. Wilson had had constantly in mind Suez, Cuba and the Bay of Pigs. But the Bay of Pigs and Suez happened because Kennedy and Eden were isolated and did not know what was going on. 'Kennedy didn't take personal care.' Every day he (Wilson) had been in full consultation. The Prime Minister must take charge of major operating, he said. 'Cecil King took charge of the Odhams takeover though he was surrounded by abler ministers than Bottomley,' he said. 'I run the economic front in the same way.'

'A criticism made against me is that had I threatened to use British troops I would have prevented U.D.I. Perhaps the criticism is justified.'

Wilson told me he is going to come out at the right time with his 'peace' terms for Rhodesia. 'I think I trust Smith but I couldn't deal with the thugs around him.'

I did not get the impression that Wilson was in any way perturbed. He said that it was not his intention, I repeat, to use British troops on Rhodesian soil unless he knew they would be unopposed. To 'invade' Rhodesia he said you would need at least a division.

What was worrying Kaunda, he said, was his left wing, and if Kaunda was removed everything would become much more difficult.

On Monday I had an urgent summons to lunch yesterday at No. 10. We met in the private flat upstairs at 1.15. Mrs Wilson, whom I like, was there but faded away and we had till 3 p.m. Wilson very friendly and far more confident than I am about the outcome of the Rhodesian affair. He repeated to me what he had said to Hugh on Friday – that the crucial factor in the situation, hardly referred to in public, is the economic one; Rhodesia could cut off power and coal from the Zambian copper mines, with disastrous results. Wilson said he is in touch with Smith and with the Commanders of the Rhodesian Army

45

and Air Force. He thinks the latter would obey Smith but would not obey Dupont, Lardner-Burke or any extremist. He says Smith had a very naive idea of what would happen as a result of U.D.I., and when he sees the country becoming unworkable there will be an opportunity for the moderates to group themselves round Campbell, who was High Commissioner in London and who has been keeping intentionally in the background. Clearly, every day that passes makes an amicable settlement more difficult. I continue to think, in spite of Wilson's optimism, that a move like U.D.I. is unlikely to be reversible and that, as time goes on, more extreme men will take over and that we shall have a measure of chaos in Central Africa. This will come some day anyway – over Angola, Mozambique and South Africa – but need not have come now. The Rhodesian Front would have been wise to stick to the 1961 Constitution and defy us to interfere. They could have continued to enjoy their high standard of living, anyway for a long time yet.

We talked about the Bank. I said I was impressed by Cromer and if that was the sort of man he wanted, he would not do better. He said, 'In fact there is no better Cromer than Cromer?' Of course, if a different policy was in mind, then a different kind of man would be appropriate. But even then, it might be as well to see if Cromer could be sold the new policy, as it would be easier for him to implement a new policy than a newcomer.

On leaving I was urged to accept a peerage – this is the fourth time of asking. I said I wanted no title; he said it wasn't a question of a title, but my voice should be heard in the House of Lords. This follows on Longford the other day saying I had turned up my nose at the House of Lords. Anyway, I said I would think about it.

Saturday, December 18th, 1965

A piece appeared in *The Economist* last week speculating on the position of the Governor of the Bank of England, Lord Cromer, whose term expires at the end of June. This is a long way off and it seems pointless to speculate on the future of the governorship at this early stage.

Monday, December 20th, 1965

Letter from Cecil King to Edward Heath:

PERSONAL

Dear Ted,

I am writing to say how much I enjoyed our time at Broadstairs yesterday.* I am sorry I had to leave at the interval, but we had far to go and much to do.

There has been some criticism of you among your Tory friends since you assumed the leadership of the Party. I don't think you need bother about this. You have a very difficult hand to play just now, but I am confident all will be well. Don't let your advisers persuade you to improve your image! It is right as it is.

With every good wish,

Yours sincerely,
Cecil King

The Rt. Hon. Edward Heath, P.C., M.B.E., M.P.,
F.2, Albany,
London, W.I.

Tuesday, December 21st, 1965

Warburg came to see me last night to talk about the Bank governorship. He thinks, under all the circumstances, Cromer should probably remain; failing him, then O'Brien with Parsons as deputy. I asked about George Bolton, but Warburg thinks he is too volatile.

Friday, December 24th, 1965

At lunch yesterday at No. 10 – alone with Wilson from 1.25 to 3.10 p.m. Wilson friendly, relaxed and confident. We talked about Rhodesia. He is quite confident he can bring down Smith and get him to talk terms. These would be less favourable than before U.D.I. His ideas are for direct British rule for an indefinite period, but of the order of ten years. There would be a multi-racial Cabinet from the start and a strenuous effort to educate the Africans up to the standards of literacy etc. required for self-government. He is in touch with

* Cecil King had been to Edward Heath's carol service.

47

Smith via the Governor and via the Vice-Chairman of the World Bank. He says that both Portugal and South Africa would rush to the aid of Smith if he seemed to be winning, but at the moment are dragging their feet, and South Africa seems to have blocked their funds. I said I thought the extremists would not allow Smith to give way; would put a bullet in him if necessary. Wilson says in that event the armed forces would support the Governor. He obviously has access to more information than I have, but I do not see Smith and his friends coming to heel.

Wilson was in Washington recently. He says the President looks thin and ill and works at a pressure which he thinks no man can stand. Johnson very friendly to Wilson, very unhappy about Vietnam. Wilson, with Johnson's approval, is trying to bring about peace talks.

Wilson going to Russia in February. I asked why? He says the initiative comes from the Russians. Because of Vietnam they cannot talk to the Americans, and perhaps wish to continue a dialogue with the West.

We talked about the Bank. Cromer's term of office ends in June but the directors are re-appointed from March 1st. So I suggested that the appointments should all be thought of together. Instead of launching out into the unknown over the governor, would it not be better to play safe over the governor and be adventurous over some new members of the Court?* In practice this would mean re-appointing Cromer (on balance, unlikely) or appointing Stevens – now in Washington – or Maurice Parsons. Of these, Stevens is the front runner at the moment. The only names for the Court that Wilson has suggested to me are Warburg and Poole.

Other points: Wilson said there would be an election in 1966. This is news: previously he has always said early 1967 at earliest.

He said that when he nominated Rab Butler to be Master of Trinity he was told all the Fellows would resign! There are a great many of them, but none has resigned – in fact Wilson says they have given Rab a great reception.

* The board of directors of the Bank of England is known as the Court.

48

1966

After a series of indications that the Labour Government's popularity was increasing, Harold Wilson, the Prime Minister, decided upon a General Election at the end of March. His judgment was justified by the results: the Labour Party was returned with a majority of nearly 100. The Queen's speech to the new Parliament said that the Government planned, amongst other things, to re-nationalize the steel industry and to provide a statutory basis for a prices and incomes policy; the latter issue, especially, was to prove contentious, and the movement in this direction was accompanied by considerable industrial unrest. In the event, very stringent deflationary measures, including a new pay-roll tax, a sur-charge on surtax, controls on private investment and foreign travel expenses and a freeze on wages, incomes and prices, managed, at least superficially, to limit balance of payments problems and restore the pound to apparent health. Beneath the surface, however, in the official and business circles in which Cecil King moved, rumours of impending devaluation continued. A major decision, announced in November, was that Britain should again seek entry in the European Economic Community – the Common Market.

Within the Commonwealth, the main concern continued to be the situation in Rhodesia. The British Government came under heavy pressure to act decisively against the Smith regime and, in spite of dramatic last-minute negotiations, was finally compelled to propose in the United Nations the introduction of mandatory economic sanctions against Rhodesia; the resolution was adopted in December. Border clashes between India and China continued, the 'confrontation' between Malaysia and Indonesia came to an end, and military coups took place in Nigeria and Ghana. In Europe, France attended a special meeting of Common Market foreign ministers in January, after a seven-month boycott of Common Market institutions. In July she finally achieved her objective concerning the financial regulation of the Market's agricultural policy, the issue on which the boycott had

51

commenced. The German Chancellor, Dr Ludwig Erhard was replaced by Dr Kurt Kiesinger in November, when the coalition government collapsed in the face of economic instability and apparently increasing isolation in foreign affairs. Further afield, United States involvement in Vietnam, which the British Government viewed with reserve, continued to escalate.

During the year, in addition to his other commitments, Cecil King was appointed a part-time member of the National Coal Board.

Monday, January 10th, 1966

Am in Paris for three days – with leisure to write about last week.

When I last saw Wilson I suggested a meeting of the really capable industrialists to get suggestions on making British industry more efficient. Brown, many months ago, had ignored this proposal, but Wilson took it up and arranged a dinner for the 6th. I was asked for suitable names and suggested a number. The party consisted of about twelve, half Jews and half Gentiles. Most of them were my suggestions but three I had not myself met – Schon of Marchon, Prichard of Perkins Diesel, and Thorn of Thorn Industries. The dinner was 7.45 for 8 p.m., but there was no serious discussion until we reached the Cabinet room at 9.50. It was late and several of the guests were tired. The party broke up at midnight, by which time everyone was tired. The two best performers were Beeching – now back at I.C.I.* – and Weinstock of G.E.C.† (much the youngest present). Nothing constructive emerged, but then Wilson did not conduct the meeting in a way that would have produced any useful result. He seemed pleased to have them all to dinner, pleased to find that some met each other for the first time, but that was about all.

At the end Wilson made a long, rambling speech, almost incoherent at times, talking about forming an industrial consultative group that would 'give a lead' – the usual verbal stuff with no hint of any action. He treated me as a guest of honour throughout and was very friendly. I asked him at dinner about his trip to Lagos (he is there now). He didn't want to go but felt it was the only way of keeping the Rhodesian situation in his hands. On Rhodesia he was as optimistic as ever. I still do not see how Smith will be allowed to give in – even if he wants to.

At the Bank on Thursday a crisis was revealed, of which no hint has leaked out. Callaghan has invited the Vice-Chairman of the New

* Imperial Chemical Industries Ltd.
† General Electric Company Ltd.

York Reserve Bank to see him. Cromer thinks this puts him in an impossible situation and has threatened to resign unless all negotiations with Central Banks go through his hands. On this issue Cromer is clearly right, but I feel it will almost certainly ensure his retirement in June.

Blankenhorn, the German Ambassador, came to lunch on Monday. It was a really interesting lunch. He says Erhard is a weak man, a bad politician, and will not last long. He will be succeeded by Barzel. He does not think Strauss will be a menace. He thinks both in Germany and in America there have been voices urging the primary importance of atomic weapons for Germany – and reunification. He does not think the Germans want atomic weapons. He thinks Germany needs a couple of generations of integration into a democratic peace-loving Europe before she can be relied on not to break out. For this reason English integration with Europe is essential. He regards de Gaulle as a misfortune Europe has to live through. His attempts to present France as a world power are naturally getting nowhere. No other part of de Gaulle's activities is sufficiently consistent to produce results.

Tuesday, January 11th, 1966

Was given lunch yesterday by Charles Gombault of *France-Soir*. Present: three of his senior editorial people plus Mendès-France, the best of the post-war French premiers, and Mitterand, de Gaulle's rival for the presidency in the recent election. Mendès-France throughout the lunch deferred to Mitterand and appeared to regard himself as a back number (though I understood him to say he was only fifty-eight). They agreed that de Gaulle has a passion for power that overrides every other consideration.

Peter Stephens, the *Mirror* correspondent in Paris, says that in the last resort he thinks the de Gaulle regime may be kept in office by force: though the President is quite free of any taint, his associates are corrupt and would go to any lengths to stay in power for fear of the consequences if they were out of office. The recent kidnapping and supposed murder of Ben Barka, a left-wing Moroccan political leader, by the Moroccan Minister of the Interior in a villa just outside Paris is an appalling example of what goes on. Ben Barka was

54

arrested by the French secret police and carried off to this villa where he was apparently murdered by the Moroccan Minister's own hand. De Gaulle was angry; the two police officers are held in prison; protests have been made in Rabat and there it is likely to remain. Why the French police should get embroiled in this way is not clear. One suggestion is that it is a quid pro quo for help from Morocco in the drug traffic. However that may be, it seems that no heads will roll as the French Minister of the Interior is involved and de Gaulle does not wish to change him. Meanwhile there are three lots of secret police, supposedly dealing with foreign espionage, but actually keeping an eye on anti-Gaullists. One group is responsible to de Gaulle; one to the Premier, Pompidou; and one to the Ministry of the Interior. They all engage in phone-tapping and all that.

Monday, January 17th, 1966

Before leaving Paris last week, I had lunch with Jean Monnet, for whom I have the greatest respect, and some affection. He does not think the General can wreck the Common Market. France benefits too much. The General's opposition to British membership is due to deep personal hostility to this country. He said de Gaulle is not interested in economics and therefore the economic side of the Market can carry on, but if the Market intervenes in political matters it restricts the General's powers and therefore he will have none of it. He regards the General as entirely self-centred and quite indifferent to anything but his own power and the maintenance thereof. Monnet wants Great Britain to call a meeting of European powers and to offer to share with them our nuclear know-how. I said the present Government would certainly not do this. I may say I was not at all sure it was a good idea anyway. But Monnet kept on returning to the idea, saying this would take the initiative from the French and would put us once again in the centre of the European picture. He belittled the importance of the Ben Barka affair, which has now grown still further by the alleged suicide of Figon, a witness of the actual murder.

Thursday, January 20th, 1966

George Brown to lunch. He was really at his best – warm, amusing,

55

energetic. He was coming next Thursday but brought the meal forward, it appears in order to tell me that Wilson is deciding to enter the Common Market! He has obviously been moving in this direction for some months but this is a big leap forward. It is apparently due to the India–Pakistan agreement arrived at in Tashkent* and the subsequent advice of John Freeman, our High Commissioner in Delhi. The Commonwealth provides no basis for a policy – so, into Europe.

I asked about the election. George is against a March election and says the alternative is, in effect, October. I suggested May or June, but George said this is not really practical politics, except in an emergency. I said I thought Wilson a bad administrator with a weak Cabinet. As time went on these facts would assert themselves, so it would be wise to go to the country as soon as possible. He said the Cabinet changes were so limited because Wilson has decided of set policy not to promote any of his young men! He says if he promoted any, the others would be jealous! On the other hand, of course, if he promotes none they will all be restive. He says Callaghan is in favour of reappointing Cromer, while George is strongly against. I wasn't quite clear about his position – he seemed to prefer Eric Roll if that was at all possible. On prices and incomes, George seemed not to see the situation in as gloomy a light as I do. He thought earnings had gone up 6 or 7 per cent, not 8 per cent (which is the official figure), and seemed to think productivity could be put up to $4\frac{1}{2}$ per cent and then all would be well. At the moment it is about 2 per cent, and more likely to fall than rise. The new Bill giving effect to the 'early warning' on price and wage increases will be published in February and is likely to lead to Frank Cousins's resignation.† George said that recently Frank had been quite impossible.

I asked about Rhodesia. The latest news seems to be that sanc-

* Concluding the 1965 India–Pakistan war.
† In 1965 the Labour Government had undertaken to introduce a so-called 'early-warning' system compelling unions to submit proposed wage claims to the Prices and Incomes Board for adjudication. Although a Bill was published before the General Election in March, it was not proceeded with, largely because of dissension in the Cabinet on the tense issue of Government intervention in wage negotiations. Eventually in July an amended Bill was published, giving the Government power to require wage, price and dividend increases to be submitted for review, and effectively imposing a four-month delay on any settlement. The Minister of Technology, Frank Cousins, resigned just before the publication of the Bill, on the grounds that the incomes policy was a 'contradiction of the philosophy upon which our party is based'. Before taking unpaid

tions are not bringing Smith down and that force will have to be used – from the middle of February. I said this would split the country. George said that Wilson was so committed to bringing Smith down that the failure to do so would destroy him. I said the unity of Great Britain was more important than Wilson. George evidently did not agree, but anyway hoped it would not come to that.

Friday, February 11th, 1966

Hugh Cudlipp had lunch with Wilson yesterday: Wilson very friendly and very confidential. The meeting lasted two hours and Wilson told all. The election is to be March 24th or 31st. The Cabinet has not yet been informed and the announcement will be made immediately on Wilson's return from Russia – I think on the 24th. The railway strike is being taken over by Wilson from last night. Wilson was planning to arrive at a settlement, which he has already worked out, by 5 a.m. on Sunday morning. Hugh told him that this, though dramatic, was bad timing, so the hour is to be 8 p.m. on Saturday to dominate the front pages of the Sunday papers! Why was he taking Frank Cousins to Russia with him? Was it to prevent him resigning just before the election? Precisely so.

Wilson is planning to take the country into the Common Market. George is scared of announcing this now as it might split the party. Wilson is not afraid of this and was planning to send Gerald Gardiner, the Lord Chancellor, to spread the glad news round Europe. Hugh objected that Gardiner was quite the wrong man to send – that he would not attract any publicity, so it is to be Callaghan. Gardiner was reluctant to go as his wife is dying of cancer and he wants to be with her as much as possible. This will give Wilson grounds for withdrawing his invitation to Gardiner. Rhodesia: Wilson is confident he can prevent this pot boiling over until after the election.

Friday, February 18th, 1966

Saw Wilson for forty-five minutes last night at the House of Commons. I thought he was tired and less buoyant than usual. He told

leave of absence to become an M.P. in October 1964, Frank Cousins had been General Secretary of the Transport and General Workers' Union, the largest trade union; after resigning his seat, he returned to his union and led the extra-Parliamentary opposition to the 'wages' aspects of the Bill.

me Mayhew had resigned as Minister for the Navy and Luce, the First Sea Lord, might well do the same. Mayhew is not objecting to the purchase of the American swing-wing planes but says that if we are to have a presence east of Suez we need a new carrier as well. I don't think these resignations will mean a thing; as Wilson said, there are far too many admirals, anyway.

It was plain that he intended to maintain our presence east of Suez though we cannot afford it and, anyway, are unable to cover this area in sufficient strength for it to mean anything.

I said I thought he would certainly win the election, though I doubted whether the swing to Labour would be nearly the 13 per cent in the public opinion polls. Wilson agreed and was not even quite sure he would win. The compelling reason for an election now is that Labour cannot get the 'early warning' legislation through this House and without such legislation the Prices and Incomes policy would be at a standstill. I didn't probe him on this point as he is always pretty off-hand about prices and incomes, regarding this as largely George Brown's province. He will not come out in favour of Europe before the election as this would split his party – two-thirds for, one-third against. He is, however, to send Callaghan round the European capitals involved asking about ways and means. The main problem, Wilson said, was imported food. The Common Market levy would add 65 per cent to the cost of imported Australian wheat and the result would be an increase in food prices of 7 per cent. This would cause trouble on the wages front, though the money saved on agricultural subsidies would be used to keep down the cost of living.

I expressed a low opinion of many of his ministers and the need for introducing new blood. He said he would have four vacancies (two of them Soskice and Griffiths, but he gave no inkling of the others). Would it be an idea to use the four vacancies to introduce young men – or to reduce the size of the Cabinet? I said why not eight vacancies and have four new young men and a smaller Cabinet, which would have room for additions later? But he said there could be no changes till after the election. I said Douglas Jay and Fred Lee were failures. He didn't defend them, nor did he suggest they may be going.

I asked about his trip to Russia next week. He doesn't know why they want him to come, but they are laying on a terrific reception, so presumably it serves their purpose in some way.

Crossman came to lunch yesterday. Unexpectedly he is becoming a rather good minister. He has courage and ideas, though how much will get done remains to be seen. He is appointing a Royal Commission to advise on the whole future of local government and asked me to sound Beeching on his willingness to accept the chairmanship. Subsequently it appeared that Beeching has far too much on his plate and cannot look at the job.*

Crossman says no decisions are made by the Cabinet. By the time matters reach the full Cabinet, they have gone beyond the point of no return. But he is enjoying himself getting on with his job.

He says the set-up in the House is very unsatisfactory – Bowden and Short (the Chief Whip) are little more than clerks and Silkin is the obvious man to have in charge of business. Here again Wilson likes to have nonentities around him.

Sunday, February 27th, 1966

It seems now to be agreed that the election is to be March 31st. I understood Wilson to say it would be announced immediately on his return from Russia on the 24th, but now it is expected tomorrow. For once his timing is at fault: it will be an anti-climax.

During the week, on Tuesday, I saw Heath at his flat – very friendly: he offered to come to me! I told him the election was to be the 24th or 31st and urged him to lay off attacking the Government either on its defence policy, in which it is moving, however timidly, in the right direction, or on Rhodesia, on which he is on weak ground. Why not stick to inflation, which is what will ultimately bring Wilson down? Heath argued that stressing the gravity of the financial situation would look like rocking the boat, while he was hoping to reunite his party on the other two issues.

As the two Governments are hardly on speaking terms, I thought it would be an idea to invite over thirty leading French editors to meet the leading British editors at I.P.C. expense. We started with

* The Commission was appointed under the chairmanship of Lord Redcliffe-Maud. See p. 324n.

seats at a Gala Performance of the Royal Ballet on Tuesday and ended on Friday with lunch at the Royal Academy to see the Bonnard exhibition. There were two days of serious discussion at the Café Royal and the whole thing went off very well. Both sides really got down to brass tacks and it seemed to some of us that we had started something. Many of the French editors had never met each other; some had never been to England. They certainly went away with a more favourable impression of us as Europeans than they came.

For quite different reasons, we are now organizing a German conference of a similar kind. The idea of this one is to bring Britain and Germany closer together and help overcome their present feeling that they are the pariahs of Europe. We might try another conference for the Iron Curtain countries later in the year.

Thursday, March 10th, 1966

The election is still in the future; only one or two preliminary shots have been fired. The Tory manifesto short and quite good; the Labour one long-winded. Heath on T.V. last night rather impressive.

However, two events may well leave a mark. The pound has been slipping these last few days for reasons that do not altogether appear. In spite of the Bank's support, the Rate has been going down. So last night I was summoned to the Bank, as were the other directors, to be told that the Governor had recommended an increase in the Bank Rate to 7 per cent (from 6 per cent) but that Callaghan would have none of this – partly on very understandable political grounds, and partly on other, vaguer, grounds that Cromer could not – or, anyway, did not – particularize. So we were all asked our opinion individually. I said I knew nothing of the banking aspect of this matter but that I was temperamentally in favour of acting sooner rather than later and, anyway, doing something rather than nothing. If the pundits at the Bank wanted an increase, and if it was the Court's statutory responsibility, I was ready to support the Governor. Any such action by the Bank in the middle of an election would, of course, be taken as an attempt by the Bank to influence the voters. However, I thought we could wear that one.

I was the last director to see Cromer and later he went on to see the Chancellor and Wilson. After *three* hours they refused to agree to the raise in the Rate and he gave in, advising us this morning that to string along with the Government would do sterling less harm than defying them. I said to one or two of them that I disagreed, and, at the meeting, that anyway I hoped we should make it plain if the policy failed that it was not ours. I gathered from Maurice Parsons that what with forward contracts falling in and spot money going out the loss this month might well be £200 million – and this is a good month.

We had a piece this morning in the *Mirror* attacking Frank Cousins who encourages his union to defy the Government's Prices and Incomes policy while he remains in the Cabinet. Apparently Wilson believes he is less dangerous inside the Government than outside – or he may merely be scared of firing him.

In the office, Hugh and I had reckoned that Wilson has four good ministers – Healey, Jenkins, Callaghan and Brown, in that order – and two that were fair – Crossman and Crosland. When I asked —— [a senior civil servant] yesterday whom he would name, he chose the same people in the same order. I asked him about Stewart, but he said he had been absorbed by his department and lost sight of. Anyway, he cannot stand up to Healey in Cabinet committees (which is what others say).

Sunday, March 20th, 1966

The election has, as yet, hardly got under way. Labour lead by about 12 per cent, which should mean a majority of a hundred and fifty or so, though I doubt this will materialize. Though Wilson is thought to be doing well, his campaign is not working out as he intended. I think he hoped to run it on his housing policy – many new houses, relief for mortgage interest, leasehold enfranchisement, and so on. This has hardly been mentioned. More and more the campaign is being fought on the Common Market and the need to curb the trades unions – the two issues I suggested to Heath should be put in the Conservative manifesto when he was asked to draw up a new one by Home.

The *Mirror* policy has been as critical of the Government as any paper, though we have not supported the Tories. How could we when we were hysterically pro-Labour at the last election only seventeen months ago? But my aim has been to break loose from any close connection with the Labour Party, as I think both on balance of payments and on Rhodesia Wilson is going to run into horrible trouble before the end of the year.

As I have mentioned earlier in this diary, I was told by George Brown that Wilson intends to join the Common Market. However, the Labour manifesto, with its pledge to continue deficiency payments for agriculture, seemed to rule out any serious negotiation. Nevertheless, Hugh was in touch with Jim Callaghan over an article for next Sunday. In the course of conversation, Jim said they were really taking the plunge. Wilson would give the green light in a speech at Bristol. Hugh asked Callaghan to ask Wilson to put in a phrase of a positive kind, suggesting some enthusiasm. In case this message didn't reach Wilson, who was in bed with a heavy cold, he sent a similar message to the P.M. via Trevor Lloyd-Hughes, the press man at No. 10. Then we all waited for the speech. It turned out to be the same old Gaitskellite guff: we would go in, if the terms were right. Complete independence in foreign policy and defence was to be insisted on, plus the right to buy food in the cheapest market; also no interference with Empire trade. None of these terms is available and it is hard to see what Wilson is playing at. He naturally got attacked for being anti Common Market in a speech which was supposed to represent the opposite.

At the Bank on Thursday Maurice Allen gave the usual monthly run-down on the economy. It seemed to me rather optimistic and I said so to him after the meeting. He said he had been as optimistic as he could – and, anyway, he was talking about the past, not the future. He said the latest (secret) Treasury estimate of the balance of payments was that it would be worse for 1966 than 1965 and that we should still be running a deficit in 1967. Nothing of this has leaked out: Callaghan is still promising a balance for this year and a start on repayment of debt next year. In fact it was on the strength of an undertaking to this effect that the last lot of borrowing was brought off.

As I think the outlook is pretty bleak, I thought it wise to see Heath this morning and tell him what Maurice Allen had said on Thursday and also about the tussle over the Bank Rate the previous

Thursday. Naturally Heath was very busy, but I had five minutes or so with him in his flat at the Albany. He seemed in good heart, though depressed that nothing he has to say about the perilous state of the economy is getting across.

At this moment in time – to use the current jargon – the outlook fills me with dismay. Wilson seems to me to have no administrative ability and his political ability is limited mostly to the Parliamentary scene, and then to very short-term tactics. No problem gets solved, but a great impression of decision and activity is created. Europe will be negotiated but without result, as Wilson and Stewart have neither the authority nor the ability to carry it through. What is so daunting is that his failure is likely to be evident while he still has a large majority in the House. Politicians are so discredited that there would be a warm reception to the Nigerian and Ghanaian idea. In their recent revolutions *all* politicians without exception have been sent packing!

Tuesday, March 22nd, 1966

Hugh [Cudlipp] had lunch with Callaghan in a private room at Brown's. Callaghan, though a fellow Welshman, did not impress. He says the Government is definitely going into the Common Market and that the pledges were only given to keep Barbara Castle and her friends quiet until after the election. Apparently Wilson thinks that after a successful election he will be able to eat any number of words with impunity. Frank Cousins wanted to resign after his return from Russia, but was persuaded to stay on and be Minister of Technology in the new Government. George Brown may not be in charge of the D.E.A.* and may well not have a place in the new Government at all.

Callaghan is determined to have a yes-man at the Bank and apparently thought of me in that role! He is now thinking of O'Brien.

C. said very little about the balance of payments; quite a bit about the Common Market, and quite a bit about ministers in the new Government. Gordon Walker's prospects are not good as Wilson regards him as someone with a hoodoo; nothing ever goes right for him. Hugh suggested Robens as a possible minister to negotiate our way into the Common Market and this seemed fairly acceptable.

* Department of Economic Affairs.

Wilson's attitude to us is that he is sure of a big majority and so hasn't to bother about the *Mirror*. At a later stage he will find – as Macmillan did – how impossible it is to govern with no press support.

Wednesday, March 30th, 1966

The election is nearly over, with polling tomorrow. I think the general opinion is that Heath increased his stature in the last three weeks, while Wilson lost some of his. The newspapers have been contemptuous of the show put up by the politicians: the opinion polls indicate a large majority for Labour – 120 or so.* The figures can justify any guess from 20 to 200, but I am hoping for not more than 80. We have had no word from Wilson since the election was announced – a contrast to the almost tearful requests for help last time. I take this to mean that he knows he is going to win the election and is showing us where we get off.

We have come out for Wilson at the end, after being very critical in the early stages. This is attributed to my friendship with Heath, but, of course, has quite other reasons. Wilson in seventeen months has shown his lack of the qualities needed in a prime minister – particularly foresight and administrative ability. I think he will lead the country into a frightful mess, and our constitution does not provide for a situation in which a prime minister with a large majority leads the country astray. But I think the voter feels that seventeen months with a majority of two is not a fair break for Labour and they should have a longer period in office with an adequate majority. Unfortunately, our electoral system is so highly geared that a small majority of votes can lead to a large majority of seats.

Wednesday, April 6th, 1966

The names of Wilson's new Cabinet came out last night. The two fresh names are Cledwyn Hughes (Secretary for Wales) and Richard Marsh (Minister of Power). I have thought well of Marsh for some time and encouraged him to stay in politics when he looked like seeking a job outside. I have done this for three men – Robens,

---

* In the event, the result of the election on March 31st was: Labour, 363; Conservative, 253; Liberal, 12; Republican Labour, 1; Speaker 1. Thus the Labour Party had an overall majority of 97, after the lowest poll (76 per cent) since 1954.

George Brown (both in 1954), and Marsh about four years ago. Events seem to have justified my choice!

Though Wilson has kept on Lee, Bottomley, Greenwood, Jay and a number of duds, this Government is better than I had expected. The new administrative arrangements are not impressive: George at the D.E.A. to be in charge of the economic aspects of the Common Market, while Thomson at the F.O. deals with the political aspects. George at the D.E.A. is in overall charge of prices and incomes, but the day-to-day administration is left to Gunter, Jay and Peart. Neither of these compromises will work.

Pickering of I.P.C. had some talk with Taverne last night. He was just back from 10 Downing St and said the *Daily Mirror* campaign had lost the Labour Party 750,000 votes. The same figure was given to Hugh by Trevor Lloyd-Hughes, so evidently this is Wilson's estimate.

John Beavan saw him this morning to arrange an interview for tomorrow. Wilson very friendly; sent nice messages to Hugh [Cudlipp]; said he was writing to me and has agreed – at my invitation – to speak at the Jubilee Dinner of the N.P.A.* So evidently our Harold knows on which side his bread is buttered!

David Bruce to lunch on Monday. We get on very well. He said he thought Wilson was over-optimistic if he thought Johnson would back the pound more or less unconditionally in return for verbal support over Vietnam. He thinks the Northern Vietnamese and the Chinese are playing their cards extraordinarily badly. If only they would come to the conference table, they would inevitably get what they want. He said he wished he was political adviser to the Chinese Government! He would have the Americans out of Asia in no time. He said the American Government is desperate to get out of Vietnam, but for reasons of prestige cannot just walk away.

Reggie Maudling here to lunch. An intelligent man and a nice one – I like him; but no comparison with Ted Heath as a Conservative leader. Realized that the old Eton and Brigade of Guards image just won't do, and that the future lies with Tories of the Heath, Maudling, Macleod, du Cann type. As I expected, no hint of dissatisfaction with the leadership provided by Ted.

* Newspaper Proprietors' Association.

On April 13th Harold Wilson sent Cecil King a hand-written letter from Scilly. It was to express, 'with the very warmest thanks', his appreciation of the 'tremendous help' the Mirror group provided in the election. 'The Mirror with inevitably a more subtle approach than in 1964, came through magnificently, just at the right time.' There was certainly no indication in the letter that this subtle approach could have cost the Labour Party 750,000 votes.

Friday, April 15th, 1966
Letter from Cecil King to Harold Wilson:

Dear Harold,

Thank you for your very generous letter of the 13th.

It had been clear for some months that if there was an Election you could be returned with a good majority.

The more restrained support we gave you on this occasion was partly due to misgivings over the implementation of the Prices & Incomes Policy, partly due to misgivings over your European attitude, and partly due to the wish to avoid a landslide which would leave you with an unwieldy majority and no effective opposition.

Hoping to see you before I leave for Australia on the 27th.

Yours very sincerely,
Cecil King

The Rt. Hon. Harold Wilson, P.C., O.B.E.,
10, Downing Street,
Whitehall, S.W.1.

Tuesday, April 19th, 1966
Had an hour with the P.M. at No. 10. Was asked for the first time to go in through the Cabinet office in Whitehall. This reminds me of Wilson when he was Leader of the Opposition; he liked leaving the *Mirror* office in my car, a Rolls Royce, but always got out before he reached the House and on the journey wore spectacles!

Wilson, cheerful as ever, says Smith is now the prisoner of his wilder men. They want him to step up the transition to a police state. Wilson has had various emissaries in Salisbury. They have seen the

Secretary to the Cabinet, but not Smith. I said I didn't see what 'talks' could be about. There can be no compromise between white and black supremacy – only negotiations on timing, and this he had been offered before. So far from moving towards a negotiating position, he was moving away by his efforts to diminish the very small educational facilities for Africans. Wilson is trying to persuade Verwoerd to reduce supplies of oil to Smith – pointing out that if he is not careful, he will bring the United Nations down on him.

The Prices and Incomes policy does not seem to be going all that well in the trades union world, so Wilson is going to go round the annual conferences of the big unions and plug Prices and Incomes. I said this would have no effect on the employers unless restrictive practices were attacked in the Government sphere. He said things are really moving in the B.B.C., where some time ago they were told they could not have an increase in the licence fee and have since been cutting out some of the fat.

About Europe, he said he thought we should be in in two to three years. The negotiating would be done by Thomson and not by George Brown. He said the F.O. wants to support the Five against France. He does not want to take sides, particularly as the French are intent on maintaining a separate foreign and defence policy, which fits in best with British (i.e. Wilson's) ideas. Of course, the whole picture would change when de Gaulle goes.

The main impression left by Wilson is of an optimist basking in a sun of his own imagining.

We talked about the Bank: clearly Cromer is not going to be re-appointed. The three candidates are O'Brien, Parsons, and Stevens – I should say in that order. I put the case for Parsons.

Jim Callaghan came to lunch. Obviously full of doubts on what to do about the economy. He raised the question of the Bank and implied, as Harold had not, that Cromer might be reappointed. I don't take this seriously.

Jim, in general, much less euphoric than Wilson; inclined to gloom, in fact. In parting, he asked if I had found Wilson in a mood to make decisions. So this lack of decisiveness on Harold's part is brought up once more.

Monday, April 25th, 1966

On Thursday, at the Bank meeting, Kindersley rose and said he had called on the Chancellor, with Babington Smith, to express their views about the governorship, as Cromer had written a letter before the election saying he wished to return to private life. Clearly Cromer could have been induced to stay but knowing the form preferred to resign. By writing his letter before the election (it could always have been destroyed) he put himself in the clear. O'Brien is to be governor and Parsons, deputy. Probably it would have been best to keep Cromer on, but in view of his relationship with Wilson, this was hardly practical. The outsiders were, rightly, eliminated.

Tuesday, May 10th, 1966

Am in Melbourne after a week in Sydney and a day in Canberra.

I have not yet seen any of the English papers on the Budget. The principal changes were the restriction on investment in the sterling area and the pay-roll tax at 25s. per man per week, less a rebate of 32s. 6d. on any men engaged in manufacture.* Corporation Tax is to be 40 per cent, which is higher than was originally expected. At this distance, it does not look a very bright idea. It will undoubtedly put up prices and hence wages. Any effect in pushing employment into manufacturing out of services will be marginal, and it increases still further the complications of the business world, which is still battling with the Corporation Tax and the Capital Gains Tax from last year. This looks to me like the Hungarians again.† The main problems facing the Government are what to do about the fast-rising wage bill. This is left untouched: the modernization of the

* The idea of this tax, officially known as the Selective Employment Tax, or S.E.T., was partly to raise revenue and partly to move labour from service industry into manufacturing. For this purpose, the tax, after collection, was refunded with a bonus to manufacturing industry, and without a bonus to certain other industries such as agriculture and the nationalized industries. Services which suffered most included the distributive trades, entertainment and hotels, professional services such as accountancy, and clerical staffs, even in industry.

† The 'Hungarians' were two Budapest-born economists, Dr Nicholas Kaldor from Cambridge, who joined the Cabinet Office as economic adviser particularly concerned with external trade, and Dr Thomas Balogh from Oxford, who became special adviser to the Chancellor of the Exchequer on economic and social aspects of taxation. Their appointment as advisers created some controversy in 1964.

trades unions is only a subject for speeches. So presumably inflation will continue and the mess we are in will worsen.

Friday, May 27th, 1966

Events at home are quite dramatic. The seamen have in fact struck and, after a week's delay, a State of Emergency has been declared. No steps have been taken under the emergency – presumably, to allow a breathing space for negotiation. The Government has been so weak with railwaymen, postmen, doctors and whatnot, that they evidently felt they had to stand and fight at last. But the seamen are not numerous and their strike can do an infinity of damage. I should have thought the Government has chosen to fight – or been forced to fight – on unattractive ground.

The Budget proposals were kept a total secret and there was no leak on the pay-roll tax. The impression seems to be that it was rushed and had far more snags than the Government realized. They also seem surprised by the vehemence of the opposition and the loss of Parliamentary time. Last year Wilson told me the Cabinet had no idea of the problems involved in the Corporation Tax, and the consequent length of the Finance Bill. He was going to insist on a very short Bill this time. Instead, we have a third innovation in two Budgets – with Inland Revenue clerks already threatening to go on strike because of the overwork involved in the Capital Gains Tax!

Friday, June 10th, 1966

Denis Healey to lunch. I hadn't seen him for two months and wanted to check up. He said the seamen's strike was unavoidable – Hogarth, the General Secretary of the National Union of Seamen, had been in favour of accepting the employers' offer and was overruled. The issue will now have to be fought out. He said the Cabinet was given no hint of S.E.T. until the day before the Budget. It was only known to Callaghan, the P.M. and George Brown. Denis made no attempt to support it. I told him I thought the main issue before the Government was how to keep wage increases within the productivity increases. The latest figures dealing with the end of last year were wages up $9\frac{1}{2}$ per cent; productivity up 2 per cent. If this continued to be true, the pound would be devalued, Wilson and Callaghan discredited, and the man who would emerge would be Denis. He said he had no ambition in that direction, thought Wilson would last, and that his ultimate successor might well be Dick Marsh, whom he has known since he was a tea-boy at Transport House. Denis was anti Common Market, but says we are all Common Marketeers now; that the new hymn is 'Inward, Christian Soldiers'! He doubts whether we can actually join while de Gaulle is around – i.e. for three or four years. In the meantime we are improving relations with the Five, notably with Germany.

I don't think Denis has any high opinion of Harold Wilson, but he is scrupulous in not making any criticism himself. At the same time, some of my more critical remarks passed unchallenged.

Sunday, June 19th, 1966

Two items since my last entry: Marsh to lunch on Monday and Hugh Cudlipp's talk with Wilson on Tuesday.

Marsh has taken on Fuel and Power and the Steel Bill, an enormous area of administration for a complete beginner. I am a great believer in Marsh. I must say I was encouraged by my lunch: he certainly has all the right ideas (including contempt for George Woodcock). The actual occasion for the meal was to offer me a part-time membership of the Coal Board – mainly for me to act as a counterweight to Robens, who intimidates the present members.

Denis Healey was forecasting Marsh as a future P.M. If politics continue on their present course, this is a distinct possibility – but will they? Marsh was strictly loyal to Wilson, but his general criticisms of the administration showed he has no illusions about him.

Nothing concrete emerged from Hugh's talk with the P.M. He was friendly, and as optimistic as usual. There was nothing much to say about Rhodesia or the shipping strike, except that the Government would stand firm. He was mainly concerned about the back-bench revolt on the east of Suez policy, which he reckoned to crush at the Parliamentary Party meeting on Thursday – as he did. This, however, was more by asserting his authority as P.M. than by the strength of his arguments.

Monday, June 20th, 1966

Ted Heath to lunch today. I am beginning to see what people mean when they call him cold. He is not cold, but he is certainly not forth-coming, when he has every reason to be just that.

He agreed that Wilson is a disaster and thinks the estimate of the crash coming in somewhere between three months and three years too long. It cannot come in three months, or be postponed for as much as three years.

Sunday, June 26th, 1966

Wilson sent for Cudlipp this week to tell him about the Communist manipulation of the seamen's strike. The whole episode was rather odd. Without any warning, Wilson announced in the House that the seamen were organized by 'a politically motivated group'. It was all 'my lips are sealed' kind of stuff. He afterwards met the lobby correspondents and told them a little more, and then it was time for Cudlipp's visit. Wilson's information, presumably from the Special Branch, was that a group of three Communists meets every morning to run the strike.

Wilson has been much criticized by his own people for this 'Red smear' and has promised to give the names on Tuesday. It appears that only Gunter knew he was going to make his statement, which is generally thought unwise.

Meanwhile, Cudlipp thought it might be an idea if I wrote Wilson a long letter – not in any hope that it would bring about a change of heart, but to have my position on record. I will file a copy of the letter with this diary. It is, by implication, exceedingly critical. I find that most well-informed people in the financial and industrial world expect a crash later this year. When I say some time between three months and three years, they think the longer period quite out of the question. I find these things usually take longer than is expected, but I cannot see Wilson surviving his five years. It is astonishing how much his prestige has dropped in the short time since the election.

Letter from Cecil King to Harold Wilson, dated 25th June:

My dear Harold,

You may think we have been drifting apart and that the support

71

you have been having in our papers is less enthusiastic than it used to be. So I am writing this letter to show you how things look to a friendly outsider who wants you to emerge as a great Prime Minister. I am sure you have the same wish to be a great servant of our country, but you may not see as clearly as I do the dismaying effects of any lack of success on your part in attaining such a goal.

Already people are talking of a British de Gaulle or a National Government. These are counsels of despair and surely show the urgent need for you to become the man of the hour.

1) Your Government will stand or fall by its ability to control wages and so inflation. Until this is done – and it must be done some time by someone – no British Government can have a consistent domestic policy nor an independent Foreign Policy. We have given all the support in our power to your Prices and Incomes Policy, but this has not so far had any success in the control of incomes, and only limited success in the control of prices – and the latter, without the former, is worse than nothing. Clearly your policy quite rightly began on a voluntary basis, but experience with the same policy in the time of Stafford Cripps and of Selwyn Lloyd showed that a voluntary control of incomes would only work for a short time and under favourable circumstances. Early last year I offered the opinion both to George Brown and to yourself that a measure of coercion should be worked out to stiffen up the Incomes Policy as soon as it began to flag. I also was – and am – strongly of the opinion that this policy must be supported by a powerful propaganda campaign on T.V. and in the newspapers. It must be brought home to every man and every woman how important your policy is to her shopping basket and his pay packet. At present it seems to be thought in many quarters a whimsical hobby of George Brown's. It would be of enormous help if you would put your great personal prestige and that of your office behind this campaign.

2) The Common Market. This is not the best British foreign policy – it is the only one. I quite see that any definite moves are out for the time being, but feel that in the meantime much may be done to show the Continentals that we feel we are a part of Europe, and to instruct our own people in the nature and consequences of this great change in our outlook – the greatest for centuries.

3) Our continued presence in Arabia and South-East Asia is an anachronism – and one we cannot afford. It does not matter what is said by any English Government, we shall have to pull out of South-East Asia, (a) because we have no vital interests there any longer and (b) because we have not got the resources to stay. When we pull out and how we pull out are open to discussion, but not whether. You are, I know, running down our commitments there, but this is too slow in view of the alarming state of our Balance of Payments.

4) Your policy on Rhodesia is clearly the only possible one – though unlikely to be a clear-cut success. So, as I advised you last year, I thought – and think – it a mistake (a) to involve your personal prestige in a happy outcome of a dangerous situation which has been building up for forty years or (b) to raise hopes – which were always likely to be disappointed – of any early and honourable settlement.

5) A Prime Minister's job is mostly administrative and the machine is too big to be run by any one man. So it is important not to fall into the trap that Macmillan, Eden, and Home fell for, by trying to be Foreign Secretary as well as P.M. The result was that the country had a part-time Foreign Secretary in No. 10 and no P.M. And this brings me to another point – that your success depends on the administrative abilities of your team. While some are great successes, and some don't matter, there are others with offices far beyond their capacities – I refer, in particular, to Michael Stewart, Douglas Jay, Frank Cousins, Barbara Castle, and Arthur Bottomley. They may be great Parliamentarians – I don't know – but as Ministers in charge of departments they just won't do. It is also perhaps hard for you to realise the damage done to your administration by the employment of Mr Kaldor – or the loss of Lord Beeching. There is said to be much excellent material on your back benches, and even if some of your young men were failures – to have tried them out would enhance your prestige.

6) But above all, what the country needs is leadership – a clear account of what sacrifices you demand of the country, and firm decisive action in implementing the policy you have decided on. You are master of the House of Commons – you can equally be master of the country if you will tell us all what we are to do and put the implementation into the hands of people who can carry it through.

73

We, at I.P.C., can be a great help and are very willing to be just that, but you are the conductor of the orchestra: we are only one of the players.

With my good wishes,

Yours very sincerely,
Cecil King

The Rt. Hon. Harold Wilson, O.B.E., M.P.,
10, Downing Street,
London, S.W.1.

In a letter of June 27th Harold Wilson replied to this letter of the 25th. He said that he was 'most grateful' to Cecil King for writing 'so fully on the problems as you see them'. He suggested a meeting, which was duly arranged.

Thursday, June 30th, 1966

After Court, a long talk with Maurice Allen. I sought his opinion, to be fortified for my lunch with Wilson on Monday. Allen says (1) the latest figures coming up are worse than ever and (2) that our reserve figures are faked, thanks to the co-operation of the Americans – a very powerful weapon they hold over our heads. I asked what should be done. He said in default of some large increase of productivity, of which there is no sign or likelihood, the Government should (1) run down its overseas commitments much faster than it is doing, (2) enforce a wage freeze, (3) introduce control of imports. A wage freeze by itself just now would not be enough, as it would not operate quickly enough, and we have, at most, eighteen months. I said I saw no chance of this Government eating its words to the required degree, and that therefore I was thinking of the post-Wilson period, which frankly appalled me. He said he had had the Governor of a Central Bank in his room yesterday who had politely said just that. I said I had foretold a crash at some period between three months and three years from now, but my informants thought three years was much too far away and three months was more like it. Allen seemed to think nothing drastic would happen this year, but he thought it out of the question for us to carry on as we are for three years.

74

Friday, July 1st, 1966

My first day at the Coal Board and, later, —— [a senior civil servant] to lunch. Last night at the Bank reception to say farewell to Rowley Cromer, where I met Eric Roll and exchanged a word with the P.M. Roll was saying how necessary it is for some *strategic* thinking. When can we have dinner together? I thought the P.M. and Mrs Wilson looked tired, but that was about all. Ruth [King] was horrified – she said Wilson looked a broken man – bigger, warmer and nicer, but he now knows he can't do it.

Tuesday, July 5th, 1966

My lunch with Wilson yesterday lasted one and a half hours, and was a deep disappointment. I didn't feel I got through to him at all; that I had been invited as a flattering gesture to keep me quiet. Though Cabinet changes consequent on the departure of Cousins had been announced on Sunday, he made no reference to these. I said I should have thought it better to dismiss Cousins rather than wait for him to resign – at a moment selected by him, not Wilson. Wilson said that, nevertheless, Cousins had resigned at a moment altogether convenient for him (Wilson). This is clearly nonsense. The gist of my letter, and of our talk, was the necessity to control wage increases if the country is to be got back on the rails. I reminded him that at the beginning of last year I had urged on him the necessity of thinking up some kind of teeth to put in the Prices and Incomes policy. Now the 'early warning' Bill has been published and is likely to become law by about December. As a measure it will be ineffective and is in line with the usual motto of successive British governments – too little and too late. Wilson said the Government had been thinking of a wage freeze; how was it to be implemented? I said I supposed either a tax or a court order. He said he preferred the former and I agreed – in fact I had gone into the matter last year and had been given to understand that a sort of surtax could be made to work. This would involve taking in tax the whole of any wage increase that had not been approved by the Prices and Incomes Board.

I said that at the present rate his Government might scramble through this year, but not next. Wages were up 10 per cent and productivity 2 per cent; the deficit for this year was serious and there would be one for next year. Much had to be done and soon. Apart from a possible wage freeze, Wilson merely said he did not accept the Bank's figures.

On Europe he said he was more hopeful than he had seemed in public and thought we should be in in two years or less. I interpreted this as soft soap to please me.

He said the present talks on Rhodesia were initiated by Smith and are getting nowhere. He plans, before the Commonwealth Prime Ministers' Conference in September, to have stated publicly his terms for Rhodesia on a take it or leave it basis. If the terms are rejected, which is likely as Smith is in the hands of his extremists, Wilson will transfer the sovereignty of Rhodesia to the United Nations and wash his hands of the whole business – more or less what I advised him to do in 1964.

I said I had written to him in a state of considerable alarm. His fall should not bother me as I am not a member of the Labour Party, but when I came to contemplate the post-Wilson possibilities, I was so alarmed I thought I should write. To this there was no reaction! Actually what bothers me most is that Parliamentary prestige is at a very low ebb and we cannot carry on like this without a demand for a dictatorship, which might be a great success in the short term, but which we should ultimately come to regret.

He was very ready to talk about the seamen's strike, which he claimed to have stopped. He also said he had the Communists on the run.

Relations with the U.S. are not so good, as Johnson does not like criticism and Wilson felt constrained to dissociate himself from the Americans over the bombing of Hanoi. Johnson has been urging us to send troops to Siam to contain the guerrillas there, but this we have declined to do.

The one spark of realism that came into the whole discussion was when he said he had suggested to Callaghan for inclusion in the Budget a proposal for a teenagers' tax, the money to be collected and credited to them and payable on marriage or at twenty-one. He didn't know what had happened to the idea, but he had heard no more about it.

In my conversation with Wilson he seemed to be trying to make me say that what we wanted was a dose of unemployment: that if we had a hundred men for ninety-five jobs productivity would be better than having a hundred men for a hundred jobs. I said what we wanted at the moment was a hundred men for a hundred jobs, and not a hundred men for a hundred and fifteen jobs, which is what we seem to have in the part of industry known to me. In the printing industry productivity agreements are more possible when surplus workers are sure to get other work immediately, than when there is unemployment. I didn't try pontificating about sections of industry of which I know nothing and stuck to the experience derived from Reed's and I.P.C.

Whitelaw came to lunch. I like him. In spite of a rather naive appearance, a very shrewd and capable human being. We agreed on the foolishness of Heath in trying to down Wilson in a verbal exchange, but Whitelaw thinks he would be a superb prime minister. A lot of criticism comes into the Central Office from party workers – mostly inspired by the *Daily Express*, which is their favourite reading. Though Max [Aitken] appears to think his paper is pro-Heath, it is in fact viciously anti – partly a left-over influence of Beaverbrook and partly the influence of Derek Marks, the editor, who is an old friend of Maudling.

Mike, with two other journalists, had an hour each yesterday with Pompidou and Couve de Murville (Foreign Minister), who are here on a state visit. They both made it clear that there is no prospect of admitting Britain to the Common Market at this stage. They are not convinced that the Government means business, and there is no question of us joining while we are so deeply in hock to the Americans. They would like to have us in as a set-off to the Germans, but only when we have given evidence that we don't want to join just to break it up and that we shall become loyal members on the lines already laid down. That Wilson is not really very keen is true, but the suspicion that we should join as a sort of wooden horse to betray Europe to the Americans is a constantly recurring theme from the French but has no substance.

Wednesday, July 6th, 1966

Pat Blackett to lunch. He is now President of the Royal Society, but works part-time at the Ministry of Technology. He liked Cousins but evidently found him very difficult. Cousins hates the House of Commons and makes no attempt to disguise or modify the fact. Some of his speeches begin rather well but are apt to break off into gibberish. He spent long hours communing with himself in an attempt to decide whether or no he should resign. On the whole Blackett thought the ministry was doing a good job – it had saved the computer industry – and could perform useful functions in industry, such as the reduction of the number of manufacturers of transformers to one-third of what it is now.

Saturday, July 16th, 1966

On Wednesday, at I.P.C.'s annual general meeting, I made a speech on the same lines as my letter to Wilson. It was run in full in the *Mirror* and *Sun*, and extracts appeared in the other papers on Thursday. What was my astonishment to get a message from Wilson on Thursday evening congratulating me on the speech, which he described as 'quite first-class'! But for one or two minor points he said he agreed with it all! As the gist of it was an attack on Wilson as P.M., I was at first completely baffled. But subsequent events seemed to show that there was a crucial Cabinet meeting on Thursday morning and that my blast had been useful ammunition for Wilson in his battle with his opponents (mainly George Brown, it is said). This is so typical of Wilson – not to bother about what I was trying to say, but seeing the immediate usefulness of my speech in a current argument.

Last night I had John Stevens to dinner. He is the Treasury Representative in Washington and is over to brief Wilson on his forthcoming visit to Johnson. He had seen Wilson twice yesterday and was quite up to date. He said Johnson had made it clear to Wilson that the pound was not to be devalued and no drastic action east of Suez was to be undertaken until after the American elections in November. In return the pound would be supported by the Americans to any extent necessary. Wilson's statement dissociating himself from the bombing of Hanoi and Haiphong had not been particularly resented, but Denis Healey's statement that we are hoping to sell bombs to the U.S. on condition that they are not used in Vietnam had roused Johnson to fury and to send a message to Wilson that

the Americans were not a 'bunch of Pakistanis', this last put through the British Embassy on the Telex machine!
Later
A call from Hugh Cudlipp to say the statement of the Government's new measures is to be made on Wednesday afternoon. This is apparently because of the continuing run on the pound on Friday. It seems extraordinary that the Government did not realize the situation would not hold for a fortnight. Now any measures agreed on are likely to be rushed – and, as a result, ill thought out.

He also passed on a message from the P.M., sent before he left for Moscow, that (1) the situation is under control, (2) he and the Government really mean business and (3) much of this stems from, and is thanks to, Cecil King's speech.

We take this to mean 'Don't attack me until you hear what I have to say on Wednesday'. The criterion will be what, if anything, he does about wage inflation.

Monday, July 18th, 1966

Was asked to call at the Bank and have a word with the Governor and did so at 4 p.m. O'Brien had seen Callaghan and the P.M. on Friday, and George Brown on Saturday. The gist of his conversations on Friday was that money was flowing out fast and that unless something drastic was done soon, they could say goodbye to the exchange rate of the pound. This had the effect of bringing forward to next Wednesday the date when an announcement is to be made. Various items of a package deal were discussed: £100 million off nationalized industry expenditure and, therefore, presumably mainly off power stations; £100 million – afterwards cut to £55 million – off overseas expenditure; use of the Regulator;* a tighter squeeze on hire purchase; and a strengthening of the 'early warning' Bill to amount perhaps to a wage freeze.

When O'Brien saw George on Saturday, George was all for devaluation on Wednesday: devaluation or he would resign. There was to be no more deflation without devaluation. In the P.M.'s absence,

---

* The Chancellor of the Exchequer was able to increase or decrease certain taxes by up to 10 per cent at short notice, in order to 'regulate' the economy. An increase of 10 per cent would, for example, be anti-inflationary, in theory at least.

George has been trying to rally support in the Cabinet for his view. The P.M., on the other hand, has deputed Balogh to tell ministers of the objections to devaluation. George told O'Brien that there was no chance of Wilson coming forward with an adequate package. In any case, O'Brien said the opposition in the Cabinet to an adequate package would be fairly formidable. He said it was clear that George was hoping to use this occasion to oust Wilson – presumably to replace him by George himself – a move that is grossly premature and one that would not operate to George's benefit anyway.

Saturday, July 23rd, 1966

Well, we had the package on Wednesday. The Regulator in use; surtax up; H.P. terms stiffened again; purchase tax up 10 per cent and so on. But on the crucial issues, not so good. No check to social services – school meals the same, prescriptions the same. The cut in Government spending to be £100 million, and on nationalized industries £95 million. Overseas expenditure to be cut by £100 million, but no details and no date. Finally, a six-month wage freeze and a twelve-month price and dividend freeze. So at the Bank on Thursday opinion was that the package was more severe than had been expected and no one was prepared to say positively it would not work. But no one, on the other hand, believed it would work. The crucial issues are (1) how to stop soaring wages and (2) how to reduce the Government's overseas expenditure. The six-month wage freeze will do nothing effective about the first and nothing much is being done about the second. The reasons for the Government's negative policy on these two issues: fear of the trades unions on the one hand; subservience to Johnson, at least until the November elections, on the other.

In spite of this package there was further selling of sterling on Thursday and the situation still looks pretty dicey.

On Thursday evening the N.P.A. gave a dinner with the P.M. as the guest of honour. As Chairman of the N.P.A. I was the host and sat between the P.M. and Mrs Wilson, with Ruth the other side of Wilson. She had not had any conversation with him since we spent part of the day with them at Chequers over a year ago. R. saw a marked deterioration – fatter, worried, more bewildered, and so *small*.

In spite of the gruelling week W. had had, he was just the same, apparently living as usual in cloud-cuckoo-land. Having been caught – with his whole Government – in a gigantic miscalculation in public, he appeared to shrug the whole thing off. The fact that the pound is still very uncertain would seem to show that this Government has entirely lost the confidence of the financial pundits of the world. The *Mirror* in public – and myself in private – have been very critical of Wilson, but he thanked both Cudlipp and me for being helpful! I don't see myself how Wilson and his Government can recover from the shock they have had. I expected trouble, but not so soon, and so supposed they would get through this year. But they are in such bad trouble and still have the worst five months to go.

Sunday, July 24th, 1966

Had lunch at Much Hadham with Mark Norman. Among other guests was Louis Franck, chairman of Samuel Montagu, and regarded as one of the ablest of the merchant bankers. He had recently been on a round of Central Banks – Belgium, Holland, France, Switzerland and Germany. This was an unofficial visit, with two others – but at the behest of the Bank of England. He said there is bound to be another crisis this year. He had thought, like me, that the first one would be later this year and the second next year, but the first has come so early, the second is certain to come before 1967. He said our reserves have now all gone and we are operating on borrowed money – moreover, all the money borrowed recently has to be repaid in gold.

I have only met Franck once before – at lunch at Montagu's. He seemed to know a lot about me, and said that some future government would have to have a large business element. In such a government he foresaw prominent places for Robens and myself.

Franck commented on the fact that the pound had not recovered after the announcement of Wilson's package. He said the previous selling must have been by people who held sterling – not speculators.

Tuesday, August 2nd, 1966

Spent an hour with Ted Heath this morning – at his request. Mike had lunch with him yesterday. The principal item that emerged from the lunch was that Pompidou had come over here with an invitation in his pocket for a State visit of the Queen. But he was so disgusted with his reception by Wilson that the invitation was never extended! He and Couve de Murville returned to France convinced that Wilson does not mean business over joining the Common Market. Ted was depressed, but seemed to me out of touch. He opined that if Wilson fell his successor might be Michael Stewart or Gunter! I should have thought neither of these has an earthly. Ted had had a good relationship with Cromer and knew more or less what was going on, but he does not know O'Brien. He was – I believe correctly – under the impression that our financial situation is a good deal worse than we have been allowed to know.

Thursday, August 4th, 1966

The morning spent, as usual, at the Bank. At the beginning, before we entered the Court room, I asked O'Brien whether the statement on Tuesday, that our reserves had fallen by £25 million, was put out by the Bank or the Treasury. He said it was the Treasury. I said I was relieved as the announcement was greeted with derision by every newspaper except one (the *Guardian*). O'Brien said the alternatives were dissimulation or panic. At Court and after, there was more talk on the subject, from which it appeared that there was much criticism of this figure at the C.B.I.* and the N.E.D.C.† meetings yesterday. O'Brien said it had been a very bad week, but that the exchange situation had eased after the announcement. Robens was very critical and I said I thought lies were dangerous, as some day you will need to be believed and will only be laughed at. Market guesses went up to £200 million, but I rather gathered from the figures we were given that something like £80 million went out last week. If this guess is correct the total must be more than £200 million.

Friday, August 5th, 1966

The daily and Sunday editors saw the P.M. and Callaghan at 10 Downing St last night. Christiansen (editor, *Sunday Mirror*) reports that the P.M. gave a highly misleading account of his meeting

* Confederation of British Industry.
† National Economic Development Council.

with the bankers: he said they were unanimous in thinking the measures taken were adequate and that none of them referred to the possibility of devaluing. They may not have referred to it, but it was certainly in their minds, and certainly two of the three B. of E. directors did not think the measures adequate. Jim Callaghan followed on and said that the whole thing was a wicked French plot to bring down the dollar by bringing down the pound first and making France the financial capital of the world. This is said to be an obsession of the P.M. and Callaghan, but I hear it from no other source, and consider it unlikely. Jim's forecast was that the deficit for this year would be as great as for last – which the Bank has been prophesying for months in spite of denials by Jim. He hopes to see us break even in the first half of next year and move into the black in the second half. Christiansen reports that Wilson thinks the greatest delusions were being suffered by de Gaulle and Ian Smith, but Christiansen wondered whether it was not Wilson who has the delusions. He sounded very tired; Jim, on the other hand, sounded buoyant and aggressive.

Wednesday, August 10th, 1966

George Brown to lunch, in a state of hardly suppressed excitement. It is to be announced tomorrow that he is to have the Foreign Office, while Stewart goes to the D.E.A. I told him the appointment would have a bad press, which he had pointed out to the P.M. He even mentioned that his Jewish wife would receive unfavourable comment from Arab countries. George had told Wilson he was coming to lunch with me and had received permission to tell me about the changes twenty-four hours in advance. I gathered there were to be no other appointments, but he did not specifically say so. In the course of one and a half hours' conversation, I tried to find out what George thought the reason was for this change. I think that to avoid further friction between the Treasury and the D.E.A. the latter had to be down-graded, hence Stewart. But now the inadequate Stewart is left to push through the Prices and Incomes policy, while the tactless George is left with the foreigners!

George said there had been a three-hour confrontation between himself and Jim (sitting facing each other across the Cabinet table) over the devaluation of the pound. Normally votes are not taken at Cabinet meetings, but this was voted on and ended (I gathered) sixteen to eight, with Crossman, Jenkins, Greenwood, Castle and Crosland voting with George for devaluation. He didn't give me all the names, but I think I got these right. He seemed to think (George is not always at all clear) that as money was still pouring out – as much as before Wilson's package – there will be devaluation in October. If this is Wilson's plan then, according to George, he would naturally want to get devaluer George out of the D.E.A. in good time. I don't follow the argument. I said I thought Wilson had passed the point of no return, so I was more interested in the succession than in Wilson's manœuvrings before his departure. The situation in the Government has now changed: the succession is being discussed. George recognizes that he is not a runner and considers the two candidates to be Jenkins and Crosland, in that order. He thinks, however, that they are not well-known enough in the party and will not take enough trouble to get known. I pointed out that Wilson will go, owing to the government of the country being in a horrible mess; there won't be time to get known among the grass roots. However, this kind of thing has evidently not been thought out. I asked about Denis Healey and was told he was too arrogant and had made too many mistakes lately. He has certainly made mistakes, and his position over our military expenditure east of Suez is none too clear. But his arrogance stems from a stronger character than either Crosland or Jenkins, and strong character is what would be needed in a jam. I asked about a National Government but this has evidently received no thought yet in those quarters.

Thursday, August 11th, 1966

The Cabinet changes were announced last night – apart from George and Stewart, they are Bowden to Commonwealth Relations; Crossman, Lord President and Leader of the House; Greenwood, Housing; and Bottomley, Overseas Development. These changes were greeted with loud laughter in the House when they were known! The reasons seem to be (1) promotion for Greenwood (known to Wilson to be useless) and Crossman to placate the left wing of the Labour Party Conference in October; (2) the removal of Bowden and Short from managing the House, where they were no longer acceptable to the back benchers; (3) the removal of George from the D.E.A., where the clash with Callaghan could be allowed to continue no longer.

The Bank as usual in the morning – a quieter week but money still going out. After Court a long piece by Maurice Allen on the outlook. Wilson had said, either to the bankers or to the editors at No. 10, that the economy would produce a surplus of £300 million in 1967. It now appears that whatever he said, the figures he was quoting state that, as a result of the measures of July 20th, the balance of payments for 1967, would be *improved* by £300 million. But this has to be read in conjunction with figures brought together earlier in July which suggested a deficit of £237 million. So that taking the two figures together, the outlook would now be for a favourable balance of £63 million, which is an insignificant amount well within the margin of error. But whereas the £237 million figure was arrived at by the Treasury and Bank of England working together, the £300 million figure was prepared by the Treasury alone and is regarded by the Bank as very optimistic and quite unreliable. So you may say the outlook for next year is for a continuing deficit.

Later I had a talk with Maurice Parsons alone to ask if George Brown's surmise that his removal to the F.O. might be part of a Wilson plan to devalue in October had any foundation. Probably not, but Parsons knew of disagreement in the Cabinet on the subject of devaluation.

Mike had lunch with —— [a senior civil servant], whom he does not know well. He was surprisingly frank and said he and two or three of the most senior civil servants were appalled at the way things were going, particularly at the lack of decisions. He said more and more civil servants were compelled to initiate policy, which was no part of their function, but in the absence of ministerial decisions there was no other course.

Saturday, August 13th, 1966

Denis Hamilton came and talked politics – comparing notes on the future. He tells me that both Macmillan and Rab Butler foresee a National Government and assume that they will be invited to join it!

85

I should imagine that any National Government that is formed will be in haste to show it has no connection with such ineffective has-beens. There seems to be a current of opinion leading to a National Government of non-politicians rather than a government with a Labour P.M. and some non politicians participating. Of course any development may well be in two moves (or more, for that matter).

Thursday, August 18th, 1966

Denis Healey to lunch yesterday. He told me that when George Brown resigned, he (Healey) was to have had the D.E.A. The Michael Stewart idea was evidently a later one. Healey spoke up for Stewart, whom everyone likes and respects, though that hardly qualifies him to be Foreign Secretary.

This morning at the Bank, Robens aghast at the idea of Stewart at the D.E.A. – he can't possibly run that department.

Tuesday, September 6th, 1966

Am in Washington. First port of call this morning was to see Helms, the head of the C.I.A.* We had a rather cloak-and-daggery start: a telephone call to Ralph Champion said I would be picked up at my hotel by a 1963 Buick, number so-and-so, driver wearing a cap! We drove off to the C.I.A. building in Virginia, into a garage under the main entrance, and stopped beside a man standing by an open lift door. I was taken upstairs and was told I was early, but Helms emerged immediately and took me into what I suppose is a waiting-room – entirely neutral except for three maps of Vietnam on the wall. Helms, a professional intelligence man, is very pleasant to meet and highly intelligent, couldn't have been more friendly and at my departure asked me to come again.

Naturally we talked generalities, but some points emerged. From all contacts with Ho Chi Minh, and at all levels, the answer they get is that the Vietnamese got the French out of Indo-China in 1954 and will get the Americans out in the same way. There is talk of coming to terms with the Russians to end the Cold War – but how? What terms? The Americans have so far failed to learn of any basis for such talks. I said I had read that the reason is that the British and

* Central Intelligence Agency.

86

Americans are traders – ready to take less than they would like. The Russian character has been determined by the Russian winter, which leaves no room for compromise.

He said the C.I.A. looked after the defectors, who brought out the difficulty of dealing with Russians and Chinese. Neither seemed able to adapt themselves to living in a free society. The Russians seemed unable to integrate themselves into American society and were a constant source of worry. The recent defection (widely reported) of a young Chinese diplomat in Syria presented another version of the same difficulty. Though he defected because he didn't like where he was, and was quite ready to give any information, his story merely read like editorials from the official Chinese *Red Flag*.

I said I thought there must be difficulty in monitoring all broadcasts, reading all newspapers, bugging all embassies, in coping with the sheer volume of material? He said this was a good question and in fact they could only cope by severely limiting the material for study. He said that the monitoring of the telephone lines in East Berlin (reported at the time: they were tapped by means of a tunnel*), though it produced useful material, involved a whole crew of men. He surprised me by saying that the C.I.A. is not a spy service like M.I.6,† but is an interpretive service using material from whatever source, including, I gather, their own cloak-and-dagger work. He said he employed enough Ph.D.s to man a university, men with first-class intellects who thought they were serving their country this way better than by getting higher salaries elsewhere.

I said American policy seemed to be to support extreme right-wing personalities with the inevitable bad results. He said Chiang Kai-shek was a special case bound up with the China lobby and domestic politics, but in other cases the American Government had had to support whatever men it could find. They had given some support to Sukarno in Indonesia because there was literally no one else. He had himself had a look at Hatta, once widely mentioned as a possible alternative, but he was just a non-runner. Those deeply committed to the Russians were no use to the Americans. I said it was

* The tunnel was built from West to East Berlin in 1954–5. It was discovered by the Russians in 1956.
† The British Secret Intelligence Service.

widely believed, particularly in Asia, that the C.I.A. pursued a policy very often antagonistic to that of the State Department. He said this was not so, but there had been some appearance of this in Laos at one time: this was due to the fact that the Pentagon and the State Department had followed divergent policies and the President had supported the Pentagon and had instructed the C.I.A. to do likewise.

He thought our Secret Service quite good, having regard to their resources. The French were pulling theirs round. They had had two – one operating in the French empire and the other elsewhere – and they had had difficulty integrating the two.

Wednesday, September 7th, 1966

Notable visits yesterday were to Mike Mansfield, Senate Majority Leader, Henry Fowler, Secretary of the Treasury, and William Bundy, Under-Secretary of State in charge of the Far East (Burma to Japan, including Australia and New Zealand). Henry Fowler had around him a lot of his top brass, five in all. He is a dim little man and had little to say. I was received as a director of the Bank. He said the U.S. and the Continental Central Banks were giving the Treasury a further amount of swap credits, which would be announced next week. They were sorry the City had not the same confidence in the future of sterling that the Central Banks had. I said the City had no confidence in the Government as a whole and that I thought it would not last another year.

Mike Mansfield, Senator from Montana, is a very nice man, obviously honest, but neither strong nor particularly able. What I found interesting was that in his suite of offices there were three pictures of Kennedy but none of Johnson! Johnson, when in the Senate, chose him as his deputy because of his dimness and now finds him exasperatingly weak, though critical.

William Bundy is very like his brother [McGeorge] to look at – obviously exceedingly intelligent and very nice. I asked why the Chinese allowed Hong Kong to continue. Bundy said it was the source of half their foreign exchange. He thought its position was now more secure than it had been. I asked about the Chinese invasion of India. It seemed so pointless at the time. He said they succeeded in humiliating the Indian Government and impeding their progress at a time when they were doing well. I said surely a better card to play was that the Chinese were the champions of all Asians. He said the Chinese regarded with contempt all non-Chinese, whether Asians or not. I asked why the quarrel with the Russians? Bundy said he thought it was genuinely ideological. I said the Chinese in the past had not been given to ideological debates. He said he did not see any other grounds for the embittered relations between the two countries, though the cutting off of aid in 1958 by the Russians had not been forgotten.

Thursday, September 8th, 1966

Had a very busy day: Scott, Senator from Pennsylvania, followed by Rostow, the President, lunch at the *Post*, McNaughton and Kuss of the Department of Defence, and, finally, McNamara with Representative Bolling coming to dine presently.

The President had just received Ne Win, the Burmese President, and was about to give lunch to Steinbeck, author of *The Grapes of Wrath*. He received me in a tiny room adjacent to his oval office where I had met Kennedy. The curtains were drawn, Bill Moyers, the President's Press Secretary, was present and there were two telephone switchboards and three T.V. sets. which kept on giving out bursts of music and having to be suppressed. Johnson seemed tired and reluctant to see me, but warmed up later and made it difficult to go. I suppose I was with him half an hour. He is a big man, not attractive, obviously able. I got the impression he is trying to run straight, much embarrassed by his murky past. He is obviously obsessed by Vietnam and finds it difficult to talk or think of anything else. He seemed to judge people by their willingness to stand by him, so he spoke very warmly of Harold Holt (who is a pleasant nonentity), of Bob Menzies (much abler than Holt, but a lazy snob), and critically of Lippman, Mansfield, and others who do not support him over Vietnam. He said so many people criticized him over Vietnam but were not prepared to say what they would do if they were in charge. What would I do? I could only hedge, as to come flat out and say they should pull out is going further than, as a guest, I should. He was pleased to see that Wilson's poll had picked up: apparently he is a great one for polls. I said it would soon fall back again! There were long silences. Nothing very definite emerged from the conversation, but I was intensely interested to meet Johnson. He is out of his depth, but more convincing that I expected.

Scott, the Republican Senator from Pennsylvania, is an able, witty, intelligent man, said by Bolling to be the ablest Republican in either House. He had been talking to Donovan, a journalist from the *Los Angeles Times*, who had just completed a six weeks' tour of the country, and said that Bobby Kennedy has more support than anyone else, including the President. He thinks this support is due to a subconscious wish to expiate feelings of collective guilt for the murder of Jack Kennedy.

While wending our way to the White House, we were held up by the motorcade of Johnson escorting Ne Win to Blair House. It really was a grim sight, with two Secret Service men in mufti standing on the car bumper behind the President, as well as motor-cycle outriders, a car full of cops, and marines lining the route! While in the White House we were under constant observation from Secret Service men in mufti – usually with one hand on a gun in their pockets. I felt that any sudden or unexpected movement might well bring a bullet.

At Defence, McNaughton (in charge of international affairs) and Kuss (in charge of arms sales) were uninteresting, but I was very impressed by McNamara, as I was before. He is not only a *very* able man, he is also a nice one. His trouble in the present situation is that he is an excellent administrator but no politician. After talking to so many people about Vietnam, which is everyone's preoccupation, it is clear that the major problem is that the Americans have no understanding of the Vietnam mentality – and vice versa. Perhaps, naturally, McNamara is over-impressed by the 1,800 helicopters, the 1,200 planes, the 300,000 men, the $900 million they have spent on the port in Cam Ranh Bay. He thinks the hostile Vietnamese, North and South, are losing, in killed and disabled, about 100,000 men per year. The population is such that they can keep it up indefinitely, but will their morale allow them to? I said I thought it hard to understand why the North Vietnamese would not negotiate. Obviously it would be done in bad faith, but it would seem a good card for them to play. But the Chinese, surely, were doing splendidly, ready to fight to the last Vietnamese? McNamara would not accept this and said the tremendous build-up of American forces within five hundred miles of the Chinese border must seem to them a most serious threat. I said surely only if they go too far, and they can have no intention of fighting the U.S.? It is hard to prevent the war escalating, as further pressure by the Americans will force the Russians to contribute more, which will force the Americans to do more, and so on. The Russian anti-aircraft missiles have been very ineffective so they may think it necessary to bring in Russians to man them.

I said one theory (actually from Patrick Dean) was that South Vietnam was just an excuse and that the Americans were building up a string of bases for the military containment of China. He said there was nothing in this idea: the Americans wanted to get out of Vietnam as soon as possible. They wanted us to stay in South-East Asia as they have no intention of becoming the world's policemen. I said their power and their control of the sea cast them in this role whether they wanted it or not. He said the great American public wouldn't play. There was always an isolationist element in the country and this might re-emerge. I asked if the war was likely to spread to Siam or other adjacent territories, but McNamara thought not, at any rate not to any significant extent. Here they speak of the Siamese Government as if it were a real one, but my recollection of Bangkok a few years ago was of a totally corrupt regime propped up by the Americans.

Friday, September 9th, 1966

Called on General Wheeler, Chairman of the Chiefs of Staff at the Pentagon. The last one I met some years ago was Admiral Radford, a very tough, impressive character. This man is equally tough; perhaps not quite as big. Very friendly. Rather naturally he was interested in the military aspects of the war, though conscious that the political aspect was more important. He rather surprisingly agreed that McNamara was a great administrator but not a politician. He had no particular information to impart but was yet another of the characters in this city who make me feel the team here is far more effective than the one at home.

Saturday, September 10th, 1966

Am off to New York this p.m., but have yet to mention half an hour at the State Department with George Ball yesterday and dinner with Sir Michael Stewart (second man at the Embassy) last night. The dinner was quite friendly, four British, four Americans, all men. The Americans were George Ball, Johnson (I think political adviser to the Ministry of Defence until recently, but now Ambassador designate to Japan), Denning of the U.S. Treasury, and Mann, formerly State Department, but to become political adviser to General Motors. The outstanding character was George Ball, whom I like and who talks a lot of sense.

When he had left, Killick of the Embassy Chancery and Stewart were saying how much he was disliked by successive British governments: they thought perhaps because he told them too many home truths! Ball's main theme was that the Germans were showing signs of restlessness, particularly young Germans. They had been promised a prominent part in an integrated Europe, but they were still awaiting implementation of this promise. As France, under de Gaulle, became more and more nationalistic, so Germany would do the same – not in a military sense, but she might well start looking to the East, not having got enough from the West. De Gaulle, pretending that France is a world power, could only make an impression by wrecking-tactics. For Britain to get into Europe (1) would be a constructive move from Britain's point of view and (2) should have a moderating effect on the nationalisms of France and Germany. He thought both we and the French should give up our atom bombs, as otherwise it will be impossible to stop their proliferation. I said I thought the immediate problem was the financial mess we are in; the French can hardly be expected to welcome us in until this has been cleared up. He said if this were the only obstacle, he felt sure the U.S. would be prepared to help. Ball has, of course, always been strongly in favour of our joining the Common Market.

Sunday, October 2nd, 1966

Have been back from the U.S. for more than a fortnight. My last interesting meeting there was with McGeorge Bundy in New York. I like him and his very quick brain. He said Helms of the C.I.A.

had rung him up about seeing me – he was very nervous, but Bundy reassured him! I suppose he was afraid I would ask unsuitable questions – or be indiscreet. Bundy said he had had the same fears when I came to see him for the first time.

Sunday, October 9th, 1966

This has been the week of the Labour Party Conference and of my visit to Berlin to be present at the opening of Axel Springer's new office there.

The Conference seems to me to be completely out of date. You have a lot of ignorant people, with some crackpots, holding forth on every subject under the sun. The Government listens and intends to pay no attention. I was thinking today that whatever the constitution may say, we now have presidential government. The prime minister of the day need pay no attention to his ministers, nor to the House of Commons, as long as nothing goes seriously wrong. If it does, he is removed and almost immediately forgotten, while someone else takes his place. All the talk about Wilson's – or Home's or Macmillan's – mastery of the House of Commons is meaningless. While he is P.M. he automatically masters the House. The day he leaves 10 Downing St he ceases to matter.

The Springer do was on a grand scale with the President of the Republic, the Vice-Chancellor, the Mayor (Willi Brandt), Kokoschka, the artist, Karajan, the conductor, and Prince Louis, the head of the House of Hohenzollern. But the guest most asked for his autograph was Max Schmelling, the retired boxer! Springer is a fanatic on the reunification of Germany and has built his new office, costing £9 million, bang on the Wall as a gesture of his faith in the future of Berlin as the capital of a united Germany. He has also, as a measure of expiation, presented a library to the Hebrew University of Jerusalem.

Springer is a curious man – only fifty-four now. He controls most of the newspapers and some of the big magazines and so is a potentially powerful figure, but his politics are said to be erratic, different in different papers and largely ineffective. He told Hugh Cudlipp he had a house in Switzerland and a fast boat, the latter to take him to Hull in time of trouble if the Swiss haven did not look too good!

93

Tuesday, November 8th, 1966

Quite a burst of activity these last few days – Louis Franck to lunch on Friday, the Lord Chancellor, Lord Gardiner, to dinner yesterday, Crossman to lunch today, and a brief word with George Brown at the Russian reception yesterday evening.

Louis Franck was pretty pessimistic. Like so many others he thinks we are heading for a dictatorship, owing to the failure of Parliament, not only in this country, but in France, Belgium, Holland, Germany and Italy as well. Thinks we shall have to end up with a government mainly of technocrats.

George thinks he will screw up Wilson to make a joint statement with him about joining the Common Market.

The Lord Chancellor rather silent but *very* nice; made quite a speech on saying goodbye, saying he agreed with every word the *Mirror* had said during the last year, and had found no other source of opinion with which he could agree nearly so well. Considering that he is an important member of the Government and that for the last twelve months we have been very critical, I was greatly surprised. He startled Mike before dinner by asking if my room was bugged!

Dick Crossman came on from a three-hour talk of Cabinet ministers on Rhodesia: how to get Wilson off the hook without being too humiliated. One thought is still to hand over sovereignty to the U.N. (Wilson has suggested this idea to me in private but has ridiculed the idea in public). Another thought is that Smith should be encouraged to declare a Republic. When it is apparent that we have not succeeded in dislodging Smith, the matter will be taken up by the U.N. and there will be a vote for mandatory sanctions on Rhodesia and probably, subsequently, on South Africa. Should we veto this? The general position is that Wilson has completely misjudged the situation and we are all now in a mess. I didn't get any clear idea of what Crossman thought should be done.

Crossman would prefer England to be a cosy offshore island, but realizes that the current of opinion is too strong towards the Common Market. He is trying to persuade the P.M. to make a definite commitment at the Mansion House where he is speaking on Monday night, Crossman's point being that there is probably more political mileage in being for than against, but none in merely dithering.

He showed great admiration for Wilson's tactical dexterity, but said he had no foresight, no interest in the administration. When Crossman was asked to move from Housing to Lord President, Wilson could not see that this meant scrapping eighteen months' work, and that his successor would have to start again from scratch.

I said I thought the prestige of Parliament was low and falling. He agreed, and said the new M.P.s had learnt this from their constituents and were very worried about it. Dick did not seem to have any ideas to counteract this.

He thinks well of Barbara Castle, of George Brown, and of Jim Callaghan; did not mention Denis Healey, but said Wilson is well aware that if he lost office, Jenkins is a very possible successor.

Thursday, November 10th, 1966

Wilson has come out this afternoon with a pretty definite declaration of his intention to join the Common Market. Hugh Cudlipp was summoned at 2.30 p.m. to 10 Downing St to be told the glad news. He met George Brown as he was coming out, who said he was a 'Common Market nut' and that he was fully satisfied with the declaration: 'The juggernaut had started to roll, and nothing could now stop it.' It is a big advance for Wilson, but will not be viewed with the same enthusiasm by our Continental friends. However, it is a step in the right direction. Hugh was quick to point out to me – undoubtedly correctly – that Wilson is in trouble in Rhodesia and in a mess at home and this is, in part, a gigantic red herring to distract attention.

Saturday, November 19th, 1966

Ian Macleod came to lunch yesterday – my first long talk with him for years. He had little to say and did not react notably to my views. His arthritis is worse; he cannot stand for long and his neck and shoulders are way out of line. He seemed to think that Smith had so many reasons for seeking a compromise that a deal with him *must* be possible. I never thought one was possible and the Government spokesmen all say that nothing has come out of all the talks. I gather the latest demand is that if Africans, with increasing education, win more seats, the whites shall be empowered to create more safe white seats and so stay in front!

Last night at the reception for Ayub Khan, President of Pakistan, here on a state visit. I have met him before. He looks like a tall, good-looking, rather effective general, which I suppose is what he is. He is too dark to be English, but his features and manners are very English – military version. Heath was there, a good deal thinner – Ruth thought overworking and tired out. Wilson looks smaller and more insignificant than ever; he is clearly dwindling and quite out of his depth. George Brown was there, and in good form: off to Moscow on Monday with a plan to bring the Americans and Russians together over Vietnam. George thinks he is on the threshold of a great coup. But I can't help wondering why the Americans and Russians should need George as an intermediary!

Gore-Booth was there. He said that we are now on the move into the Common Market. I said, as a cynical newspaper man, I was afraid Europe was being used as a huge red herring, trundled across the stage to distract attention from failure in Rhodesia and on the home front. Gore-Booth and his very attractive wife both said, 'But the red herring, having been trundled across the stage, cannot be trundled back again!'

Friday, December 2nd, 1966

Had nearly an hour this afternoon with George at the F.O. The last time I was in the Secretary of State's room it was in Butler's day. George had had the windows opened, had had a fire lit in the grate (both of these innovations after many years!). He had also removed the picture of George III and had had Palmerston put in his place. He had said about three weeks ago he wanted to see me as a matter of urgency, but our meeting got put off and when we did meet this evening he had nothing in particular he wanted to talk about, so I embarked on Rhodesia. Wilson and Smith are at present on board a cruiser* in the Mediterranean negotiating while a very considerable storm is blowing. A cruiser in a storm for a pair of landlubbers must be a very unsuitable venue for a conference. I said I did not see what

* H.M.S. *Tiger*.

thcy could negotiate about as Smith had been offered both by Alec Home and by Wilson progress towards self-government over ten years, and African advancement to be hastened by a crash programme of secondary education to be paid for by the U.K. I didn't see how any British Government could go further than this – perhaps even this was promising more than could be performed in view of the fact that ten years is a very long time in Africa these days.

George said they would certainly go no further than this – hardly as far – as they were insisting on a government with some black faces, and physical steps (of some undefined kind) to be added to make certain a written undertaking was in fact honoured.

I asked if Smith could possibly get away with such terms. He said he thought the chances were five to four on rather than five to four against.

He was very annoyed that Callaghan, in a speech to the Parliamentary Labour Party, had indicated that pressure had been brought to bear on the Cabinet by the Treasury and the Board of Trade to secure a settlement, as these two departments knew how serious an effect on our balance of trade mandatory sanctions would have. Though this is true, this is obviously not the moment to blurt it out in an unimportant, impromptu speech.

While these pressures are being brought to bear on the Government here, pressures have been mounting on the Government in Salisbury, where it is thought impossible for them to sustain a boycott of a second year's tobacco crop. The South African Government has been in close touch with the F.O. – as much as twice daily – and is also bringing pressure to bear on Smith. George is planning to go to New York on Tuesday to tell the United Nations what we are doing and why – whichever way the decision goes.

I asked about Cabinet changes and George said his latest information was 'the New Year'. It would not be important as Wilson would certainly not move the duds in important offices – Jay, Greenwood and Stewart would certainly stay where they are – and shuffling around Bottomley, Lee and Co. would not affect anything.

He spoke about the Common Market, on which he had been exchanging cables with Wilson on the *Tiger*. The idea is that they should go to France in January, but somewhere else first. What about

97

Belgium? But Wilson thinks this might have objections as they would have to meet Hallstein and the Common Market officials – so it will probably be Italy. I said this approach would not be successful, because Wilson has neither the drive, the personality, the conviction, nor the administrative ability to pull it off. While he was telling George he was flat out for the Common Market, doubtless he was leaving people like Jay and Peart with the impression that there was many a slip betwixt cup and lip – and, anyway, any agreement was a long way off. George asked if I really thought this? Because if I was right, he was being had for a sucker. I said it didn't matter much because Wilson was such a bad P.M. he could not be expected to last. He said this was intriguing, but now he had to greet the Argentine Ambassador, so we must meet again after he had returned from New York.

Sunday, December 11th, 1966

The last week has mostly been taken up with sound and fury over Rhodesia. Picking one's way through the violently partisan statements by all concerned, it appears that Wilson, at his meeting with Smith on the *Tiger*, was convinced he had to make a deal with Smith, and when he left the ship he was confident he had done so. The terms are difficult to interpret, as much was left vague, but they appear to amount to a sell-out. The original terms offered to Smith by Home, and later by Wilson, were majority government in ten years and, meanwhile, a crash programme of secondary education for the Africans at British expense. In the terms on the *Tiger* there was no reference to African education and the ten years had grown to a possible fifteen. It is difficult to see why these terms were not accepted, and at least some accounts suggest that Smith and a majority of his Cabinet were prepared to accept but were overruled by the right-wing members of his party.

O'Brien (of the Bank) told me he had dined with a friend who was on the *Tiger*, after his return. Whereas Wilson was confident he had negotiated a deal, the friend said it was clear to him before Smith left the ship that the answer was No. The whole thing was very humiliating for Wilson, who had planned this Churchillian conference on a cruiser. It was to have been a profound secret – only to be revealed when success was announced. In fact, this whole build-up only accentuated the failure. There is one advantage in going so far to meet Smith, and that is that Wilson can fairly claim he tried very hard. To distract attention from the failure, in the debate he launched a ferocious attack on Heath, who answered back in kind. The main result of the exchange was to delight Labour M.P.s and unite the entire Conservative Party behind Heath. It is agreed in the Sunday papers that a much more acrimonious period of Parliamentary politics is ahead.

I had a long talk with O'Brien on Thursday. He had told us at Court that there had been, as expected, a run on the pound when it was known that the Rhodesian negotiations had broken down. This had been about half as bad as had been expected, and half of this half had come back on Wednesday and Thursday morning. Nevertheless the outlook is not good.

In our private talk later he harped on the rising tide of Government expenditure – now likely to be up by $6\frac{1}{2}$ per cent in real terms. Callaghan apparently takes the line that he is not to be criticized, as anything anyone could do he is doing. This line is, of course, quite untenable. He is only doing what he, a lightweight, can do in the present Cabinet. According to Robens he took the same line in the Neddy meeting this last week.

Tuesday, December 20th, 1966

Had Tony Crosland to lunch yesterday – doing quite a good job at the Ministry of Education. He always seems to me highly intelligent, but an unstable character. I have known him off and on for a long time. He was very frank yesterday.

Crosland seemed to think day-to-day business was adequately conducted but the underlying problems of the country were not being tackled; thought Wilson would win the next election but not the one after. If he dropped dead, Crosland thought the only possible successor at this moment would be Callaghan. This, not because he is a good Chancellor (Crosland said he was an outstandingly bad one), but because of his performance in the House, which is apparently impressive. Crosland did not think Callaghan's standing would remain high for long and thought, in due course, the likely successor

99

to Wilson would be Jenkins – or himself! From all kinds of quarters one hears more and more of Jenkins but no more of Denis Healey. Today Chapman Pincher, of the *Daily Express*, who is usually well-informed, says the Ministry of Defence is in a state of chaos, because decisions, even when made, are so often countermanded, and none of the three Services knows where it is. Chapman Pincher is dependent on friends in the Services to tell him what is going on, and may well be grinding one of their axes. Denis Healey may be the victim of Cabinet changes of mind, having regard to our 'world role' on the one hand and our need for economy on the other. But I do not get the impression of the steady unfolding of a Denis Healey plan on defence.

Friday, December 23rd, 1966

Kenneth Robinson, Minister of Health, came to lunch yesterday – at his suggestion, as he recalled. He offered me the chairmanship of the National Council of Health Education. I said I would let him know after the holiday. The work would be mildly interesting, but I cannot take on any more.

Robinson is a nice man, devoted to his job and apparently very good at it. He said he saved a lot of time devoted by several colleagues to wishing they were in No. 10! I asked him about prescription charges, on which he is quite unrepentant: said they were a particularly regressive kind of taxation hitting the sick poor. But, of course, the objection to free prescriptions is that so many are unnecessary anyway. He said this raised an entirely different – and very thorny – subject. Should doctors have complete freedom to prescribe? At present they have this freedom and set great store by it. But is this right? I recalled the fuss they had made over a proposal for a total ban on heroin. Robinson evidently felt that doctors were too ready to prescribe and to sign certificates for days off work, but didn't think charging for prescriptions was the answer.

Wednesday, December 28th, 1966

Had tea with George and Sophie Brown at Dorneywood, the house given to the Foreign Secretary of the day by Lord Courtauld-Thomson. I had suggested a meeting to hear about George's interview with de Gaulle. He had suggested lunch, but I wanted to be back in the office after the holiday, so it ended up as one and a half hours at tea-time. According to Sophie, George is in better health because he is enjoying himself and has a settled department instead of having to create one, as at the D.E.A. He obviously enjoys every minute of being Foreign Secretary, the world travel and all the trimmings.

The General was apparently wearing very thick pebbly glasses and was friendly: spoke beautiful French and kept George for an hour. He was very alert and on the spot, but very noncommittal. At one point George asked whether they couldn't discuss their mutual problems in connection with the Common Market. The General said France had no problems – she was in! This sounded to us like a crushing snub, but George wondered what it meant! The General also said he didn't see how a maritime power like England could join a group of continental powers like the Six. I cannot see that there is anything in this last argument.

George said a Government shuffle was coming. He evidently thought that Fred Lee (whose office has disappeared) and Frank Longford would depart. Wilson has said he will reduce the size of the Cabinet: at twenty-four it is about six too big – but George doubted whether the reduction would be more than one, or at best two. George had put forward the names of a number of young back-benchers who should be given a chance. Wilson replied coldly that they had all been involved in the 'July plot'! No one but Wilson (and presumably Wigg) can discover any plot, though Callaghan and Brown made it evident that if Wilson fell, their hats were in the ring.

George went to Moscow with a three-stage plan for ending the Vietnamese war, endorsed by the Americans. The Russians were cagey, as was Rusk when George subsequently saw him in Paris. Evidently neither party was going to commit himself to George as a go-between. But George interpreted this caginess as evidence he had started something!

At no point was there any hint of the financial trouble the Government is facing – nor any suggestion of the formidable problems that confront the country and the Government on every side. The impression given by George – as by other ministers – is that it's wonderful being a minister, long may it last.

George was very amusing about Michael Stewart, who had impressed him by his fluency in Cabinet when Foreign Secretary. He now learnt from his old friends at the D.E.A. and from his new friends at the F.O. how little they thought of him. Apparently, because George has at the F.O. a minister of Cabinet rank (George Thomson), Michael Stewart wants one too.

I reminded George that last time we met, Wilson was on the *Tiger* and that he had said the terms to be offered Smith would be less favourable than those offered before U.D.I. – to wit, majority rule in ten years and meanwhile a crash programme of African secondary education at British expense. He said the terms *were* less favourable because they all depended on a referendum, and the Africans would certainly have turned them down. Meanwhile a Defence Council would have been set up under the Governor which would control the armed forces. As the commanders of the three services were all anti-Smith this Defence Council would have provided us with a military presence which would have been decisive in the later stages. This all strikes me as being too clever by three-quarters. The military commanders may be anti-Smith, but they are unlikely to be pro-African, and to advance a plan with a view to its being rejected by the Africans would not have worked. George said that Smith had really accepted the terms when he left the *Tiger*, and the Cabinet, the following morning, did the same. It was only when Lardner-Burke came in from Johannesburg at midday that things moved the other way. But, I reflected, wouldn't Lardner-Burke have broken off his holiday earlier if he had had any doubts over the way things were going? Anyway, now George envisages demands in the U.N. for a blockade of South Africa – and should we or should we not use our veto?

1967

The domestic scene in Britain was dominated by the developments which led to the decision to devalue the pound in November. Although there were some favourable signs, it was clear that the balance of payments position remained weak, in spite of high unemployment, and it seemed beyond Britain's capability to combine full employment with a satisfactory balance. This general situation, combined with the closure of the Suez Canal on the outbreak of the Arab–Israeli war in June and the effects of dock strikes in Liverpool and London, made devaluation inevitable. The Government's efforts, in the course of the year, to stabilize the economy caused its popularity to drop sharply, as was shown by a series of defeats for the Labour Party in by-elections and local elections. Major Cabinet changes took place in August, when the Prime Minister took personal charge of the Department of Economic Affairs, in place of Michael Stewart. Two weeks after devaluation, the Chancellor of the Exchequer, James Callaghan, exchanged posts with the Home Secretary, Roy Jenkins. Britain's renewed efforts to join the Common Market met with an effective French veto in November, when President de Gaulle announced that he was not prepared to start negotiations on the issue.

Internationally, as ever, wars made the headlines. Israeli forces were victorious in the six-day war against Egypt, Syria and the Lebanon in June; the situation in Nigeria degenerated into full-scale civil war between the Federal Government and Biafra, the secessionist Eastern Region; and the war in Vietnam continued. Britain followed its 1966 decision to withdraw its forces from Aden as soon as South Arabia became independent in 1968 with the announcement that all British troops would leave Malaysia and Singapore by the mid-1970s; the withdrawal from east of Suez would then be complete.

Thursday, January 5th, 1967

Quite a spate of political meals this week: Reggie Maudling, Monday; Ted Heath and John Stevens, Tuesday; the Bank today. I was to have had lunch with the P.M., but he is in bed – or is he? Reggie really had no news – except that he was sounded out by Callaghan about becoming Governor of the Bank. It was not quite clear whether or no he was actually offered the job.

Ted Heath was tired, thinner, older, sadder. He had no particular news: reacts very little to anything I say, though he did assert that his electioneering policy in March had been suggested by me and adopted by him – i.e. Into Europe and Down with the Trades Unions (more or less!).

John Stevens was mildly interesting. George Brown – anyway, according to Stevens – made quite a good impression on Johnson, but a very bad one at the dinner in Detroit, in the Washington Embassy (where he had a flaming row), and at a dinner in New York. Stevens said he thought Johnson would support the pound this year, almost come what may. The dollar is weakish owing to the Vietnam war and Johnson cannot afford to see the pound go down.

I sat next O'Brien at lunch at the Bank. At the time of his appointment he seemed to be pro-Government, naturally enough, but now he sounded despondent and disillusioned. I said I wondered where the newspapers had got the figure of a £200 to £300 million surplus on the balance of payments for 1967. He said he thought £100–£200 million would be nearer the mark. I pointed out that Maurice Allen had suggested a small deficit. This, O'Brien agreed, was also possible. Maurice Allen, sitting the other side of me, said exports were doing better than had been expected and investment by industry was also not too bad. He thought it was too late for any substantial cuts to be made in Government expenditure.

Sunday, January 15th, 1967

Quite a political week. We gave a film party on Tuesday and I had Jim Callaghan at my table; dinner with Bill Carr and a long talk with Ray Gunter on Wednesday; Denis Hamilton to lunch on Wednesday; and lunch with the P.M. alone at No. 10 on Friday.

Gunter said controversy was raging at the moment among ministers on what was to be done when existing freeze legislation* ran out in August. Gunter is afraid that coercion will lead to more coercion, and then what? At the same time we cannot get back to the state of things before July 20th. Perhaps it would be best to have a period of voluntary freeze policed by the T.U.C.† and the C.B.I. If that didn't work, there would be a stronger case for coercion.

The P.M. was very friendly. I had two hours with him but very little emerged. The purpose of the lunch seemed (1) to flatter me and (2) to convince me that he really is going all out on the Common Market. His conversation was, in the main, long stories of how clever he was, doing this or that. He asked me what I thought he should do next about the Common Market. He so obviously did not want my opinion, that I brushed this off. Otherwise he asked me no questions, nor invited my opinion on anything.

Trying to sum up the impression Wilson made this time, I should say he looks older and slower. Is still – at least superficially – very self-confident: the balance of payments will be in surplus to the tune of £300 million this year; his and de Gaulle's are the only two stable governments in Europe, etc. etc.

No mention was made of Rhodesia; rising Government expenditure was rather airily dismissed; defence cuts of £300 million were promised and by 1970 defence would be down to £1,750 million at 1964 prices instead of the promised £2,000 million. The Government changes were explained as an attempt to bring in some younger men in place of the over-sixties. I spoke well of Houghton and said I was sorry he had gone. Wilson said he couldn't keep a man of sixty-eight in the Cabinet when men of sixty-four were being removed in the middle ranks. This is, of course, pure nonsense. Why exchange a

* The six-month wage freeze and twelve-month prices and dividend freeze introduced in July 1966.
† Trades Union Congress.

useful little man of sixty-eight for a total dud, like Gordon Walker, of fifty-nine? Some of the changes were transfers at under-secretary level. This was to give young men like Shore 'more experience', though what useful experience can be picked up by moving a man from one ministry to a totally different one after six months is hard to see. It emerged again that Wilson has no administrative sense of any kind. Callaghan seems to have none either. He was saying on Tuesday that he would be happy to be at the Treasury for another year to complete his programme, but after that he would have finished his contribution! In fact, after three years a much abler and more energetic man than Callaghan would be just beginning to be effective.

Denis Hamilton was saying that his first inspection of *The Times* reveals an even greater vacuum than even he had expected.* There is absolutely nothing there. He will have to build from the ground up. The first signs of improvement were a turn-over article on Friday, from the Parliamentary Correspondent, saying how empty most Parliamentary forms have become, and a very good leader yesterday praising George Brown. The leader is, in my opinion, too enthusiastic, but what it says is sensible and well put. Ted Heath, on the other hand, on T.V. on Friday evening, in a programme, 'Where Power Lies', was putting out all the old bromides, asserting that power lies where it is supposed to lie – in the House of Commons; in the ministries; in the P.M. If this were really so, there would obviously have been no programme.

Monday, January 16th, 1967

A last gleaning from my talk with Wilson: the raising of the school-leaving age will have to be postponed by at least two years.

Saturday, January 28th, 1967

Have been in Rome three days, after four days in Madrid, and have interviewed or talked to three ministers (Finance, the Budget and Foreign Trade), the proprietors of the two principal Rome papers, *Il Messaggero* and *Il Tempo*, Quaroni, former Ambassador in France

---

* *The Times* had been sold to Lord Thomson on September 30th, 1965. Denis Hamilton was the editor of the *Sunday Times* from 1961 to 1967, and in 1967 became editor-in-chief, Times Newspaper Ltd.

and England, and now Chairman of the State Broadcasting Corporation, Monsignor Carew of the Vatican Secretariat; had to dinner Malagodi, Secretary of the Liberal Party; I had interviews also with Nenni, the Socialist leader; Shuckburgh, the British Ambassador; Carli, the Chairman of the Central Bank, and sundry others. After so much talk over such a short period one can only get impressions. From London Pope Paul seems to be a ditherer. On the spot this impression is fully confirmed. Everybody is polite about him, but no one seriously pretends to agree with his attitude and methods. On birth control he is just dithering, while the laity has in effect taken the matter into its own hands. In about six months' time it is thought a statement will be made more or less condemning birth control – but surely it will then be too late? There has been a special week of prayer for the unity of the Christian Churches, but at the same time the Pope has gone out of his way to consecrate as priests with his own hands some converted Anglican parsons – thus pointedly repudiating the validity of Anglican orders. He has done a number of similar things, and this is thought to be due, not to ill-will, but to a kind of ineptitude which proceeds from the supposition that if you pursue two contrary policies simultaneously, you will placate everyone.

What is not realized in England is that the Pope is the most potent figure in Italian politics – the Christian Democrats are in effect the Pope's own party. Perrone, of the *Messaggero*, was longing for a non-Italian Pope who would inevitably be out of Italian politics. This Pope is thought likely to go on his travels again next year. It seems to me to diminish the prestige of his office, but he likes travel.

Quaroni was not particularly interesting about broadcasting – much more so about de Gaulle, as he was Italian Ambassador to France from 1948 to 1959. He said de Gaulle's *force de frappe* was not intended to show independence of the U.S., but to demonstrate superiority to Germany. His broad policy at the moment was based on two fallacies, (1) that his influence with Russia was such that he could help Germany unite, and (2) that his influence with Germany was such that he could detach her from the U.S. – which would please the U.S.S.R. Actually he had not got this kind of influence with either party. His objection to Britain joining the Common Market was that he knew that if she did she would become the leader. None of the Five would accept Germany, and no one wanted France, but for a number of quite illogical reasons they would look to Great Britain. He doubted if de Gaulle worried about the slights he received in London and Washington during the war. He was more likely to worry over the fact that England defeated France at Waterloo!

The story going round here is that de Gaulle was asked to take part in the consecration of a new crucifix at a church near Colombey-les-deux-Eglises. When there, he was asked to write an inscription, which he did – 'From the first citizen of France to the second Person of the Trinity'!

Tuesday, January 31st, 1967

Am in Bonn for three days. Saw Willi Brandt (Foreign Minister) yesterday, and Schmidt, Leader of the Social Democrats in the Bundesrat, today; breakfast with Strauss (Finance Minister); lunch with the Ambassador;* and half an hour with Kiesinger (Chancellor) in the afternoon. What emerges is that Germany is very keen for us to join the Common Market, but has no intention (even if she has the power) of forcing de Gaulle to let us in. Kiesinger apparently did his best to get us moving long before Macmillan made his first approach – and now it is more difficult.

Kiesinger was as clear as others have been that de Gaulle does not want us in the Common Market because it would thereby be enlarged – not only by us, but by the Danes and Norwegians, and perhaps others. De Gaulle doubts if he would have the same measure of control over the enlarged Common Market as he has of the present one, and therefore will endeavour to exclude us. This is the real reason, but our present financial plight is advanced as an obstacle, along with other far less plausible considerations.

Driving around the countryside provides a great contrast with Italy and, above all, Spain. Everything is clean, orderly, tidy and *prosperous*. There is no sign of poverty anywhere – nor any sign of the war, except a very few bullet marks on the older buildings.

When I saw Willi Brandt in Berlin recently, he looked a broken-down man. Now, after two months in office, he looks a new man,

* Sir Frank Roberts, G.C.M.G., G.C.V.O.

confident and strong. I gather he likes his glass, but what I was told in Berlin, though borne out by his appearance, was greatly exaggerated. Brandt is a capable, strong, brave man, would be an ornament to any government. Strauss is an unattractive man to meet, but when he gets going (I had nearly one and a half hours with him) is very realistic and outspoken. He is obviously a man of outstanding ability. Since he had to leave the Ministry of Defence over attacks on him in the magazine *Der Spiegel*, he has slimmed, studied economics, and really taken a pull. The result is someone far more impressive than any of our ministers. He is not such a nice man as Brandt, nor such a good man, but an abler one.

As the Ambassador said, Kiesinger is like Macmillan, and so he is. There are much the same height; have much the same mannerisms; their faces are similar – they might well be brothers.

Monday, February 6th, 1967

Yesterday was the guest of the Lazareffs (editors-in-chief of *France-Soir* and of *Elle* respectively) at lunch at Louveciennes, near Versailles. Other guests were Pompidou (Prime Minister) and his wife, Couve de Murville (Foreign Minister) and his wife, Alphand (Permanent Under-Secretary at the Foreign Ministry), Hélène Rochas, the dress designer etc.; Forgeot, head of Creusot; Mlle Fabian, French film actress.

At lunch I sat on Mme Lazareff's left, with Pompidou on her right. Pompidou seemed rather grumpy; Alphand looked stuffed and was very silent. I had Mme Alphand on my left – good-looking and basically nice, though with a very artificial manner. She was always said in Washington, where her husband was Ambassador for so long, to be one of the best-dressed women in the world. She was dressed in a hideous short concoction, mainly of black leather. I said to Mme Lazareff that the Italians and Germans both said the real objection to Britain joining the Common Market was that, when inside, we should lead it, and I had no idea the French Government was so afraid of Wilson's gifts of leadership. She said, 'Can I say that to the Prime Minister?' I said, 'Yes.' It was a leg pull that might have opened up the conversation, but he remained grumpy and I had no talk with him.

I had two long talks with Couve de Murville. He was a bit sticky to start with, but then really got going. One interesting piece was that Wilson told him that this Government would last for four years, after which he would win the next election and so would be in office for eight years from now! Couve assumed that Britain was coming in, but that with our three satellites, Ireland, Norway and Denmark, this would change the character of the Common Market, which would necessarily, for a time, become a looser association. He said that what impressed them in Paris was that Wilson had completely changed his tune since he was here two years ago and the change was due to pressure of public opinion. One effect of our joining would be to increase our agricultural production until we were nearly self-supporting. He said the Common Market would be protectionist, and that we were in no position to criticize as we now had the highest tariffs in the world. They objected to sterling not as a trading currency, but as a reserve currency which concealed our deficits. Working balances would be necessary and were unobjectionable. They were surprised by the sunny optimism of ministerial pronouncements about our financial affairs, which did not seem justified. The other point which impressed the General was Wilson's argument about the larger base now necessary for technological advance. If Europe did not get together for research, we had no hope of keeping up with the Americans.

Wednesday, February 8th, 1967

Grimond came to lunch today – very relieved at relinquishing the leadership of the Liberal Party. He is very gloomy over the country's affairs: thinks we are drifting downwards with no one caring very much. Says that the parties no longer have any meaning, and sees no reason why Wilson should ever be dislodged.

Sunday, February 12th, 1967

On Friday was a guest, with about thirty others, at a lunch at No. 10 for Kosygin. I was specially favoured, as, when Wilson joined the party late with his guest of honour, it was I, in the background, who was presented first, and was afterwards propelled into a side room with George Brown and others to talk to Kosygin. Conversation under these circumstances, with interpreters, is quite futile. Kosygin is a big man, but not a great one: modest, sad, and with a charming smile. Thanks to agitation in the *Mirror* he had a reasonably cordial welcome. As he is not a Head of State, the authorities were planning to give him much less than the King of Jordan. No doubt his very warm reception in Paris also helped. I don't think the visit serves any real purpose. Wilson will, no doubt, regard the visit as useful publicity for himself.

I was interested to see Marcia Williams for the first time. She looks about thirty, but surely must be more, bleached mouse hair, quite good-looking, with a scared expression.

Wednesday, February 15th, 1967

Had forty-five minutes with Wilson on Friday evening. I was to have met him at 10 Downing St at 7 p.m., but the American Chargé d'Affaires had come to say that the bombing in Vietnam was, after all, to be renewed, and I actually had 7.25 to 8.10 with Wilson. I came to tell him about my trip round Europe and, in particular, to warn him that – soft words or no – de Gaulle was determined to keep us out of the Common Market if he could. In fact our only hope was to outmanœuvre him. Wilson, as usual, very faintly interested in what I had to say; spent forty of the forty-five minutes saying what a wonderful relationship he had established with Kosygin; how he had missed a cease-fire in Vietnam by a hair's breadth. Later, switching to the Common Market, he knew everything I had to tell him, and then went into a long account of how well he had handled de Gaulle, and how friendly he was. I have never met de Gaulle, but from anything one has read about him, and heard about him, I should imagine he would look upon Wilson and Brown with amused contempt. But that is no reason why he should not be friendly in an avuncular sort of way. I came away from 10 Downing St more depressed than usual. You cannot break through Wilson's façade of buoyant optimism. His vanity is quite astonishing – each failure is hailed as a brilliant breakthrough; realism never shows up. One must just wait for events to reveal to the world that the emperor has no clothes.

Wednesday, February 22nd, 1967

Roy Jenkins came to lunch – in good form as usual. After lunch I gave him one of my political forecasts: this government is too bad, Wilson is no P.M., our problems are not being solved, things cannot go on like this, at some point the *Daily Mirror* will have to move into open attack. Roy seemed to think that though no problem has been solved, Wilson was clever enough to continue to manœuvre, evading any real issue, until the next election, or even beyond. I said the great danger in the present situation is that deterioration might be so gradual as to be acceptable. Though this policy was possible under Baldwin, our latent strength is, I hope, no longer sufficient for a policy based on inertia. I thought a break would necessarily come, or could be created, after which there would have to be a fresh start, with new faces, some of them not politicians: Robens, Beeching, Shawcross and Sainsbury, for instance. It would be a National Government under some other name. He did not fancy the idea. Clearly he has no thought of including any Tories (though, in my opinion, this may well come). I told him I thought he and Denis Healey were the two candidates for the succession, as it would have to be Labour-dominated in view of the present composition of the House. I didn't say this, but I think probably we shall have to move over to the attack by September or October, by which time events will, I think, have weakened Wilson's position.

On Saturday afternoon Mrs Balogh came to tea – at her suggestion. She said we had met at a dinner-party at George Weidenfeld's, but neither of us remembered her. She had come to consult Ruth on her daughter Tessa, aged nine, who wants to be a ballet dancer, and me on the publication of some pieces on mental health, as she is a psychotherapist. In the course of conversation she greatly praised Barbara Castle as a minister, which was evidently the opinion she had heard at No. 10. She also said that many people thought that Wilson would be returned with an increased majority in 1970, but *she* thought it would be lower. I said I didn't think he had a chance of being re-elected at all (hoping this would be reported back!!).

Thursday, March 2nd, 1967

At the Bank as usual. While Wilson tells me the surplus this year will be £300 million, Maurice Allen tells me the latest calculation by the Treasury and the Bank is £23 million! The deficit for last year was supposed to be £350 million, but is now put at £150 million. The difference is due to de-stocking and sales of foreign securities, which have been larger than had been realized. But using this money, as Paul Bareau* said, is like eating the seed corn.

Friday, March 3rd, 1967

Denis Healey came to lunch. I hadn't seen him for some time. He was very eloquent on his success in cutting down defence expenditure. He had cut £750 million of what would otherwise have been spent. I said that even so, defence expenditure had risen. He said this was only a small rise, by next year there would be a fall. I said he had told me there would be no base in the Persian Gulf and now they were building one. He said they were only building accommodation for one additional battalion, and if they didn't keep some troops in the Gulf they were afraid Europe's oil might be held up while the various Arab powers fought it out for possession of the oil wells. The Aden situation was disquieting, and they might have to remain longer than they had originally intended. They didn't want to leave chaos behind. At present the Egyptians were one of three nationalist groups struggling for control of Aden after our departure. The South Arabian Federation – like Malaysia – was (according to Denis) one of Duncan Sandys's crazier creations.

I said I thought Wilson an even worse P.M. than Alec Home – difficult as that was! He entirely disagreed. He seemed pleased with the public opinion polls and willing to leave it at that. I said I thought people had had the Tories and desperately wanted the Labour Government to be a success. They would learn before long that it was a failure – and this was the disquieting thought. I came to the conclusion that Denis Healey has his hands full at the Ministry of Defence and does not expect any dramatic developments, at any rate for the present. He certainly does not seem to be preparing the ground for a takeover bid for No. 10.

* Paul Bareau is a friend of Cecil King's, the editor of the *Statist* and a well-known writer on economics and finance. The *Statist* was published by I.P.C.

Thursday, March 9th, 1967

A long talk after Court with Maurice Allen in his room at the Bank. The present estimate of the surplus on our balance of payments is £25 million. There are various pluses and minuses that may apply to this and, in practice, the minuses are smaller than the pluses, so the figure may end at £75 million. The estimate in today's papers is £175 million, which is wildly optimistic.

Thursday, March 23rd, 1967

Mike dined earlier in the week with Harold Lever, now Under-Secretary at the D.E.A. Among the guests was Dick Crossman, with whom Mike had a long talk. Crossman said he had just come from a Cabinet meeting on the Common Market, the first one of *six*! He said Harold could not afford another failure, but was badly in need of a success. He thought on balance Harold would make a definite bid to join the Common Market.

Today George Brown came to lunch, at his request. He sees no chance of overturning Wilson before the next election. George obviously attaches all importance to Parliamentary manœuvres, none to successful management of the nation's affairs. At present he sees Jim Callaghan as the successor, even though I pointed out that we are heading for further financial crises, which must discredit both Wilson and Callaghan. No mention was made of Denis Healey, though Roy Jenkins was spoken of as a possible runner in the remoter future.

Thursday, March 30th, 1967

Brian Walden came to lunch yesterday. I had never even seen him before. He is in his early thirties – quite insignificant to look at, but has already made quite a mark. He seems to earn his living working for a firm of public relations consultants. He entered Parliament as M.P. for the All Saints division of Birmingham in 1964 or 1966. He said that in the House there is a great divide, particularly in the Labour Party, between those over forty-five and those under. In the Labour Party the over forty-fives mostly left school at fourteen or less, while the newer intake are mostly graduates. I found that on politics, in general, he agreed surprisingly with myself. He is quite certain that present political alignments are in for drastic changes:

the old slogans and the old loyalties have no longer any meaning. Contempt for Parliament and for ministers is pretty prevalent, but particularly so among the young.

I found his forecasts depressing. He said the Labour Party's loyalty to its leader is very strong, and particularly so when he is P.M. He doubted if Wilson could be upset: he would go out with his party. He thought this would be a fairly easy year; next year very tough, with financial disaster overtaking us in the spring of 1969. What is always difficult to estimate is what people will do when the situation changes. Obviously Wilson is immovable this week, but surrounded by enemies as he is, he is surely liable to be the victim of a palace revolution if things go seriously wrong – as they will do.

Walden said he thought Wilson would make a serious effort to get into the Common Market, but would fail. This would leave the whole political situation deadlocked. He assumed that after frittering away two and a half years it would prove impossible to enforce an effective wage and price policy.

The front-page news for more than a week has been the big tanker wrecked off Land's End.* Sir Zolly Suckerman tells Mike that the experts realized that the tanker could not be floated off and should be set on fire as soon as possible. However, dithering went on for days and days, and the tanker was fired too late. It was amusing the way Wilson tried to cash in on the episode by holding press conferences and appearing on television, not apparently realizing – through lack of foresight – that this oil is bound to reach the South Coast holiday resorts whatever anyone can do; and all he will have succeeded in achieving is to identify himself with the disaster.

Tuesday, April 4th, 1967

Hugh Cudlipp, in from Moscow this morning, was astonished at the warmth of his reception by *Pravda*, *Isvestia*, and Soldatov, formerly Ambassador here and now Deputy Foreign Minister. The editor-in-chief of *Pravda*, until recently Russian Ambassador in Prague, hinted that he would like us to extend an invitation to Russian editors to

* The *Torrey Canyon*, a Liberian-registered tanker, ran aground on the Seven Stones rocks on March 18th. Her cargo of about 100,000 tons of crude oil threatened beaches on the Cornish and Devon coasts, and a major operation was mounted to destroy the oil and cleanse the beaches.

attend a conference in London similar to the ones we have held for French, German, Czech, Polish and Dutch editors. Their propaganda line is being softened and made more acceptable and they profess to see in us the means to better relations with the U.S.A. Soldatov, in this talk with Hugh, was more welcoming than our Ambassador* expected to the idea of a Europe united from the Atlantic to the Urals, and far more hostile than expected to any idea of German reunification ever.

Last night to dinner at No. 10 to meet Hubert Humphrey, the American Vice-President, whom I have met many times and like very much. The party was a dull one – I sat between two very dull women. The two speeches were so eulogistic about Wilson and Humphrey that one could only hope they were hypocritical. In a gathering of some forty or fifty people Wilson just disappears. His usual entourage were all there: Marcia Williams, Balogh and Trevor Lloyd-Hughes. Neither Wilson nor Mary [Wilson] has any social gifts and the more Wilsonian ministers you invite, the more insignificant they look.

Saturday, April 22nd, 1967

In Washington to make a speech to the American Society of Newspaper Editors. I was asked to be critical and indeed I was.

Yesterday evening I went to the Editors' reception at the White House. My purpose was to see Mrs Johnson and have another look at the President. I have been through the reception rooms before. They are very poor – appalling pictures of past presidents (even one of Mamie Eisenhower!), poor furniture, shoddy carpets. Mrs Johnson is said by Barbara Ward to be such an outstandingly nice woman that there must be some good in the President. But to shake hands with and to watch her shaking hands with others, she looks like her photographs – insignificant. Mrs Graham was saying that she has a marvellous control over herself and never shows her feelings in any way. The President was beaming benevolently. He is a big man and an able one, but unattractive. The job is probably beyond anyone's capacity – certainly beyond his. Washington is obsessed with Vietnam: they want to get out without loss of face, but cannot

* Sir Geoffrey Harrison, G.C.M.G., K.C.V.O.

see how. Meanwhile, the Government continues slowly to step up the war.

Thursday, May 4th, 1967

Quite a bit has happened since my last entry, but I have had no important personal contacts until yesterday. Whitelaw came to lunch and I saw Ted Heath at his flat in the evening. I do not think either Whitelaw or Heath had any news, but they wondered why Wilson did not go on television on Tuesday night to explain his decision to go into the Common Market. He is usually very ready to appear on the most trivial occasion. According to Whitelaw, ministers have been told not to make speeches on the subject. This sounds as if Wilson had only got the agreement of ministers to support the application on the basis of an agreed formula, and any gloss on the formula might well lead to trouble. Why Wilson should insist on keeping every one of his very weak team is hard to explain, except in terms of internal politics in the Parliamentary Labour Party. The strings that have been attached to the announcement make it hard to see how we can have success this time and the fact that half the Cabinet is known to be against the Common Market, anyway, is bound to weaken Wilson's hand still further.

Friday, May 5th, 1967

Monnet came to see me yesterday afternoon. He was to dine with Ted Heath in the evening and is seeing George Brown at some point. He thinks on the whole, so far so good, but that a lot will depend on the actual terms of the application. We shall do our best to get this in the right form by publicizing Ted Heath's opening speech on Tuesday, when he is going to deal with this very important aspect of the matter. The Foreign Office people tell Mike that the text of the application has not yet been drafted and will not be until after the debate.

Wilson made his announcement on Tuesday, but on Wednesday Bowden, a limited but honest man, now at the C.R.O., gave a press conference at which he said great regard would be paid in the course of the negotiations to the interests of the Commonwealth and that if these were not adequately protected, we should withdraw our application! Now, in a further reversal of his position, he is to speak in the debate! This Government cannot get used to the idea that if you pitch different stories to suit different audiences, there is no means by which you can prevent the wrong stories getting round to the wrong audiences.

Letter of May 5th from Cecil King to Edward Heath:

STRICTLY PRIVATE & CONFIDENTIAL

Dear Ted,

I am wondering whether you saw the Frost programme last night? I do not look in much, but this is by no means the first programme I have seen that treats Parliament, Ministers, political broadcasts – the lot – with total derision. No newspaper in my time has gone nearly so far. The sinister aspect of this is that these programmes are very popular, and the contempt they express for politicians and politics is widely shared by the public.

Clearly the present Government will contribute to this impression, but if we are to save our democratic insitutions something drastic will have to be done as soon as this is possible.

I doubt whether a Government of ministers all from the House of Commons or of peers recently transferred from the Commons will do. Won't serious efforts have to be made to bring in people from outside who do command public respect? I am thinking perhaps of people with a scientific reputation (Medawars, not Snows!), or further injections of people like Beeching.

With my good wishes always,

Cecil King

The Rt. Hon. Edward Heath, M.B.E., M.P.,
F.2, Albany,
Piccadilly, W.I.

Thursday, May 11th, 1967

Had Aubrey Jones to lunch yesterday. He is highly intelligent and able, but has little authority or weight. Probably the right man in the right job. I asked him about the end of the price and wage policy in July. He said he had worked out a plausible policy for continuing

Government restraint into the future: Michael Stewart and the P.M. approved; Ray Gunter opposed it. When it came before the Cabinet, George Brown – to everyone's surprise – spoke up strongly against the plan, which was defeated. So now from July the Prices and Incomes Board can express opinions when asked, but the Government has thrown away its power of restraint. Aubrey Jones assumes that there will be a steep rise in wages after July, which will lead to a financial crisis and another clamp-down by the Government. Politically this is not as easy as it sounds. If the Government cannot summon the authority to maintain its policy, to readopt the policy later on is much more difficult and can only be done with much loss of face.

Application to join the Common Market was approved last night in the House of Commons, all three parties voting in favour. There had been talk of a majority of 500, but in the end it was 426 – far less than had been hoped. The usual Tories voted against, but the number of Labour M.P.s who voted against was surprisingly high and there were a lot of abstentions. Quite seventy Labour M.P.s abstained or voted against. I can't believe that this reflects a sudden increase in opposition to the Common Market, but rather a lowering of fear and respect for Wilson and the leadership. George Brown seems to expect an early admission to the Market, but I would suppose a long period – say, two years of obstruction by the French. As there have been no resignations and no dismissals from the Cabinet, Wilson is not well placed to negotiate, with half his Cabinet more or less opposed to this part of his policy.

Friday, May 12th, 1967

Two items of political interest this morning: sweeping gains by Tories in the municipal elections – Conservative majorities now in Liverpool, Manchester, Nottingham, and perhaps Newcastle. Labour holds Leeds and Sheffield, but only by the skin of its teeth. Manchester goes Conservative after thirty-one years and, in general, the Tories have done better than was expected – far better than was expected only a few weeks ago.

Wilson has insisted on the dismissal of eight Parliamentary Private Secretaries who abstained in the vote on the Common Market. It is said that the minister would not in one case dismiss his P.P.S., so it was done by the P.M.'s office. I cannot imagine that this will go down very well: to let the ministers get away with near murder and to decide to do nothing about the M.P.s who voted against the Government; yet to fire the poor little P.P.S.s. This will surely seem to be the feeble, almost spiteful, discipline of a weak man.

Saturday, May 13th, 1967

The following is copied from a letter received from Hugh Cudlipp about his visit to the Prime Minister yesterday evening. It lasted one and a half hours and was at Wilson's request.

He went out of his way to say that the *Mirror* had 'done him proud' this week, meaning of course our treatment of the Common Market debate. In a side remark he said he thought it odd that we had referred to Ted Heath as 'a man of principle'.

The theme of the whole of our talk was his art and success in approaching the big problems 'politically'.

'I told you in Liverpool that I would get the right Common Market decision at the right time, but that the political in-fighting had to be done by me in my own way. What better result could there have been? Remember your front-page article on February 27 – and it has all come about, and with a three-line Tory Whip into the bargain.'

He told me that in Paris de Gaulle had said to him at dinner: 'I accept your absolute sincerity on this question. I believe that you intend to moor your ship of state along the coast of Europe instead of in mid-Atlantic.' (Sorry about the cliché, it's de Gaulle's!)

I brought up the question of Jay and Peart. 'Again,' he said, 'this question has to be handled politically and I know how to handle it. Before the Cabinet had definitely decided on our Common Market policy I could not rightly complain of Ministers expressing contrary views – this is a democracy. But once the policy was accepted by the Cabinet the position changed. I have told them bluntly that from now on they toe the Cabinet line or go. I would not hesitate to sack them, if necessary. Jay came to see me about a speech he is making next week. I insisted on seeing it before it was delivered.'

His confidence is immense, dangerously immense.

He clearly wasn't worried by Labour's overwhelming defeat at the local elections. 'I predicted it,' he said, 'it came as no surprise to me. Everything is working perfectly to timing – the three phases: first, the emergency measures to clean up the Tory mess; second, the hostility of the public; third, the recovery.'

I asked him what line he was going to take on his journey to Canada and Washington in a fortnight's time, and he said something of significance. There would have to be blunt talking in Washington. Wilson is concerned about L.B.J.'s continuing escalation of the Vietnam war. I did not get the impression that Harold was desperately concerned about the question from a moral point of view himself, but concerned about the concern of many members of his Party, and also of public opinion here.

'The question of disassociating the British government from this policy might well arise, if not in Washington then sometime soon.'

Thinking politically again, he said, with a knowing look, 'Of course a new policy on these lines towards Vietnam and the U.S. would stand us in good stead in Europe, wouldn't it? And at the right time, too. You've got to think politically.'

I said I had two points to raise – more psychological than political.

The first was that politicians are to blame themselves for the low standing of their profession in the eyes of the public. I instanced the Moran Diary,* which established that Churchill had been propped up in power by Butler and Salisbury long after he should have been put out to grass, merely so that his name and reputation could be exploited in a coming election. Also mentioned Anthony Eden's lie to the Commons about Suez and other recent episodes. And then came to Harold's conversion to Europe.

'Instead of saying that the situation has changed, which it has not, why not admit in public that you were wrong?'

He saw the point immediately. This was right up his street. 'Yes,' he said, 'I see that. I will establish that at least one politician, and a Prime Minister at that, is honest with the public. I will do it on television – that's the place to do it. I quite see your point.'

* Lord Moran's account, taken from his diaries, of Churchill's life and illnesses. *Churchill: The Struggle for Survival 1940–1965* (London: Constable, 1966).

The second point I raised was a criticism frequently made of him that he is too much of a tactician with no strategic plan. He hotly denied the charge, and it was obvious that the accusation irritated him. The reverse was the truth, he said, and instanced his handling of the Common Market issue as evidence. I suggested that the only way he could succeed in refuting the charge was to prove that he did have a strategic plan. He agreed to do a major interview with John Beavan on questions from Beavan and myself in a fortnight's time and accepted the headline: WHERE ARE WE GOING? AND HOW WILL WE GET THERE?

When the Nutting series appeared in *The Times** he knew that Eden was in the country and let it be known that if Eden wanted to see him he was quite willing. Eden did in fact see him at Downing St. I asked if Eden denied the major charge – that he had lied to the House. 'No,' he said, 'Eden said there were inaccuracies. He repeated that several times.'

Macmillan had also been to Downing St to see Wilson on the same question. What they were discussing, of course, was had there been a breach of a Privy Councillor's obligations?

A day or two before I saw him I had sent him the full details of our press arrangements with the Russians. He was extremely interested in this, and considered it a most important breakthrough. I told him that I had had two hours with Soldatov, who was obviously working on Russia's future policy towards Europe. I told him the story which I told you when I returned – Soldatov's reference to the Common Market and the future, his criticisms that the Common Market was too small and was discriminatory against the U.S.S.R., and his vision (quite seriously expressed) that one day it might include the U.S.S.R. Wilson was intrigued about this and it was quite clear he had not heard this concept before.

He told me that John Freeman is coming to see him soon. He is concerned about his future on a long-term basis and wants to resign so that he can take part in the new television programme companies. Wilson, however, is thinking of Freeman as Ambassador

* Anthony Nutting was one of two junior ministers in the Eden Government who resigned as an expression of their opposition to Anglo–French military action against Egypt (the other was Edward Boyle). Nutting published his views in a series of articles in *The Times*.

in either Moscow or Washington, and feels that some such offer might well change Freeman's thinking.

He is giving a knighthood to Richardson, Editor of the now-failing *Sunday Citizen*. I think I was quite right not to take that knighthood: it's an ill omen.

Wednesday, May 17th, 1967

Rowley Cromer came to dinner at Hampton Court last night. He anticipates financial trouble by September. In the long run he expects trouble with the trades unions to end in violence. He is off to Portugal today for Baring's to try and negotiate a very big contract in Mozambique, but has arranged all his interviews himself without reference to the Embassy. In Tokyo, when Cudlipp saw the Prime Minister, the Ambassador asked if he could come along too as it was his only chance of seeing the P.M. In Moscow, Cudlipp saw Soldatov, now Deputy Foreign Minister, for two hours: he was very frank, including asking if, in time, Russia could join the Common Market; the Ambassador said he had had no chance of such a frank conversation with anyone. When I was in Spain, the Ambassador said he was so glad I had come as it enabled him to lay on the lunch-party for ministers and others whom he had no chance of seeing in the ordinary way. Finally, someone passing through Bonn lately was told by Roberts, the Ambassador, that 'those damned Kings had been through lately'! When asked why he referred to them in that way, he was told, 'because they saw people I cannot'! There must be something very wrong with our diplomatic service or our policy, or both, if our ambassadors are unable to see politicians who are available to passing newspaper publishers and merchant bankers.

George Brown was attacked in a mild way in the *Sunday Telegraph* for unseemly behaviour with Princess Margaret the night before. We were critical on Monday and the *Express* on Tuesday. It looks as if the newspapers are making up their minds to give old George the works. To do so would gravely embarrass Wilson, who would either have to sustain a totally discredited Foreign Secretary – or dismiss him, and have a very dangerous enemy. In any case, George is incapable of sustaining the long negotiations on the Common Market, which may well continue into 1969. Mulley, the minister immediately in charge, is a nonentity who is neither here nor there.

I asked Rowley why Kaldor and Balogh kept their jobs. He said he had told Wilson on one occasion that hundreds of millions of the sterling outflow could be attributed to lack of confidence in these Hungarians on the Continent. Wilson said he had indeed heard this. But they stayed. Rowley is of the opinion that they are kept because if they went they would be dangerous critics of the Government, joining with Labour left-wing back-benchers. This rings true to me. They have, of course, less than no influence with the outside public.

Wednesday, June 14th, 1967

It must be a month since I wrote this diary last. Since then I have spent a fortnight in Czechoslovakia and a week in Romania; we have also had the Arab–Israeli war. I don't like being behind the Iron Curtain, but we were given a wonderful welcome by *Rude Pravo* in Prague and were well looked-after in Romania.

I saw a variety of bigwigs in both countries, including the First Secretary of the Communist Party in both capitals: Novotny (also President) in Prague and Ceauşescu in Bucharest – both quite intelligent but nothing special. I thought the outstanding people I met in Prague were Švestka (Editor-in-Chief of *Rude Pravo*), Pohl (Governor of the Central Bank), and Sucharda (the Minister of Finance). In Romania I was most impressed by Pungan, their ambassador in London.

The Israeli war lasted six days, in which time the Israelis completely disintegrated the armies of Egypt, Jordan and Syria, reoccupied the Sinai Peninsula, the whole of Palestine west of the Jordan, and a slice of Syria. It was an extraordinarily well-planned, well-fought campaign, from a military point of view entirely decisive. The Israelis want now to arrange a peace treaty with the Arabs from a position of strength. The Russians, who appear not to have wanted any fighting, but to have counted on the Egyptians coming out on top if there was any, want to mobilize the United Nations in a huge propaganda campaign against Israel, the United States and Great Britain. At the moment any settled peace looks a long way off.

In the early stages before the fighting began, Wilson, speaking to the E.T.U.,* said how the Straits of Tiran must be kept open, plainly implying that this would be done by force if necessary. The Americans and French conspicuously omitted to say anything. If the Israelis had not won so swiftly, we might have been in an awkward fix. The only result of this declaration was to have Britain linked with America as the 'aggressor' and to have our shipping excluded from all Arab ports and our oil supplies stopped. It seems to be assumed that these embargoes will be lifted any day now – but will they? If they are not, we shall have to pay a lot more for our oil, and this at a very awkward moment in our financial affairs.

Sunday, June 25th, 1967

Meanwhile, in domestic politics an absurd situation has developed over the D-Notice tribunal.† Wilson accused the *Express* of publishing information in contravention of a D-Notice. We disputed his opinion and, by the resignation of Lee Howard (*Mirror* editor) from the D-Notice Committee, forced Wilson to appoint a tribunal of three Privy Councillors, Radcliffe, Selwyn Lloyd and Shinwell, to inquire and report. They reported in favour of the *Express*, so Wilson has put out a White Paper repudiating his tribunal and reiterating his accusation. He arranged a debate and forced his party to accept the White Paper. This has brought down on him the condemnation of all the newspapers and has made him look a fool. The whole matter could have been ended by an apology by Wilson in the first place, but now it will rumble on for months in a way highly damaging to the P.M. In the debate on June 22nd, instead of opening as he should have, Wilson wound up. This gave no opportunity for anyone to question what he said and the last five minutes, speaking

* Electrical Trades Union.

† The D-Notice arrangement was a system whereby notices were issued to editors and other communications agencies providing general and occasionally specific guidance on the kinds of information which should not be published in the interests of national security. The notices, issued by a committee composed partly of officials and partly of nominated representatives of the press, were merely advisory, but in practice were rarely defied, if only because an editor who did so might find himself at risk in relation to the Official Secrets Act. In February Mr Wilson mentioned in the House that the *Daily Express* had defied a D-Notice with a story concerned with the collection by the Government for intelligence purposes of copies of international cables filed in the U.K. Parliamentary and other pressures forced the appointment of a committee of Privy Councillors under Lord Radcliffe to inquire into the incident. Their report was published in June.

against the clock, he devoted to an attack on Colonel Lohan, a civil servant, who is secretary of the D-Notice Committee. His accusations were vague, but the intention was clearly to divert attention from himself to the shortcomings of Lohan. The result is the worst press any P.M. has had in my day, notably the contemptuous references in *The Times* to attempted character assassination. It may be that Wilson is quite pleased. He made his speech and got his vote. This may be all that he can see. But to unite the entire British press behind the *Express* is quite a feat anyway, and press contempt for Wilson is not likely to evaporate.

Had Robens (in great form) and Beeching to lunch this week. Both assume this Government is heading for a crash: this year or next. No one can see what happens then. Neither Jenkins nor Denis Healey is improving his position. Jenkins seems a weak liberal at the Home Office and most of Healey's defence plans seem to have come unstuck. No other personality is enhancing his position. Marsh has far too much on his shoulders and, according to Robens, is showing it.

Our progress to Europe is not going well. Wilson saw de Gaulle in Paris. The visit was mistimed and served no purpose. Brown darts about making pronouncements when silence would be more effective. Robens says Sophie [Brown] has several times implored Robens to try and persuade George to retire. They have no home life and George is increasingly short-tempered.

Saturday, July 1st, 1967

It has been a very heavy week and so have had no time for this diary. Blankenhorn, the German Ambassador, came to lunch on Wednesday. I like talking to him as he is intelligent, well-informed and indiscreet. He told me he had had a cable from Kiesinger that morning asking what the special relationship between England and the U.S. amounted to today. I said I thought a certain amount of sentiment and historical background, largely confined to the eastern seaboard. An Englishman may feel almost at home in Boston, but a stranger in a strange land in Los Angeles. The American attitudes to such fundamentals as death and women were so different from the English ones that the development of the two countries must proceed on quite divergent lines. During the last war and for a period afterwards the special relationship had some political significance, but I thought none now.

Blankenhorn also told me that he had seen a report – he didn't say so, but it sounded like a transcript – of the conversation between Wilson and de Gaulle at their recent meeting. De Gaulle had given Wilson a glittering reception at the Grand Trianon, and then, having illustrated to his own satisfaction the importance of de Gaulle and the nullity of Wilson, took him under a spreading chestnut tree and fairly clobbered him. The Ambassador's view was that the meeting should not have taken place at all. It was, in any case, mistimed. De Gaulle apparently said there were two of the Six that had partial relationships with the U.S. These could not be eliminated if Great Britain joined the Common Market. So we should have to be kept out at least until these pockets of Americanism had been cleared out. Blankenhorn also mentioned in passing that he had had a talk with Alec Home, who had said of the general political situation, 'This can't go on.'

Pam Berry gave a party on Thursday evening for Mrs Graham of the *Washington Post*. I was there early and talked mainly to Senator Javits, who was pressing the merits of a North Atlantic free-trade area. However, later in the evening, Hugh Cudlipp was there. Dick Crossman came up to him and, later, Elwyn Jones (the Attorney-General) buttonholed him as he was leaving. The theme of both men was that press criticism had Wilson distracted – in particular our leader on Tuesday. The implication was that if we, and the other newspapers, keep on like this we shall break him. George Brown is in similar plight, though this week's *Economist* comes to his rescue.

I had a long talk with O'Brien on Thursday. My theme was then, and had been on Monday with Parsons, that Callaghan's optimism was fully represented in the newspapers, but the Bank's more cautious (i.e. gloomy) view was hardly represented at all. Clearly the official line would prove to be nonsense, and so would it not be wise for it to be known more widely that the Bank's attitude was quite different? I had suggested giving a couple of dinner-parties and inviting Parsons or Maurice Allen, perhaps even the Governor, to meet a couple of editors. This was not approved, but I think some of the editors will be seen singly. In any case, an earlier suggestion of mine that the Governor and some of his people should meet the principal City editors over dinner from time to time has been adopted. There are likely to be three such dinners every six months.

Friday, July 14th, 1967

Denis Healey to lunch – in boisterous form. On previous visits he has always professed indifference to the idea of promotion to 10 Downing St. But not so today. He was, of course, cautious, rated Roy Jenkins's chances high, but left me in no doubt that his hat is in the ring. Of specific news he had little. Wilson was quite uncontrollable and impervious to advice over the D-Notice affair. He and George Brown were restrained only with difficulty by the rest of the Cabinet over the Middle East. They wanted to come out far more strongly in the early stages in favour of Israel. He said George, with all faults, did have his value. Nobody but he in the Labour Party could have forced through the decision to join the Common Market and to leave Singapore.

He said the decision by the French to drop collaboration on the swing-wing plane was very opportune for us. We should have had to drop it ourselves, I gather. He had heard a good deal about the interior of French politics from Messmer, whom he had been dealing with over the swing-wing plane. The General is getting more and more remote from reality, more and more dictatorial. His policies are all failing, but he still has a great nuisance value – the power to say No. His ministers and his party are intriguing among themselves for the succession, but he can go on more or less like this for several years.

Monday, July 17th, 1967

David Bruce to lunch, as always in good form – anyway, when we lunch together. There was no mention of American politics. He said the Americans did their utmost to restrain the Israelis, but the Israelis (very sensibly) thought they had had enough. He did not think any solution could be approached for a long time. Meanwhile, the Russians, in spite of their appalling miscalculations, think they may be able to use the whole episode to improve their position in the Mediterranean.

Bruce took some part in an engineering survey of Mesopotamia and said it is the largest area of unoccupied corn land in the world. There would be no difficulty in irrigating it and settling a million Arabs thereon, but the Arabs wanted to keep their Palestinian refugees as a propaganda weapon.

Tuesday, July 18th, 1967

Geoffrey Rippon to lunch. I had not seen him for quite a time. He seemed to me a good minister, i.e. a good administrator, but he lacks any perceptible political sense. I think the only unexpected idea he put forward was that Alec Home should be the leader of the Conservative Party. The reason he gave was that he is the right age! Geoffrey is doing quite well at the Bar, but seemed to have no idea why the Tory Party has condemned the Prices and Incomes policy. They will have to have one if they take office, so why make things more difficult for themselves by condemning it in advance? Meanwhile, Tony Crosland hits the headlines by complaining of cuts in the social services when, to me, he said he wanted to double the cost of school meals but got no support. It may be he only wanted this money to spend in his own department and had no interest in overall economies. But, anyway, by coming out like this when the whole matter is under discussion in the Cabinet might suggest that he, too, has designs on No. 10.

Thursday, July 20th, 1967

At Ellis Birk's on Tuesday evening, met Tony Crosland and had a long talk with Dick Crossman; last night met a number of ministers at a party at the Zoo given by Solly Zuckerman. All in all, I must have talked to the more important half of the Cabinet (minus Wilson) in the last few days. I think, speaking in general terms, the morale of the Government is collapsing. Crossman seemed to me bewildered and harassed, exclaiming at length on the impotence of the press. As he returned to the subject so often, I took it that he was getting rattled by press hostility. He said Wilson had been misled by his civil servants over the D-Notice affair, and, in Crossman's opinion, he should have fired them. I said he had only to read a few lines of print to see if the D-Notice was in fact infringed by the *Express* and, if he had done so, he would have seen it had not been. He said the P.M. had no time to check. I said, not even when you are launching a direct attack on a daily newspaper? He dismissed daily newspapers as of no political account. However, at the end he said, 'Well, Harold has six months to pull the whole thing together and make a success of it. If he does so, your criticisms will be irrelevant and, if he does not do so, he will be finished and your criticisms will be irrelevant also.' I said, 'Do you think he has six months?' He said, 'Well, four months then.'

Last night George Brown was present. He asked to be asked to lunch so as to tell me about recent happenings. I said, 'You fought a fine fight to get us out of Singapore.' He said, 'Yes, I and my friends brought that off, so you can say I control the Government.' I greeted Jim Callaghan at the party and some time later was sitting on a seat looking at an African elephant. Jim came up and said, 'When I retire I suppose I shall be doing this.' So I said, 'You are a young man: you won't retire for a long time.' He said, 'My retirement will be forced; it will not be of my own choosing.' The conversation continued for a short time and I moved away. Ruth, afterwards, said, 'You realize Jim came over specially to tell you he was being fired, don't you?' I said I thought he was just making conversation. However, this morning I told Maurice Parsons that yesterday, in talking to Jim Callaghan, I got the impression he might have the skids under him. Maurice said, 'He has. I think he will be relieved to lay down his office. He has found it very harassing.' I said the Government's morale seemed to be crumbling and that the Cabinet was far from being a band of brothers! He said that was how it looked from their end.

At Court it was a gloomy story of big purchases of gold, rising interest rates, weak exchanges, sagging gilt-edged. After Court, George Bolton said we are now faced with two inescapable future events: devaluation of sterling and the collapse of British Government credit.

Tuesday, July 25th, 1967
Mike, at my instigation, had an hour with Alec Home yesterday. He

told Mike he would have preferred Reggie as leader of the Conservatives: he thought lazy men came off better in a crisis! He thought this country would not pull itself together until there was a serious crash of some kind. He also thought the time had come to put paid to George Brown.

Lasky (editor of *Encounter*) came to lunch and said he recently returned from the U.S., where he had met McGeorge Bundy, who is at present head of a group to advise the President on the Middle East. McGeorge Bundy told Lasky the President was furious that he was not given advance notice of the Israeli attack. Asked what the U.S. Government expected, McGeorge Bundy said they rather anticipated an Egyptian victory, but could do nothing about it – except take some Israelis off in ships. This sounds to me nonsensical. Mike understands the C.I.A. gave the President notice of the Israeli attack and prophesied a quick win over the Egyptians, which is why Johnson played the whole episode very cool.

Wednesday, July 26th, 1967

George Brown to lunch at his request. He was very voluble and friendly and stayed two hours. He said Bowden is leaving the Government owing to his wife's ill-health. Fleet St rumour is that he is to become chairman of I.T.A.,* while Charlie Hill becomes chairman of the B.B.C. because of the death of Lord Normanbrook. Later in the conversation George said Douglas Jay would not be in the Government much longer. I said Callaghan had given me the impression he was on his way out. George said he is not being forced out, but he may suppose that devaluation is inevitable and, if that comes, he will certainly resign. George said he thought there was a race between a financial crash and joining the Common Market. He thought we should just make it. (1) I think any joining is a long way off, and (2) it will lead to great difficulty in the short run, though I am confident that it is the only policy for this country in the long run. It is certainly no answer to our immediate financial problems.

I asked about the Middle East. He had read an intelligence appreciation this morning, and had had two hours with Eban, the Israeli Foreign Minister, on Sunday. The Russians have restored

* Independent Television Authority.

half the Egyptian air force, but few bombers, and a quarter of their tanks. The Russians were determined to avoid any fresh outbreak of hostilities but, otherwise, were waiting for a policy to emerge. Before the Israeli war the Russians felt they could control the Egyptians and the Americans were controlling the Israelis, so when the Israelis destroyed the Egyptian air force on the ground, the Russians thought they had been double-crossed, and took some persuading that neither we nor the Americans had been parties to the attack.

I asked if the Russians were using the episode to establish themselves as a naval power in the Mediterranean. He said 'apparently not', that they have fewer warships in the Mediterranean than they had before the Israeli attack and that these were of a more defensive character.

All in all, George was obviously enjoying himself. He had no understanding of, or interest in, the weakening position of the country, the Government, or the P.M. He seemed to have no real grip of anything – and certainly is quite undisturbed by our financial prospects.

Saturday, July 29th, 1967

Dick Marsh to lunch yesterday. He seems to me one of the best ministers, in spite of his inexperience. He has an impossible job: coal, steel, gas, electricity, nuclear energy, plus being an M.P. and a Cabinet minister. A superman could not possibly cover the ground effectively, as he very clearly sees. He complains that he is expected to make decisions on important matters when his knowledge is only what could be put on the back of a cigarette-card. He then has to co-ordinate the policy of his ministry with other ministers, whose knowledge is even less. He thinks the Cabinet – which at present can only allow two or three minutes to each item – should be reduced to eight or nine members, each of whom would be chairman of a cabinet dealing with external affairs, finance, or whatnot.

He says it is impossible to get full-time directors of nationalized industries at the salaries he is allowed to pay. This seems to be his biggest worry. Recently a nationalized board considerably overspent without authority. So he had up the chairman and reproved him. As the chairman was leaving he patted Marsh on the shoulder and said,

'I know you had to say all that, but I won't hold it against you' – or words to that effect. Marsh was indignant and said, 'If you really think that, our conversation has been wasted.' He told his officials to summon the whole board, to reprove them all. The officials were aghast: said you can reprove a chairman if you don't do it often, but you can't summon the board. However, Marsh, quite rightly, insisted, summoned the board and tore a strip off them. The chairman is, in consequence, resigning in October. He should have been dismissed. The only worry in Marsh's mind is how to find a successor at £11,000 p.a.

Over North Sea gas and all that, Marsh suggested calling in the two Government directors of B.P.* to talk things over. The officials violently objected and said he couldn't do such a thing: there was a long standing agreement that H.M.G. would not interfere in the affairs of B.P. However, Marsh insisted, and is to see them. I mention these two episodes as they seem to me so extraordinary. Marsh was obviously correct and the officials were clearly being ridiculous, but it must be difficult for an inexperienced minister to do the right thing with such timid and misconceived advice.

Tuesday, August 1st, 1967

Tony Crosland to lunch. I had met him briefly going into Ellis Birk's party a fortnight ago when he seemed to have grown in self-confidence. However, today he was the old Crosland, excellent brain, small, uncertain personality. He said Jim Callaghan had put up a very clumsy fight for economies and if he had been a bit more subtle (or 'devious') could have contrived more cuts. Both Jim and the P.M. were against raising the school-leaving age, but really made very little effort and the decision has (quite wrongly in my opinion) been made to go ahead. Altogether, on this issue, Crosland was rather cock-a-hoop: the Cabinet had agreed to all the expenditure he wanted. He proposes to raise the price of school meals again – it has just gone up from 1s. to 1s. 6d., against an average cost of 2s. 6d. He also proposes in time to get students educated on loans which have afterwards to be repaid.

On the more general matter of the Government and the future,

* British Petroleum Co. Ltd.

he was frighteningly optimistic. As with George Brown last week, our financial troubles do not loom large; they enjoy being ministers; Wilson is immovable and will be P.M. up to the next election and beyond. Why worry?

Thursday, August 3rd, 1967

Denis Hamilton to lunch yesterday. He said Wilson was very cross with *The Times*; had come to lunch, was very critical in conversation with Denis Hamilton, emphasizing his points with cuttings he had brought in his pocket. He said that in future *The Times* representative would not be admitted to his briefings. Denis said that would suit him well, as if his man were excluded he would be able to publish the substance of the briefings – with attribution. Wilson, having made no progress with Denis, had a crack at Roy [Thomson], saying is this all the gratitude he got for pushing *The Times* acquisition through the Monopolies Commission? However, Roy pleaded that he was not a political animal and did not interfere with his editors.

Mike dined with Rees-Mogg, editor of *The Times*, last night. He said Wilson would clearly not stay the course – the whole situation was crumbling around him.

O'Brien drew me aside after Court to talk about the political situation. He is acutely unhappy, living from day to day. He hopes Callaghan will stay at the Treasury as he has learnt so much in the last two and a half years. He is afraid that the idea of devaluation has gathered so much momentum that it may prove irresistible. What did I think of the political outlook? I told him: he made no demur, but passed on no news of his own.

The Aberfan Report* is out this afternoon and, against my advice, Robens is planning to offer his resignation. The laugh in the situation is that the Government is to put out a statement, I think this afternoon. It is being drawn up by the Ministry of Power, but

* On October 21st, 1966, a rain-soaked slag-heap slipped down the side of the Aberfan Valley in South Wales and engulfed houses and a school, killing 144 people. A judicial inquiry, under Lord Justice Davies, was appointed. The report, published on August 3rd, 1967, criticized the National Coal Board and censured Lord Robens, its chairman, for his early denials of responsibility. Lord Robens tendered his resignation, which was not accepted.

Wilson has insisted that the words, 'the Prime Minister' shall appear in the first line!

Friday, August 4th, 1967

Press comment on the Aberfan Report is more hostile than I should have expected. Clearly Robens will have to offer his resignation; even more clearly it should not be accepted. I think the Report shows personal hostility to Robens. Alf tells me the reason why warnings were not sent further up the line was that the local people knew the tip was in the only possible place and if that were disallowed, the pit would be closed. If it were, all interested parties would be out of work, as there is no alternative employment in the neighbourhood.

Tuesday, August 8th, 1967

The news today is substantially that of the meeting of the Coal Board yesterday afternoon. The meeting was called for 4 p.m. and I think there are eight members of the Coal Board, including myself. It is difficult to draft a statement with a committee of eight, but what was my horror when I discovered that Robens had summoned the divisional chairmen and others, so we were twenty-six! The meeting went on and eventually I left at 7 p.m. when the important decisions had been made, the essential drafting finished. But what with telephone calls to some affected parties and refreshments, the meeting finally broke up at 9.30 p.m. – after five and a half hours. In this long time one decision was taken – not to fire the men named in the Aberfan Report. On this there was no difference of opinion. The rest was the drafting of a very simple statement. The whole thing could have been well done in an hour. At about 6.45 p.m. Robens read out an exchange of letters he had just had with Marsh, in which he offered his resignation and Marsh deferred consideration of this until the end of the month. The actual wording of the reply had to be submitted to Wilson in the Scilly Islands!

Saturday, August 12th, 1967

Cudlipp had some talk a few weeks ago with Mountbatten at some dinner. Hugh asked him if it had been suggested to him that our present style of government might be in for a change. He said it had.

Hugh then asked if it had been suggested that he might have some part to play in such a new regime? Mountbatten said it had been suggested, but that he was far too old (sixty-seven, I think).

Tuesday, August 22nd, 1967

Pondering the political scene yesterday, it seemed to me that the problem is no longer our affair and our Government's. The whole world seems to be sliding downhill. In China, in Vietnam, in the Middle East, in Central Africa, in Nigeria, things are going very badly. Even the United States is in dire trouble with a war it cannot win and riots by Negroes in cities all over the United States, trying to give publicity to grievances that are indeed real, but might well take a generation or more to alleviate.

Our relations with Johnson are deteriorating; our relations with the Russians are negative; our relations with the Chinese could hardly be worse. We have antagonized both sides in Nigeria and both sides in the Middle East. Events in Rhodesia are proceeding without regard to this country. Where *do* we go for honey?

Thursday, August 24th, 1967

At the Bank, having missed the last two meetings. The Governor was not particularly expansive, though he did mention in passing that recently £25 million went out in two hours and – according to Maurice Allen – that was not the worst two hours recently.

After Court, I had a long talk with Maurice Allen, who was even gloomier than usual. He said our reserves were even lower than they were in the crisis of July last year. Almost anything might push us over the brink.

On balance of payments, the latest, highly secret, estimate at the Treasury is that we shall be £300 million down on the year. This is made up of £25 million plus in the first quarter, minus £25 million in the second quarter and minus £300 million in the last two quarters. The most recent estimate was minus £200 million, the difference being due to a higher estimate of the cost of the Israeli–Arab war. The Government, however, is likely to put out quite different figures by bringing in 'unidentifiable items'. This is partly pure invention and partly 'leads and lags'. They put the 'unidentifiable items' in the first quarter at £150 million plus, and the second quarter at £95 million plus, in this way making a plus for the first half-year of £245 million. Maurice Allen thought the £150 million had some foundation because there had been such a large minus in the last quarter of 1966, but he thought the £95 million for the second quarter pure invention – or nearly so. In the second half-year these 'unidentifiable items' are normally minus and wipe out the pluses in the first half-year, but it is open to the Government to discover (1) that there were no net 'unidentifiable items', so that the £245 million is intact at the end of the year, or even (2) to discover that there have been further credits under this head in the last six months of 1967.

I said surely all this faking of figures merely postponed the evil day, and would make it worse when it came. His argument was that even if you are going to be killed shortly, there is no point in committing suicide now; that any factual representation of our financial condition would push us over the edge the same day.

Allen was at a meeting of permanent under-secretaries to discuss a White Paper which is to take the place of the National Plan. But this is to come out in the early winter and can hardly be produced without some figures of Government expenditure. Callaghan has said expenditure is to be 'reined back', but has given no facts. I said I understood the Government 'cuts' were to look at last year's expenditure – say £100 million – and consider the £10 million additional expenditure that had been contemplated, so that the 'reining back' would consist of reducing the £110 first thought of to, say, £107 million. Allen said, 'Not so.' If last year the figure was £100 million, and it had been intended to let this run up to £110, they found on really looking into the matter that the expenditure was running away with them and now looked more like £130 million. Now, as a result of ruthless(!) cuts, they were endeavouring to bring this figure back to £110.

Tuesday, August 29th, 1967

After a lot of speculation, the Government changes were announced last night. Douglas Jay goes; Crosland moves to the Board of Trade; Gordon Walker to Education; Willey goes; Bottomley goes; Bowden goes to I.T.A.; George Thomson gets the Commonwealth Relations

Office; Mellish, Works and Buildings; Prentice, Overseas Development; Stewart leaves the D.E.A. and is First Secretary without portfolio; Shore gets the D.E.A., subject to the overriding authority of Wilson, who takes the main responsibility for the department. It is difficult to know what to make of this lot. One had expected Wilson to clear the decks for the Party Conference in October, but in what way could these changes help? Of course, Jay and Bottomley ought to go, but moving Crosland means the third Minister of Education in three years. Patrick Gordon Walker is quite useless and has no particular political complexion. Crosland will not impress the business world – even less will Shore, who, though forty-three, gives the impression of being a clever undergraduate. I should say his ceiling would be as a university lecturer in economics. However, he is a friend of Wilson and that, presumably, is enough.

The reaction of the newspapers this morning is unflattering – both *The Times* and the *Express* (in a piece by Maurice Edelman) suggest that if this new team cannot produce results, Wilson's own position will be in doubt.

Hugh Cudlipp's reaction is that Wilson's assumption of the direct responsibility for the D.E.A. may well prove to be the mistake of his life. Some people, on the other hand, think this is a move to phase out the D.E.A., which has clearly been a failure. It is very unlike Wilson (1) to kill his own brain-child and (2) to kill off a department headed by himself. I should have thought the move is more likely to have been due to a mixture of defiance and vanity, but now he has taken the hot seat, he will be made to sit on it.

Thursday, August 31st, 1967

It appears that the Bank did very badly last week in the exchange market: very well on Monday and Tuesday, but since 2 p.m. Wednesday the slide has been resumed. I had a long talk with O'Brien after Court on other Bank matters, but naturally the general state of affairs came under review. I think he has given up hope of maintaining the exchange value of the pound. He thinks under pressure ministers are thinking more of full employment and less of our financial position. O'Brien seemed to be already adapting himself to the new situation – a mild devaluation of 10 per cent or so might give our economy a shot in the arm without inviting retaliation. I said but supposing it falls away to 30 per cent? He said that would spell disaster in any language. But apparently it is quite uncertain what Rate could be maintained with our non-existent reserves.

Friday, September 8th, 1967

Iain Macleod to lunch. He reminded me that when we last met I had told him there would be a deficit on our balance of payments for 1967. I had also said Wilson was slipping. He had believed neither at the time, but now saw I was right. He had little news to impart: was afraid our position as a nation would deteriorate without any dramatic event to enforce changes. We discussed possible successors to Wilson and he said he would accept Denis Healey as leader of a Government of National Unity, but doubted whether the Tufton Beamishes of his party would. On the other hand, Roy Jenkins, who would personally be more acceptable, might not be the right man in a crisis.

Friday, September 15th, 1967

De Courcel, the French Ambassador, to lunch today. He had not been here for many months. He is an attractive man and was more expansive on this occasion. On the Common Market the complaint was that there had been no follow-through. In June last year Wilson had told Pompidou that we had decided to join the Common Market. It was then agreed that the matter should be examined by experts. But nothing was done then or since. De Courcel was obviously puzzled by Wilson and Brown's trip round the Continent early in the New Year. Of course, all this is typical of Wilson's love of gesture, with no follow-through. De Courcel clearly thought the process of joining the Market would take anything up to six years, and should start now. The time should be devoted to aligning our financial, agricultural and other policies with those of the Six. I said it was said that the F.O. was strongly anti-French. He said, 'That is so – and it is strongly pro-American.'! There have been many occasions when the British Government could have pursued an American or a European policy. It has followed an American one. Even in matters like taxation it has gone off at a tangent – e.g. Selective Employment Tax

– instead of trying to bring British taxation into line with Continental practice. He thought our financial difficulties alone would take a long time to overcome, and clearly we cannot join the Common Market until we are out in the clear. He offered the opinion that joining the Common Market was the only policy available to us. The argument that still weighs very strongly with the French is that the Common Market is not a big enough economic base on which to compete with the Americans. To this end the accession of Great Britain would be a great source of strength.

Monday, September 18th, 1967

Had lunch with Jim Callaghan – alone, at his request, at 11 Downing St. He explained that the meeting did not take place at Wilson's suggestion and that he would not have arranged a meeting on Wilson's behalf.

We talked first of the Common Market. He said that there is nothing more to be done than they are doing. It is true Chalfont is unconvincing, but there is nothing much anyone can do at this stage. There is, of course, quite a lot – for instance, in the way of aligning our agricultural and taxation policies with those of the Market. Even that might make no difference for the present. The Common Market is thus the only possible foreign policy, but there is no headway to be made now or in the immediate future. There is no point in quarrelling with the Americans. They have a stranglehold on us, as we have on them (have we?). Singapore we are leaving in the mid-1970s. We are staying in the Persian Gulf for a time to enable King Faisal of Saudi Arabia to sort things out before we leave. We have been in the Far East for two hundred years (actually much longer), so to allow us ten years to get out is not excessive. I said all that is fine if we have the money. But we haven't. Jim seemed to be saying we should sell some of our overseas investments to pay for the run-down.

And why were we so hostile to Wilson? I said because he is a failure. To this he naturally said he could not agree. He was standing by Wilson, who was doing his best. I said Wilson had started off with the greatest goodwill on all sides and had had a better break even from the right-wing press than Macmillan ever had. But he could not wait to throw it all away, though he had claimed to be a wizard in

143

handling the newspapers. Jim acknowledged all this. He said Wilson was trying to do the right thing – prices and incomes and all – and had a success in handling the Labour Party that no one else could have had. This was a democratic country and there were limits beyond which ministers had not the power to go. I said the Prices and Incomes policy had never been explained to the populace, though I had urged this on both Wilson and Brown.

So would I join the Government? He had no authority for making the suggestion (is this true?). I said when the Government was formed I thought Robens, Sainsbury and (possibly) myself were inevitable, as we had experience of administration and so few others had. I had been asked before they took office by Jim and George Brown if I was prepared to help and I had said yes. I had therefore accepted a directorship of the Bank, a membership of the Coal Board and of the National Parks Commission. Was this really the best use to which they could put my experience and ability? He said that the F.O. was occupied by George and the Treasury by himself, so I couldn't have those. I said, 'But why should I join a sinking ship?' Jim said it wasn't sinking and they would win the next election. I said, 'Not a hope.' I said if they offered me a place in the Government, I would consider it (but I didn't take back what I had said about the sinking ship!). I recalled that I had been offered the job of understrapper to Douglas Jay, which I should have regarded as a bitter insult if I had been of a vindictive nature. He said I should have been Lord of Exports. I said such an idea couldn't work – look how Wilfrid Brown, who did take the job, had vanished! He said this was Brown's fault.

The meeting was quite amicable, and when leaving he said we must have lunch again soon.

They are obviously very worried by the press. I said it was critical, but would soon be hostile. He said it was hostile already! They are also very worried about the Labour Party Conference. I doubt whether the suggested offer of a seat in the Government will be followed up. Maybe they hope it will keep me quiet.

He is to send Harold Lever to see me to talk about the Stationery Office. The Bank – i.e. presumably O'Brien – has complained of my hostile talk of the P.M. This is amusing as my views are to be found on the front page of the *Mirror* whether I utter them in person or not. Presumably I must now be more discreet at the Bank.

Friday, September 22nd, 1967

Denis Hamilton came to lunch today. Apparently Wilson thought that having given some small assistance to get *The Times–Sunday Times* merger through the Monopolies Commission, he would have the paper in his pocket. Anyway, soon after the merger he had Denis to lunch and specified by name four members of *The Times* staff who were to be dismissed. Denis gave me their names, but I did not know any of them. Wilson accused all four of being Tories. He didn't apparently realize that no newspaper director could possibly accede to such demands. Even had he been planning to get rid of any of these men, Wilson's demand would have forced Denis to postpone any action. In fact Denis was noncommittal and did nothing – hence Wilson's hostility to *The Times*. He sees James Margach every week, but all this has done is to weaken Margach's position in the *Sunday Times* office. He will be transferred elsewhere before long.

Sunday, September 24th, 1967

Christopher Soames at lunch a few days ago was talking of Roy Jenkins as a not very convincing leader of a coalition government. He asked, 'Is he the sort of man you would want to go tiger-shooting with?' I said, 'No.' He went on, 'I wouldn't go mouse-hunting under a sofa with him.'!

Tuesday, September 26th, 1967

Ted Heath for lunch, the first meeting for some months. He arrived tense, serious, and exceedingly difficult. After one and a half hours he left laughing, but what a lunch – the most difficult I have had in years. He was obviously deeply hurt by newspaper criticisms and the opinion polls, but battling on nevertheless. Was very critical of the newspapers always pulling down, never building up. I said this was due to prime ministers over the years resenting any praise for members of their governments, as such praise implied a right to dictate Cabinet appointments; so newspaper praise of an individual politician tended to be the kiss of death. He wouldn't agree that Parliament and the parties were held in low esteem; or that we were heading for a National Government. The present Government would disintegrate before 1971; there would be an election, the Tories would win, and on we should go.

I had intended to point out that Barber was too insignificant to make an impression on the public – so was Walker, Shadow Minister of Transport. Why not make more of Soames? Or bring in Cromer or Beeching? But Ted's mood was such that there was no chance of saying anything of the kind: the newspapers and T.V. were united in denigrating politicians. I said the newspapers and television were controlled by such a miscellaneous assortment of people that if they agreed on anything it was unusual – and they might be right. Ted would have none of this. The newspapers were sheep and followed each other – and so on and so on. What emerged was (1) that Ted is deeply hurt by all the criticisms, and (2) that he seems to have no understanding of the political atmosphere as I see it.

Friday, September 29th, 1967

Roy Jenkins to lunch – at his suggestion. He seems to be gaining confidence at the Home Office: has secured the promotion of some better civil service material. He says Denis Healey tells him he would like to have the F.O. or the Exchequer, but does not want to be P.M. I don't know how seriously to take this, though in talking to me, too, Denis said he would like to be Chancellor but not P.M.

Jenkins thinks Wilson will get through the Labour Party Conference and should probably scramble through the winter. Trade might pick up in the spring and there might be an election. No problem has been solved, so even if he won the election, we should soon be back in square one.

I told him how gloomy the Bank people continue to be. This seemed to surprise him, though he spoke as if he saw some of the figures.

A catastrophe might remove the P.M., but he thought opinion in the Parliamentary Labour Party was violently against any kind of coalition. I doubted whether you could revive confidence with the Labour Party alone, even under a new P.M.

Hugh recalled a conversation he had with Wilson on Tuesday at the party at No. 10. Wilson said Heath should have surrounded himself with a Praetorian Guard of Old Etonians to please those Conservatives who resented his middle-class origin. Wilson himself had formed his Government by merging elements from his own Left and from the Gaitskellite Right, and so had secured harmony in the party. Needless to say, this has been regardless of the administrative skill of ministers (or lack of it)!

At lunch at A.T.V. yesterday, I had some talk with Norman Collins, who has a considerable position at Conservative Party Headquarters. They are in despair over Ted, and have no opinion of Barber as the new Chairman of the Party because (1) he is out of the same social drawer as Ted and (2) he has no personality (Jenkins says he is not even good in the House).

Meanwhile, Wilson's relations with the press get worse and worse. On the eve of the Party Conference he is denounced on the Left by the *New Statesman* and *Tribune*, and on the Right by *Socialist Commentary*. We have had four pieces this week in the *Mirror*, the first reviewing Max Nicholson's book condemning the civil service, *The System*, and the others rather more friendly to Wilson than we have been of late, on the grounds that you catch more flies with sugar than with vinegar, and, anyway, the Conference next week is not our best moment for attack. There will be plenty of others. We laid down a list of things that have to be done, knowing full well that Wilson will not, and with his limitations cannot, carry them out.

Tuesday, October 3rd, 1967

Letter from Cecil King to Edward Heath:

STRICTLY PERSONAL

Dear Ted,

When you came here last Tuesday I was distressed to see how grievously you had been hurt by press and other criticisms.

I should like to convince you that there is so little that is personal in this. The British public is unimpressed by the Tory record 1951–1964. They neither want to hear about your party nor its leader – any leader. Some are still hoping Labour will make good. You and I know they won't. You will then have a British public disillusioned by both parties and by the failure of Parliament to provide the Government the public wants – and doubtless, in time, will insist on having. If you play the political game on the lines that Trollope would have understood you will get nowhere. But if we are to get ourselves out of our difficulties, you are obviously one of the key people who can direct events.

But to do this you must somehow protect yourself from being too much hurt and be prepared to think of politics in national terms. Politics do not begin and end in the House of Commons.

I enclose a cutting from last Wednesday's *Telegraph* that illustrates what I was saying on Tuesday. Newspaper editors and directors are as public spirited as Members of Parliament. Being onlookers they see much of the game. It is surely wiser to pay attention to what they say – particularly when they are substantially in agreement – and not put it all down to a desire to increase circulation (of which, at least, the *Telegraph* and *Mirror* stand in no need).

With every good wish,

Yours sincerely,
Cecil King

The Rt. Hon. Edward Heath, M.B.E., M.P.,
F.2, Albany,
London, W.I.

Tuesday, October 10th, 1967

Since I last wrote in this diary we have had a Labour Party Conference. It had been expected that the Government would have a rough passage. But this was not so. The proceedings were dull, the delegates elderly, and there were no fireworks. Wilson made a really disgraceful speech that charmed the audience. It never referred to any of the real problems and boasted of the huge increase in spending on the Welfare State – not mentioning, of course, that all this was done on borrowed money, Jim Callaghan made the best speech of the conference, making, however, no reference to our balance of payments nor to the effects of excessive Government spending. By begging all the real issues, all went well. Papas, the *Guardian*'s cartoonist, summed it up well: George Brown, with a fig-leaf marked

'E.E.C.', and Wilson, with one marked 'Economic Policy', are otherwise naked, walking away from the Conference – Wilson remarking, 'We are not much worse off than when we came.'

Thursday, October 12th, 1967

The Bank this morning: bad trade figures, the worst for a year. The exchanges have been very quiet for a month with only small amounts of hard currency going out. The prospects for a large deficit on the year become clearer. Otherwise nothing fresh.

Friday, October 13th, 1967

Kenneth Keith to lunch in high good humour. He is just back from Sweden and says in all his journeys on the Continent the question is not whether we devalue, but when. He assumes the figure will be 20 per cent. The Finns devalued by 31 per cent this week. They had been hoping to do this at the same time as ourselves, but cannot wait. Keith is even more depressed (if possible) about the state of the economy than I am.

Thursday, October 19th, 1967

Beeching to lunch on Monday – depressed and depressing, but nothing new.

In the afternoon I had an S.O.S. from Ralph Harris asking if he could bring Joe Hyman, chairman of Viyella, to see me that afternoon. So he came for half an hour or so. He is a big bouncing Jew of forty-six, full of energy, ability and self-confidence. He now wants to enter politics and had suggested himself to Ted Heath as Chairman of the Conservative Party! The response was definitely chilly. He is now thinking of putting £1 million into the Liberal Party and taking that over. He thinks it stands for nothing at the moment and therefore could be fitted out with whatever policies Hyman favours. If he did this, would we publish a weekly paper to support him politically? Well, clearly no. However, he asked if we would deal with the commercial side of a weekly or monthly of his. Well, on commercial terms, yes. Hyman has great energy, great ability and great enthusiasm. It remains to be seen if these qualities can be diverted from a commercial into a political channel.

Tuesday, October 24th, 1967

Dinner at No. 10 last night to meet Kiesinger. I had only a formal word with him, but had some talks with various ministers. George Brown cut me dead, presumably because of a piece in the *Mirror* during the Scarborough Conference. Wilson could not have been more friendly, frequently coming up to me to exchange remarks, ending with a long piece at the close of the evening on how he had handled the Liverpool dock strike. Ruth had some talk with Callaghan on the attitude of the *Mirror*. What did I want? They had thought of offering me the Board of Trade but then I was always saying younger men must be brought in and I am sixty-six. I am writing to Callaghan today to suggest a meeting to explain things. I am also writing to Wilson to say what I think: the deficiencies in his Government are due to poor administration. I think both Ruth and I were under the impression that ministers are working their hardest and doing their utmost, but just have no idea. They are all little people out of their depth – particularly Wilson.

—— [a senior civil servant] to lunch yesterday. He says the civil service is unhappy. What they like above all is clarity: both on the policy to be pursued and the means to implement the policy. Since 1964, Whitehall has had imposed on it endless committees and other bodies that have the effect of blurring responsibility and delaying action.

Letter of October 24th from Cecil King to Harold Wilson:

Dear Harold,

As you said last night, we have not seen each other for some time and no doubt you think we are drifting further apart. So I thought I would commit to paper the basic reasons for the currently critical attitude of our papers.

As I see it, government is about 75% administration and 20% politics, the remainder being Parliamentary tactics. When you took office few of your Front Bench colleagues had any experience of administration at all. Introductions from outside such as Cousins and Snow did nothing to improve this situation: better people were available. Though many of your colleagues have revealed their inability to administer a Government Department, they still remain in office. The Civil Service is increasingly unhappy about the proliferation of committees and enquiries with so few clear-cut policies or decisions. In administration the problem is to get from the idea to the execution and it is in this area that your Government is so weak.

Your colleagues, too, seem to lack political sense on the big issues. If they had it, our Middle Eastern and Rhodesian relationships would have been less unsatisfactory.

The area where you are supreme in your generation is in Parliamentary tactics, which is all-important in Opposition, but of so little avail when in Office with a large majority.

I realise you and your colleagues are putting everything you have into the conduct of the country's affairs, but hard work and devotion to duty are not enough. Without the necessary administrative resources the country will only stumble from one crisis to another. And without the right political perception the young will be even further alienated from our constitutional apparatus than they are already.

There is no lack of goodwill on our part, but a lack of confidence that your Government is finding the answers.

It is because I feel it is so vital to Britain's future that your Government succeeds that I am so critical. My hopes were high, and I write frankly for this reason.

Yours very sincerely,
Cecil King

The Rt. Hon. Harold Wilson, O.B.E., M.P.,
10, Downing Street,
Whitehall, S.W.1.

Wednesday, October 25th, 1967

We looked in last night at the reception at Lancaster House for Kiesinger. George Brown evaded me, but Ruth would not let him escape. When confronted, he greeted her as briefly and coldly as possible.

Friday, October 27th, 1967

No particular news at the Bank. Robens was there saying things were going badly on the industrial front – dockers, railwaymen, builders, printers, powerhouse men and now his miners were getting restive.

Denis Healey to lunch in hilarious form. He now thinks the financial outlook very threatening – should we devalue now or wait until it is forced on us? He thinks a situation might develop in which he would be called on to be P.M., but obviously thinks it unlikely. He thinks highly of Marsh, very highly indeed of Shirley Williams, and well of Brian Walden and Jack Ashley. He thought nothing of Crosland's chances of No. 10.

Apparently Healey had had a discussion with Wilson on his own future. He had said he was very willing to go to the F.O., but thought he should have a go at something else before trying his hand at the Treasury – what about the D.E.A.? Wilson had said there could be no question of moving Stewart from there. Yet three weeks later Stewart had gone and Wilson was in his place.*

Wednesday, November 1st, 1967

On Thursday night at Lausanne, Lord Chalfont gave a succession of non-attributable talks to a number of British journalists. The gist was that if the Germans would not help us into the Common Market, we could turn nasty: pull out of Berlin; pull our troops out of Germany; give the Germans no help over reunification, and so on. The journalists were appalled by this, particularly when they were urged to publish not earlier than Saturday and without attribution. They asked did the P.M. share these views? Whereupon they were told both by Chalfont and by the F.O. man that they took a long time to let the penny drop! When the story reached the *Mirror*, Hugh Cudlipp rang Wilson up, who denied there had been any change of Government policy, so we published the story and the denial. It now appears that Chalfont had been saying something similar to the German journalists earlier in the week, and Wilson had been giving a much milder version of the same point of view in a briefing on Tuesday. In any case, it is inconceivable that Chalfont would have expressed such views if he hadn't been confident that they were those of Wilson. He admitted that Brown did not wholly agree with him. Mike spoke to him at Lausanne after Wilson had spoken to Hugh and apparently after Wilson had spoken to Chalfont. This

* See page 141.

conversation ended with Chalfont saying, 'I seem to have made a mess of it.'

Meanwhile Brown, on Monday night, turned up late at a Foreign Office party and proceeded to abuse the *Mirror* and *Express* and, in particular, me. So Mike, who was there, protested and left.

Last night Roy Thomson gave a party to eighty prominent Americans and other guests and Brown was the principal speaker. He seems to have been very emotional; launched out into an attack on Roy and the *Sunday Times*. The evening ended with what amounted to a brawl between George and twenty-odd journalists. Never before has an incident caused such discussion in the lobbies. So Wilson is faced with a situation in which the Foreign Secretary and the Minister of State are totally discredited and the Permanent Under-Secretary, Gore-Booth, is regarded as weak and ineffective. If he dismisses either minister, he gravely weakens his Government; if he doesn't, the result is different but equally bad.

Blankenhorn, the German Ambassador, came to lunch. He never thought anything of Chalfont. Said Wilson handled Kiesinger badly – in particular at the dinner at the German Embassy, when he called for 'deeds not words' from the Germans to get us into the Market. Blankenhorn has been busy keeping the temperature low, as there could easily have been an explosion in the German press. He said in Germany, as here, and through Europe, Parliamentary government is losing all credibility, let alone prestige.

Thursday, November 2nd, 1967

After Court the Governor asked me to his room. Nothing specific emerged, so I suppose he just wanted to weep on my shoulder. He said senior civil servants are getting more and more exhausted and a number of possible resignations would leave the top echelon pitifully weak.

At lunch I sat next to Maurice Allen. He said Bank opinion was about sixty to forty that we should be forced to devalue this month. If we didn't it would only be because the Americans in their own self-interest had decided to prop up the pound. If we scrambled through this month, we should probably get by till the spring, but then the old pressures would return. I asked what measure of devaluation and he said the idea had been about 10–15 per cent but now the figure discussed is higher. However, its exact level would depend on the Americans – we should cease to have any standing in the matter, as we should have no reserves to support the pound at any particular level.

The storm over George Brown blows furiously; most newspapers demand his resignation. Wilson is in a very nasty dilemma. To dismiss Brown will weaken his Government; to keep him, knowing that there will be further episodes, will do the same.

Thursday, November 9th, 1967

Rowley Cromer came to lunch at the Bank and when I ridiculed Chalfont's kite-flying at Lausanne, he said the Government suggested to Washington we should stage a quarrel so that the Continentals would see how European we are! Needless to say, the Americans turned down this ridiculous idea. Money has been pouring out this last week and the situation is obviously very sticky. According to Maurice Allen this is likely to be the month, but this is not likely to be the week. Meanwhile our debt due for repayment on December 1st is to be extended for an average of one year, but the obligation for repayment – for the first time – rests on H.M.G. and not on the Bank.

Jim Callaghan last night was friendly: said it was supposed in some quarters that the critical attitude of the *Mirror* was due to my disappointment at not being given high office. I said no government post was as good as the one I have, though I had supposed in 1964 that I might well be called in to help. Jim is very nice but has neither the brains nor the education to grasp the problems of the Treasury. He said he thought we were building up to a 'climacteric' (his word); he was obviously very unhappy at the way things were going and planned to stand by Wilson, as sticking together was the only salvation for the Labour Party.

Last night at dinner Ruth sat next to Bowden, now Lord Aylestone and Chairman of I.T.A. He told her he had accepted the post because he was unhappy in the Government and wanted to get out. He told Robens, also last night, that he had found the gap between the party and the Government too wide and growing wider.

Sunday, November 12th, 1967

Had Marsh to dinner on Thursday; Joe Hyman of Viyella to lunch yesterday. Marsh hasn't a good manner, but is a nice man and able. He impresses me by the quality of his comments. He held forth on the lack of discussion on policy. He has been a Cabinet minister for nineteen months, during which time there has been one discussion of one hour in a Cabinet committee on the subject of fuel policy. There has been no discussion on a policy for the Middle East. Episodes are dealt with as they arise, but there is no central policy to which to refer episodes as they arise. He said Wilson strongly dislikes being disagreed with but said he is good at reading a document once through and absorbing its contents. He thought the best civil servants were overworked preparing endless papers for their ministers, while their normal work is neglected.

It seems that Wilson, in defiance of all reason, is optimistic and foresees a revival of his fortunes in the spring.

Joe Hyman is very able, very forceful and rich, and is bent on making an impact on the political world. He is not easy to follow, but seems to be planning a takeover of the Liberal Party. He foresees a National Government, which will not be a success, and thinks his best way to power is by constituting himself the Opposition to the National Government, using the Liberal Party as a platform. I wished him well, while declining any idea of joining or sponsoring any group he may gather round him.

Thursday, November 16th, 1967

The Bank as usual. George Bolton was the first director I spoke to. He said the Government had attempted to get a long-term loan abroad and had failed. The Americans – in view of the weakness of the dollar – were trying desperately to help. Next I spoke to Alf Robens, who has caused a stir by indicating that if the output of coal is to be run down to eighty million tons by 1980, this will need only 65,000 miners, a sixth of the present labour force. I think he is trying to get the Government to look more favourably on coal, but possibly has also in mind the fact that in the course of future politics his high standing with the miners will do him no harm!

Finally we moved into the Court room and the Governor was

155

more forthcoming than is usually the case. Money had been pouring out since May. Though the effect of the bad trade figures on Tuesday had not been quite as bad as it might have been, we had got to the end of our present resources. We could make one last borrowing on very strict terms from the I.M.F.,* but if that went, we should be quite helpless. O'Brien plainly implied that we should have to devalue on Saturday and use these final resources for controlling the situation post-devaluation. He gave no indication of the level of devaluation but said it would have to be large enough to do the trick. He thought the sterling area countries would follow us and they hoped the non-sterling ones would not. If they did our devaluation would be nulli-fied. The dollar is very weak and it might be that they would have recourse to a higher interest rate (it is already very high for them) and import quotas to protect their position. We are not contemplating import quotas. When this exposition was over, Alf Robens passed me a paper: 'Glad to see you can still smile, 1931.'

Sunday, November 19th, 1967

Friday was a bad day for the pound, partly because of an obscure answer to a Parliamentary question by Callaghan. The papers have given estimates of a loss up to £200 million in the one day.

On Saturday morning I rang up Maurice Parsons to get an appointment for Monday, as clearly some announcement would be made over the weekend. I expected it to be on Sunday, but Parsons told me it would be at 8.30 that night and that Wilson would be on T.V. at 10 o'clock. In the outcome the announcement was at 9.30 and Wilson did not appear until 6 o'clock today.† Clearly Wilson should have made the announcement himself: Callaghan told Hugh that the announcement was always timed for 9.30. There was no row about the decision, which was unanimous and taken on Thurs-day morning.

Hugh got a very polite invitation to see the P.M. at 2.45 at 10 Downing St. It was almost 'Would he consent to come'! The sum-mons appeared to be merely to keep in touch. No particular informa-

* International Monetary Fund.
† A statement from the Treasury announced the devaluation of the pound by 14·3 per cent, from $2·80 to $2·40.

156

tion was imparted and no requests were made. One might have expected a crestfallen or jittery Wilson, but not a bit of it. There was no hint that his economic policy of three years lay in ruins. The balance of payments problem had become an aching tooth, he said, and he and Callaghan, three weeks ago, had decided to have it out! His attitude, both in his talk with Hugh and in his broadcast to-night, was quite unrealistic and bore no relation at all to the Government's policy until yesterday. He is confident he will keep his party together in the House, and the Cabinet was unanimous yesterday, so all is well. The Bank Rate is 8 per cent: Corporation Tax up; S.E.T. rebate down. In other words incentives are still further reduced but social services are not to be cut, and seemingly the Prices and Incomes legislation is not to be strengthened. I shall get a line on the whole business from Maurice Parsons tomorrow, but the new policy as propounded so far does not sound as if it will work for long – the old Government formula, too little and too late.

In his conversation with Hugh, Wilson said he had an important offer to make to me. He had had my letter and had sent a message on Thursday for me to see him on Wednesday. I have had no such message and hope to be in Germany on Wednesday.

One curious feature of Wilson's conversation with Hugh was his bad language. This is quite new.

Monday, November 20th, 1967

Called on Maurice Parsons at the Bank at 10.30. I asked if it was true that £200 million had gone out on Friday, as some of the newspapers say. He said the amount was larger! He thought a devaluation of 14·3 per cent was right because devaluation by a larger amount would have been followed by similar action by so many other countries. A loan is being got together of $3,000 million, but this will only work if the requisite deflationary measures are taken at the same time. But I pointed out that there is to be no let-up on expenditure on houses, hospitals and schools, no extra charges for the Health Service, no strengthening of the Prices and Incomes policy. Surely this won't work. So far, the Government has said this is enough for now, but the measures can always be toughened up later. This is, of course, nonsense. The time to announce the whole package was over the weekend. If anything, ask for too much. It is easy to relent later. But to take harsh steps in the future that are not acceptable to the Parliamentary Labour Party now, is just not on.

Louis Franck to lunch. He says the amount that went out on Thursday and Friday was not less than $1,300,000 million. He said the whole operation was unbelievably mismanaged. The Bank Rate should not have been put up to 8 per cent, the money will be coming back tomorrow anyway. To stop the outflow on Thursday and Friday, the markets here should have been closed then, not today. He had spoken to three Central Bankers this morning, none of whom thought the Government measures would work. He said himself he thought there would be another devaluation next autumn. Australia and South Africa have decided not to devalue, so that is the end of the sterling area. The $3,000 million loan that was announced has apparently not yet been arranged. He is also worried about the gold pool, which is now in the red by many hundreds of millions of dollars. He thinks it will be abandoned, as it already has been by the French, and that gold will have a double price, as it had in the early 'fifties: the present parity for Central Banks, and a free gold market in Beirut, Hong Kong and Macao for others.

Saturday, November 25th, 1967

I have been in Germany since Wednesday and so have no personal news. Cromer made a very telling speech in the Lords, which we gave great prominence to, pointing out that Government measures are quite inadequate to prevent inflation. Peter Jay revealed in *The Times* that the Government was twice advised to devalue in past years but merely ordered copies of the reports to be destroyed. Wilson was quizzed on T.V. and made more admissions than he had in the House, where both he and Callaghan pretended that the outlook for next year was disappointing so they had decided to advise the Cabinet to devalue. Actually, of course, Wilson stuck stubbornly to the $2.80 parity until he had no more so-called reserves left. Equity prices have been erratic but are still very high; there has been a wild boom in gold, and the dollar premium, which had been 34 per cent just before devaluation, has now risen to the equivalent of 45 per cent – a totally unexpected development! The extra charges involved in new taxes and the new exchange rate will cost Reed's £10 million a year and I.P.C. £5 million.

On top of clobbering the goose which is expected to lay the golden eggs, Callaghan in his speech in the Commons spoke of a 'sinister group of dubious persons' who had decided to help with our economic affairs. This ludicrous statement refers to the chairmen of twenty of the top companies representing the larger companies, who with Paul Chambers as chairman, are to meet the C.B.I., representing the smaller ones. The 'dubious persons' include Israel Sieff, Harry Pilkington, three other B. of E. directors, and so on. They are nearly all people of the very highest standing.

The result of the crisis to date is a heavy blow to Wilson's prestige: Callaghan has come out of it as a likeable chap, honest but not much brain-power. Ted has failed to make any impact, and other Cabinet ministers have failed to emerge. The prestige of the House of Commons is at a new low level.

Tuesday, November 28th, 1967

An hour with Wilson yesterday evening. He was his usual chirpy self – relaxed, with his feet on the Cabinet table. The summons seemed to be to offer me: (1) a peerage (is this the fourth or fifth time?); (2) a Privy Councillorship; (3) he had been going to offer me the Paris Embassy, but after de Gaulle's statement in the afternoon veto-ing British entry into the Common Market there was now no point in going to Paris. I refused the honours and the interview amounted to a desultory chat. Any approach to reality was brushed aside. For instance, I said that obviously the market expected another devaluation, hence the continued boom in equities and the very high dollar premium. He said it was not a devaluation boom as gold shares had gone down that afternoon. I was not talking of yesterday's market but of the market ever since devaluation, or, for that matter, over a period of months.

Wilson said he was examining George's position and was evidently contemplating Government changes. These cannot amount to much. There are rumours that George will go as Ambassador to Washington; Denis Healey to the Treasury; Callaghan to the F.O. Alf Robens told Mike last week that he thought a National Government inevitable, with Callaghan as P.M. He didn't think any of the other candidates were runners.

Whitelaw, at lunch today, said he thought Callaghan would be more acceptable to the Tories than either Healey or Jenkins. He says Ted Heath's self-confidence, as well as his standing in the party, has risen no end, partly on his showing at the Conference* and partly on his speeches over devaluation. Over the House of Lords they will be easy over the composition, but will insist on powers – arguing, very sensibly, that you will not get important people to take part in the work of the House unless it has some power. I produced my pet idea on this subject, that the House of Lords should revert to its original purpose, when it contained all the men who were individually powerful. Why not reconstitute it as a body of 250 or 300 people representing industry, trades unions, the Churches, the civil service, the law, local authorities, etc. ? These people have great power and it might be wise to bring them into the Parliamentary ambit. In any case, if Parliamentary government is to be saved, it necessitates pretty big changes of some kind.

Wednesday, November 29th, 1967

Cromer to lunch. He is obviously contemptuous of the deflationary measures taken so far; does not think they will be carried any further; expects a crisis in April; further devaluation in July. I urged him to consider himself as a very possible 'outside' minister to come in a National Government. He is evidently not very keen, but quite easily envisages a situation when it would be his patriotic duty to stand up and be counted. He will be seeing Oliver Poole for advice and Alf Robens as the most promising of all the possible 'outside' ministers. He doesn't seem to be in touch with the Bank, but sees quite a lot of Ted Heath.

Thursday, November 30th, 1967

At the Bank as usual, to encounter a quite unexpected degree of pessimism. George Bolton started off, saying that there is to be an

* The Conservative Party Conference was held in Brighton from October 18th to 21st. Edward Heath was particularly courageous in resisting the pro-Smith views of his right wing during the debate on Rhodesia.

embargo on Argentine beef for at least three months. This will, of course, send up the price of beef, already high owing to foot-and-mouth disease. But in retaliation the Argentine, Chile and Uruguay are to impose a total ban on British imports. These are not now important markets, but we cannot afford to lose any under present circumstances.

Though the papers have reported money 'flooding in' after the devaluation, this was only true of the first two days when speculators were covering their forward sales. Since then, receipts have been disappointing. The 8 per cent Bank Rate – apparently the highest since 1914 – is necessary because even so, so little money has come in. I had some talk with Maurice Parsons in his room after Court. He said sterling-area holders of sterling are disgruntled at losing 15 per cent of their deposits and may well decide to take their money elsewhere; that confidence in sterling and in the Government is so small that a run on the pound could build up with great speed at any time. I quoted Cromer as suggesting a further devaluation by July and he clearly thought that, short of some miracle, we shall not hold the present parity until then. He said we have now no reserves and a further devaluation would mean not only the collapse of sterling, but the collapse of our economy. Maurice Allen later said that if the public knew what officials know, there would be further devaluation today.

The only ray of light on the scene is the appointment of Roy Jenkins as Chancellor, while Jim Callaghan goes to the Home Office. Hugh Cudlipp dined with Roy yesterday and found Roy as usual very friendly and receptive. He did not expect the appointment and only heard about it at 6.20 p.m. on Tuesday. He said he and Wilson are not close and that Wilson could certainly not have welcomed this appointment. Hugh devoted the dinner to telling Roy he must be an Iron Chancellor, laying down the steps that must be taken and resigning if he cannot get his way. The idea of waiting till the Budget is quite unacceptable; there is not that amount of time. Hugh thought Roy knew he was right, but doubted if he had the strength of character to impose his will on the Cabinet – a difficult job at any time, made more so by the pledges that have already been given.

Thursday, December 7th, 1967

Edward Boyle came to lunch yesterday – a nice man and intelligent, but no drive and apparently with little influence on his party. His line was that another devaluation would not only break up the Government but destroy the dwindling public confidence in politicians of any complexion. The idea of some sort of National Government was suggested by Boyle, and appears in a piece in *The Times* this morning and in the leader in the *Evening Standard*.

Bruce, the American Ambassador, came to lunch on Monday and ridiculed the story being put about by George Brown's friends that his removal from the F.O. would displease President Johnson.

Thursday, December 14th, 1967

In Lagos. For many years from 1948 I visited West Africa every eight or nine months, but this is my first visit for two and a half years. Since when there have been two changes in the regime and Major-General Gowon is the Supreme Commander. I had half an hour or so with him yesterday in his quarters at the Dodan Barracks. We were searched for arms before going into his room, but otherwise there is no evidence of a military regime. There are armed police at the Central Bank, but in general everything is normal. There is less effervescence than usual, but this may be explained by the absence of the Ibos, who have nearly all gone.

Gowon is the best type of young officer, straight as a die, upright, honourable, public-spirited. Whether he is of the calibre to keep a very large, heterogeneous country together, is quite another thing. He owes his position to the fact that he was the senior officer on the spot when Ironsi was shot,* though he is only in his thirties. It is a

* Nigeria was an uneasy federation of very different Regions. After the unrest and coups of the latter months of 1965, Major-General Aguiyi-Ironsi, an Ibo (from the Eastern Region) and C.-in-C. of the armed forces, formed a military government. Its main policy was an attempt to impose an Ibo government on the whole of the country – an attempt which met with violent resistance. Widespread unrest in the armed forces and tribal massacres took place during the summer of 1966, and Ironsi was abducted and killed. His place was filled by Lieutenant-Colonel (later Major-General) Yakubu Gowon, a northerner, but a Christian rather than a Moslem. Gowon managed to persuade the rebels to return to their units, and to negotiate the return of troops to their home Regions with Lieutenant-Colonel (later Major-General) Ojukwu, who, as Eastern Regional Governor, was in effect the head of a schismatic Ibo state. The independence of this state, Biafra, was declared on May 30th, 1967, and from that date the Federal Government sought to compel the separatist area to re-enter the Federation.

great political advantage that though nominally a Northerner, he comes from the Middle Belt, from a very small tribe, and that he is a Christian, so his background is reassuring both to the Northerners and to the non-Moslems. Gowon knows Ojukwu, the Biafran leader, well and does not trust him at all. He was not trained at Sandhurst and Gowon obviously regards him as a political soldier of an unreliable kind.

Monday, December 25th, 1967

Since my last entry I have dined at the Annans', where one of the guests was Roy Jenkins and another Arnold Goodman; and there was the Bank on Thursday. Goodman I find unattractive in appearance and woolly-minded. Roy was his usual suave self, showing no signs of pressure or any idea that this is the crisis of his life. On his appointment I wrote and asked to see him after Christmas but the meeting is fixed for the New Year, which hardly suggests any sense of urgency.

At the Bank I had fifteen minutes alone with the Governor and some talk with Maurice Allen. They do not think another devaluation in 1968 inevitable, but they think it is odds on.

While I was away, Holt, the Australian Prime Minister, was drowned and there was a Cabinet crisis here over sales of arms to South Africa. Holt was a nonentity, chosen as his successor by Menzies for that reason. But his death is bound to result in a new P.M. who will be more oriented towards America and the Pacific.

The Cabinet crisis was a confused affair which, after three Cabinet meetings, ended in Wilson saying in the House that the embargo on the supply of arms to South Africa still stands. He also said that there would have to be severe economies and no cows would be sacred. These cuts are to be announced on January 17th, two months after devaluation – a critical two months which have been just thrown away. Roy protests that he came in new and will have to examine the whole field. Apparently no preparations were made for a possible devaluation by Callaghan, and Wilson said on T.V. that no cuts would be necessary. The result of the whole episode has apparently been to devalue Wilson, who at one point only had five ministers on his side and those of little importance.

1968

In spite of the first circumnavigation of the moon at Christmas, 1968 was a bleak year internationally, domestically and, perhaps, personally for Cecil King. The wars in Vietnam and Nigeria raged unabated, tension in the Middle East continued and – especially in France and the United States – student and civil unrest posed a major threat to the established order. In the United States, where the presidential election resulted in the choice of the Republican Richard Nixon, two assassinations – of Senator Robert Kennedy, the most likely Democratic candidate, and of Dr Martin Luther King, the Negro leader – had shocked the nation and the world. As if these events were not sufficient, in August the Soviet Union, with other members of the Warsaw Pact, invaded Czechoslovakia in order to inhibit certain liberalizing reforms that appeared to be taking place in the regime. On a less spectacular level, international speculation in gold caused difficulties for many countries, including Britain.

In Britain, the decline in popularity of the Labour Government continued, partly because of its retrenchment in expenditure on the social services which brought it into conflict with its own left wing, partly because of its Prices and Incomes policy which aroused bitter hostility in the trades unions, and partly because of a general malaise which seemed to affect British actions and society. Britain's application to join the Common Market remained unsettled; the Rhodesian problem was discussed anew on another warship – this time H.M.S. Fearless – but no solution seemed in sight; and the passage of a Race Relations Bill through Parliament was dramatized by a speech in Birmingham by Enoch Powell, which led to his dismissal from the Shadow Cabinet. Because of the need for economy in Government expenditure, it was decided that the withdrawal of troops from east of Suez should be completed by the end of 1971, rather than the mid-1970s. The old feud between the Protestants and Roman Catholics in Ulster broke out again as a civil rights campaign was launched. Clashes with the police followed demonstrations by Catholics and civil rights supporters on the one hand, and ultra-Protestant groups on the other.

Cecil King's disenchantment with the Labour Government, and especially with Harold Wilson, had grown. In May, the Daily Mirror *published a leading article by Cecil King,* ENOUGH IS ENOUGH, *suggesting that Britain needed a new prime minister, and the Labour Party a new leader, and commenting on the state of Bank of England reserves. Cecil King had resigned as a director of the Bank of England before publishing the article, but it nevertheless received widespread coverage, and had a considerable effect on domestic and international opinion. In the same month, after a palace revolution in the International Publishing Corporation's boardroom, Cecil King was dismissed as chairman, and his place was taken by Hugh Cudlipp, previously deputy chairman of the group.*

Tuesday, January 2nd, 1968

Three-quarters of an hour with Roy Jenkins at 5 p.m., while Pickering had lunch with Denis Healey. Roy seemed in good heart. I said we would get no real return of confidence without a new P.M. He said in the present delicate political situation, a change for some months was not possible. But the balance of power in the Cabinet had changed in the last two months.

Denis Healey at lunch with Pickering was very outspoken. There was no political crisis, just a Wilson crisis. He had been trying to drive a wedge between Roy and himself and isolate Denis. However, he and Roy had got together to frustrate such knavish tricks. He thought Wilson's watershed had been the D-Notice affair. Up to that point his judgment had been quite good, but since then had been very erratic. His own difficulty has been that Wilson has called for defence cuts but has refused to cut any commitments or indicate a defence plan for the future. And Healey is determined to make no cuts without cutting commitments.

Thursday, January 4th, 1968

At the Bank. We are all awaiting the 17th, when Roy will reveal to the House the measures to be taken to restore our balance of payments. On the one hand it is difficult to see how the economies can be effected quickly enough; and, on the other, can the necessary cuts be got through the Cabinet and the Parliamentary Labour Party? It is increasingly being said – even at the Bank – that confidence cannot be restored without a change at No. 10. But can a change be made *in time*? It may well be that Roy's package may be the best that can be devised, but that we have run out of the time necessary for its implementation. Maurice Allen says the latest estimate for our balance of payments in 1968 is a deficit of somewhere between £100 and £250 million, which will use up fully half the loans we have for shoring up sterling. Maurice Parsons, at lunch, said if we have another successful attack on the pound, we shall have no resources with which to defend any particular exchange rate for the pound; that our trade will have to be conducted in dollars or some other foreign currency, and that under those circumstances, three million unemployed is perfectly possible. He thinks the present crisis is as grave as that of 1940 – with no Winston Churchill waiting to take over.

The dinner at the Argentine Embassy before Christmas, at which George Brown repeatedly denounced Wilson, continues to be a subject for discussion. There seem to have been other occasions where similar views were expressed by other ministers.

According to Maurice Parsons, George has been looking for a job in the City.

Friday, January 19th, 1968

The main news of the week has been the cuts which were announced by Wilson on Tuesday. They were badly received by the market. The debate included a good speech by Jenkins, an excellent speech by George Brown, and a very bad one by the Prime Minister. The position at the moment is that the cuts are quite inadequate and will leave Government expenditure 5 per cent higher next year than this. There is talk of a tough Budget, but this is two months off, which gives the spending spree every reason to continue. We are pulling out of the Far East four years sooner and out of the Persian Gulf, too. But no savings can be made in the coming year because of severance clauses, redundancy clauses, and penalty clauses attaching to our existing commitments. The current expectation is that there will be a further devaluation. At the moment only ministers think the situation will hold till next year. The relations between ministers, and between ministers and back-benchers, have never been worse. It is evident, too, from the reaction of studio audiences on T.V. that Wilson is regarded with contempt by the public.

Saturday, January 20th, 1968

Joe Hyman of Viyella came to see me yesterday evening at short notice. He is a man of bounding energy and great commercial ability but no visible political judgment. He is in touch with Robert Maxwell, who also hopes to fish in these troubled waters. He asked me to get him a peerage so that he could use the House of Lords as a platform in the crucial two months ahead. I pointed out that I couldn't get him a peerage; in any case, I wouldn't if I could, and he could make no impact on the public from the House of Lords in two months. He also said he thought the new prime minister should be Crossman, 'because he is so honest'! Meanwhile Maxwell has been pestering Hugh Cudlipp with phone calls and letters. He really will have to be given the brush-off.

Thursday, January 25th, 1968

At the Bank as usual. The situation according to Maurice Parsons is just holding! After Court, George Bolton said if he had not a sanguine character, he would be in despair. The Government has no authority and is not believed anywhere. At lunch Maurice Allen said the chances of a further devaluation in February were about fifty-fifty. I quoted the American Ambassador, David Bruce, who on Tuesday night said another devaluation would affect the whole world and he thought a crisis of that magnitude would take longer to develop, perhaps till June. Allen said he thought Bruce was in for a surprise. Allen said the next crisis was bound to come soon unless the Government were to borrow funds it knew it could not repay. By descending to that level it might be possible to fend off trouble, but not beyond the end of this year.

Roy Jenkins is regarded as far too weak, and apparently there are already views circulating in the Treasury on the lines that the export boom is not developing as it should, so perhaps it would be wise to put off the really stiff fiscal measures until 1969.

On Tuesday night we dined with the Rothermeres, where Ted Heath was one of the guests, and I met him again at a building society lunch on Wednesday. He thinks in purely conventional party terms: the other side is ruining the country; their Government will disintegrate and then we shall all go back with a sigh of relief to Tory rule. It still seems to me that some kind of a National Government is inevitable. Wilson went out of his way this evening to describe the idea as 'fatuous'. Obviously, the longer a real show-down is postponed the worse it will be. The distressing part is that while Wilson's stock sinks ever lower, the Tories gain no ground.

Thursday, February 1st, 1968

At the Bank as usual, with some talk with Archibald Forbes, chairman of the Midland Bank, at the lunch-table. The exchange situation has looked up quite considerably in the past week so that January as a month has fared a good deal better than expected. Enough dollars have come in to meet the Bank of England's forward commitments with a small margin. In February the liabilities are much greater as they represent three-month forward sales for the period just before devaluation. The attitude of the Governor is to live from day to day and recent days have been unexpectedly happy. The future is clouded by the Budget and by rising wages. To keep faith with the promises advanced earlier, the increases in taxation would have to be so large that they are unlikely to be contemplated. Having failed to bring on the Regulator when Wilson announced his cuts, Jenkins can hardly introduce any changes until the Budget. The Ministry of Labour says wages are rising at a rate of 6 or 7 per cent per annum, which is far more than productivity. So that to hold the position the Government would have to introduce a wage-stop plus a very heavy increase in taxation, some of it indirect taxes that would raise prices. No one thinks this Government can or will take these steps.

Wednesday, February 7th, 1968

Had Douglas Houghton to lunch on Monday, Tony Benn yesterday, and I sat next David Smith at lunch today (he is a director of Lloyd's and of the Union Discount Co.). The really astonishing aspect of our affairs is that, while the banking fraternity are talking about the date of the next financial crisis, ministers sail on oblivious. Houghton had no idea that we might well have a crash this month – or, anyway, pretty soon. Benn thought there might be trouble later in the year over rising wages, but this is no more than a cloud on the horizon. This head-in-the-sand attitude has its practical side: it means that apparently no one in the Cabinet is thinking ahead – after Wilson, who? They seem to think Jenkins will probably pull off his deflationary measures and then he is presumably in line for the succession. Denis Healey is not popular, but his stock might rise at a time of great tension.

There was a lunch yesterday, or Monday, at which Norman

Collins had as guests Eric Fletcher (Deputy Speaker), Shawcross, Renwick, Ellis Birk and Beeching. They were agreed that the country is in a mess and that Wilson won't do. What, however, should they *do* ? What about a joint letter to *The Times*? This did not find favour, so what about a deputation – but who to?! Eventually they decided to see if they could get Roy Jenkins to dine. It was agreed that the Tory Party is in such a mess that a purely Tory administration is no answer. But what about an *Emergency* Government? I thought this a good name for a National Government.

The papers this week are full of news from Vietnam, which is even more in evidence on the T.V. newsreels. The Viet Cong launched an offensive on a very wide front. They may have expected the country to rise in their favour, which it has not done. But it has been made evident that the South Vietnamese Government has no real standing apart from with the Americans, who evidently had no idea what was going on under their noses. The picture on television is of terror, cruelty and destruction on a huge scale. Yet this is the moment Ted Heath and the Shadow Cabinet choose to put down a motion declaring the solidarity of this country with the Americans over Vietnam. It scores a small debating point over Wilson, who leaves today for a pointless and ill-timed visit to Washington, but it reflects the exact opposite of popular sentiment, which is one of horror at the whole business.

A piece appeared in *The Director*, the organ of the Institute of Directors, this morning. Who should form a businessmen's government of fifteen men? The answer is Robens for P.M. and me for Education and Science! Other colleagues would be Paul Chambers, Lockwood and Kearton. Billy Butlin is a dear, but I hardly see him as Home Secretary!

Thursday, February 8th, 1968

Hugh had lunch with Roy Jenkins – alone. Roy very friendly and communicative. Two days before devaluation there was a Cabinet meeting at which Roy asked to be put in the picture over our economic affairs. After a whispered conversation between Wilson and Callaghan a meeting was promised – for ten days later! Wilson is very much given to votes at Cabinet meetings and when the cuts were being discussed, each one went to a vote. This is not only against Cabinet tradition, but by giving one man one vote, the more valuable members of the Cabinet are not allowed to exert their full weight. Wilson does nothing to control meetings, so that they go on interminably.

Hugh dined with Roy on the day of his appointment as Chancellor, and pointed out that he was now the most important man in the Government. He told Hugh that this gave him a shock at the time. He went home and thought about it, and realized Hugh was right. Asked why he did not do more to cut expenditure by the public, he said the reasons were (1) by checking expenditure by the public there was no reason to suppose that before the Budget any more production would be pushed into exports, and (2) it would have increased unemployment. Roy said the feeling in the Cabinet was not strong over payment for prescriptions: the biggest tussle was over defence, and he was pleased and relieved that his insistence on the defence cuts had left his good relations with Denis Healey unimpaired. In these discussions, Wilson did not help – in fact played no leading part – but at least he did no double-crossing.

Friday, February 9th, 1968

Ellis Birk looked in to tell me more about the Norman Collins lunch. In addition to those already mentioned, there were present Lord Watkinson (former Minister of Defence) and Field Marshal Lord Harding. Cromer was asked, but didn't come; it was thought he would have come if he could. The outcome is a lunch or dinner, which Jenkins has agreed to attend in the near future. Sigmund Warburg is to be invited to join them. Everyone spoke with affection and respect of Jenkins, but I think this is all late in the day. After his feeble cuts and the delay before the Budget (due to Treasury insistence) he seems to me to be writing himself off.

Sunday, February 11th, 1968

In conversation with Hugh yesterday, he recalled that Jenkins, during their lunch together, had asked what, in broad terms, was the failure of the Government since it first took office. Hugh said he thought a lack of foresight, which meant that measures like pulling

174

out of Singapore were forced on them late in the day though it had been apparent for years that it was necessary. Furthermore, the *Mirror* had repeatedly pointed out that we should be compelled by lack of means to withdraw our forces from east of Suez. Personally, I think it was an obvious corollary of our departure from India in 1947. The bases that had been established to protect our route to India no longer served any purpose, and the sooner we withdraw from Gibraltar, Malta, Cyprus, Aden and Bahrain the better. This – and departure from our base on the Canal – should have been planned in 1947. Instead of that we wait to be pushed. Roy said he accepted this criticism.

Monday, February 12th, 1968

Bert Bowden, now Lord Aylestone, for lunch. A dull man, but honest. Before Wilson took office I was told that Bowden had his ear, and was cheered, as Bowden is sensible as well as honest. However true that may have been at that time, it has certainly not been true since. He is delighted to be out of the Government and enjoys the I.T.A. Would have had to resign, anyway, as he had given the Australians and New Zealanders the most categorical assurances that their interests would be fully safeguarded in our approach to the Common Market. He did not think that either this promise had been honoured, or his assurance to Lee Kuan Yew and the Anzacs that we should not move out of Singapore until 1975.

Tuesday, February 13th, 1968

Among others to dinner last night, Cromer, Eccles and Hyman. Cromer is not a great brain but has integrity and authority, both in very short supply in public life these days. He volunteered to Ruth that he did not think we should get to Budget Day, March 19th, without the collapse of the pound. Hyman, whom I have only met twice before, is a real dynamo, but still very inexperienced. I thought he might throw his weight about, but not a bit of it.

Eccles, it was announced yesterday, is to be Chairman of the British Museum in succession to Lord Radcliffe. Noel Annan said he was the best Minister of Education ever. Last night we thought he was older, slower and more out of touch. He is to have lunch alone with Heath today. What was he to say? I said tell him not to say that the British public is solidly behind the Americans in Vietnam, which is patently untrue. After all, this last week or more we have had the war in Saigon on everyone's television set – and a horrifying spectacle it is. I said also that I think there will be some form of coalition government and even if he doesn't agree with this prophecy, he should at least be prepared for one. This led Eccles, whom I like and admire, into a long tirade on the futility of businessmen thinking they could be ministers. It requires long apprenticeship in the House of Commons. I said business and government were both administration and the trouble with nearly all ministers is that they are such poor administrators. He said a coalition was an absurd idea. This Government was collapsing. There would be a General Election and the Tories would be in for a generation. I said a purely Conservative administration would be quite incapable of solving our present problems (e.g. putting into force an effective Prices and Incomes policy) and any attempt to do so might finally destroy the House of Commons. It is curious that such ideas, which are widely accepted by all and sundry, are repudiated only by politicians, who think everything is as it was in 1906.

Monday, February 19th, 1968

Am at Menton being painted by Graham Sutherland. I like both him and his wife. It is curious that the best portrait-painter of his day does not really like doing portraits, and does not regard himself as a portrait painter. He thinks his best was of Adenauer, but is very pleased with the way mine is going.

Being in France for a bit with Peter Stephens is always a revelation of the corruption and malpractices of the Gaullist Government. There has been recently a great scandal, in which a mayor and several councillors have had to resign for corruption and fraud. Though nearly all the French newspapers are quite anti-Gaullist, this has not been reported because the mayor is a Gaullist and the newspapers are afraid. An O.A.S.* man escaped from the Ile de Ré

* L'Organisation de l'Armée secrète, a loose collection of French and European terrorist groups formed to oppose by force the granting of independence to Algeria in the early 1960s.

and the entire police force of France were turned on to hunt him down, without success. He recently turned up in Rome and gave his complete story to *Paris Match* which has not used it for fear of annoying de Gaulle. A senior judge 'retired' recently but none of the newspapers said why. This was because of a squalid scene involving himself, his ex-wife and his mistress. The wife persisted in bringing the matter to the courts and in the end he was dismissed. When Algeria was given its independence, the senior French representative in Algiers was the Consul-General. His house was invaded by thugs, he was stripped naked, paraded round the town, and sexually assaulted in each of the main squares. This was not reported, nor was any protest made. These stories go on and on.

The General's spite is very active. Though by French law General Weygand was entitled to a military funeral with a band and a battalion of infantry, he was only allowed a platoon and no band. General Juin, the only Marshal of France, had his staff cut off, the furniture removed from his official flat and his car taken away. He then threatened to bicycle round Paris in full uniform, so a car was given him – a smaller one. All these emoluments are prescribed by French law and were his by right. In addition to suppression by the French newspapers, there is, of course, a constant stream of Gaullist propaganda by radio and television – and this, too, is in direct breach of the law.

It seems to be pretty generally agreed that whatever services de Gaulle may have performed for France in the past, he has nothing to contribute now. His term of office expires in 1972, but no one thinks he could stand again. His contemptuous references to doddering old Pétain would be too readily available for use against him. Apparently he looks old – he is seventy-seven – but is quite spry.

Wednesday, February 21st, 1968

I am in a plane en route from Marseilles to Paris. Yesterday I had forty-five minutes with Gaston Defferre, mayor of Marscilles, a Deputy, a leader of the Left and proprietor of the principal Marseilles paper, the *Provençale*. He is sometimes spoken of as a future prime minister or president. He is a nice man, older than I expected (in his upper fifties at least).

I asked what he thought would happen after de Gaulle. He said he hoped after ten years and more of de Gaulle and the Right, that there would be a swing to the Left. But French finances would be in an awful mess. Debré is expected to make economies without touching the subjects reserved to the President, but as these include foreign affairs, monetary policy, defence, among the most obvious items, it leaves him with precious little to work on. I was saying that Wilson had no administrative ability and no foresight. He said no one had everything: he himself was a good administrator but had not the wide grasp of world affairs and foresight possessed by Mendès-France, who, however, was a hopeless administrator. He told me that during the war, in London, de Gaulle told him the British and the Americans were 'des salauds'. It is a pity that this opinion of his was not known more widely – and sooner. He mentioned in passing that Pompidou is no administrator.

Thursday, February 22nd, 1968

At the Bank. The deficit for last year has come out at £600 million: to break even this year we should have to do better by £600 million plus the £250 million handicap imposed by devaluation. To suggest, as the Government is still doing, that this £850 million can be achieved this year, with a further £500 million next year and in subsequent years, is totally unrealistic. Imports are rising – of manufactures, not raw materials. Maurice Allen thinks the Treasury estimates are far too optimistic.

While I was away, the *Guardian* had a big piece on the front page suggesting I was trying to organize a coalition. They also said I had sought office in 1964 and 1966. So I published a denial, which was given prominence in all the papers except the *Daily Mail*. Politicians seem incapable of understanding that when I talk of coalition I am talking of the future, not of the present. The whole episode is interesting as it would not have been given the prominence it was unless people are thinking in terms of a National Government. *The Times* even gave me a cartoon yesterday.

Saturday, February 24th, 1968

Yesterday a more detailed attack on me was made in the Peter

Jenkins column on the back page of the *Guardian*. It is thought in the office that these two attacks were the opening shots of a campaign, certainly ordered by the editor, Hetherington. The general theme is a bit confused, but is mainly on the lines that King is too powerful; we want no Northcliffes here. The *Guardian* is not an influential paper any longer and if it comes to open warfare I have all the guns in both verbal dexterity and coverage.

Saturday, March 2nd, 1968

Ruth had lunch with Mrs Denis Healey. It was a purely social occasion – the two of them – and politics only came into the conversation incidentally. In Mrs Healey's travels round constituency gatherings of faithful Labour supporters, she says they all are seeking reassurance. 'Do tell us what the papers say isn't true! It will all come out right, won't it?' Among M.P.s, Mrs Healey says a clear majority believe that Harold is so clever that at the right moment he will pull the rabbit out of the hat and prove he was right all the time. It is quite natural that devoted party workers should seek reassurance that all their efforts are not in vain. But the attitude of M.P.s is inexcusable. They read the papers and are in a position to check any statements they feel unhappy about. In any case, three and a half years of failure should have taught them what to expect.

I had a visit this morning from Hedlund, a leader on the Conservative side in Sweden. I gather he is head of the Farmers' Party. Reed's are big customers of his. After preliminary courtesies, he came to the point. Is there no way of getting H.M.G. to modify its present stand of all or nothing in its approach to the Common Market? The Swedish view is that full membership is some years off, and pressing for full membership – all or nothing now – will result in nothing. The Six were offering us tariff advantages which the Swedish Government thinks should be accepted. It was made quite clear in the course of forty-five minutes' talk that he came with the full knowledge of the Swedish P.M. (he said so in so many words), and we thought he had been *sent* by his Government. I explained that Wilson was in no way interested in the Common Market except as a ploy to help him in his Parliamentary manœuvres; that in any case British politicians, though not the British public, thought it beneath

179

their dignity to accept anything less than full membership of the Common Market which, they assumed, they would dominate. He said was this likely to be the attitude of the Government until the next election? I said Wilson would not last three years – probably not three months – and one would hope that his successors would be more realistic. He left, I was told afterwards, feeling he had had a satisfactory interview. At any rate he knew what I thought.

I also got a letter following up a call from Siggy Warburg about three weeks ago. His idea is to ask about thirty-five people of importance from five countries (assuming twenty-five would actually show up). One night they would be addressed by Moshe Dayan, Israeli Minister of Defence, and the next night by the Egyptian Foreign Minister or Haikal, the editor of *Al Ahram*, who is known to reflect Nasser's thinking. The address would be off-the-record, followed by questions – no holds barred and all questions to be answered. Warburg has been seeing Dayan and he has been in touch with Nutting, who has been in Cairo. They think that now, when the pressure is off, is the time to get some talks going. I am dubious about organizing such a gathering. I know hardly any of the people suggested and an invitation by me might (1) be refused or (2) be regarded as a Jewish move to which I was lending myself.

Monday, March 4th, 1968

The only public news is another bad day for the pound, which sank to its lowest ever. The announcement that our reserves increased by £9 million last month had no effect as it was so widely known to be untrue. I gathered that the true figure was a loss of $200 million or so.

Thursday, March 7th, 1968

At the Bank – to be elected a member of the Committee of Treasury.*
I had been there yesterday afternoon, at the Governor's request. In view of the two attacks on me in the *Guardian*, I think he wanted me to say again that if I get personally embroiled in political controversy I will resign from the Court as, under such circumstances, my continuance on the Court might embarrass the Bank. Having cleared

* The inner group of seven Bank directors (there are eighteen in the full Court). Of these seven, three are executive and four non-executive.

that point, we had a general chat about the situation, of which he seemed to me to take an optimistic view: £500 million surplus next year and all that. However, today in addressing the Court, O'Brien was very gloomy: said what a disastrous day Friday had been; how we were teetering on the brink, etc. etc. Even if we could solve our own problems, America was giving us cause for much worry.

After Court I spoke to Maurice Allen. He said there is no possibility of a £500 million surplus next year; that we have now so little in the way of available reserves that we cannot now sustain a day like Friday. He thinks the Government may seek to borrow again, but this could only be done by lying and borrowing money we should be unable to repay. A plan to requisition our dollar portfolio investments in private hands would probably crash the pound at once and it is believed that Roy knows this. The Bank people know a certain amount about the Budget and expect a very tough Budget tax-wise, but the ceiling on wage increases is not solid – more like perforated zinc, as Maurice Allen said. The situation is so dicey that O'Brien yesterday said if he spoke out he would bring the pound down. Maurice Allen thinks that we should get through to Budget Day. This could either break the pound or give us a breathing space. It can do no more. In any case, over the months ahead there are so many hurdles to jump that I do not think Allen thinks it possible for the pound to outlast the year, and it may not last another week.

Wednesday, March 13th, 1968

My first appearance at the Committee of Treasury. The Governor was much gloomier than he has ever been before. Subsequently, I had some private chat with Maurice Parsons. They say they are living from day to day – last Friday was disastrously bad and, as the Governor said, pushed us even nearer the brink. Friday is the worst day because changes in exchange rates are likely to be made at the week-end. There is a world-wide boom in gold and a lot of sterling is being sold for dollars with which to buy gold. O'Brien and Parsons both say we may get by if the Budget is tough enough, but today no Prices and Incomes policy is yet agreed, and I don't believe they really think this. In my opinion, it is all too late and it doesn't matter now what is in the Budget. I think they expect the pound to go down this month. Roy Bridge, who is the man in the Bank who deals with foreign exchange, rang up from Tokyo this morning to ask if he should come home as it was believed in Japan that the pound would go on Tuesday.

Meanwhile the trade figures for February came out at midday showing exports down, imports up, and a deficit of £70 million.

At the N.P.A. in the afternoon and had some talk with Drogheda to protest at the *Financial Times*'s leader on Saturday saying there was no threat to the pound. And then had a long talk with Denis Hamilton just back from the U.S. where he saw Johnson yesterday. He says Johnson looks tired out and utterly depressed. The New Hampshire primary election result is out this morning, with McCarthy getting 42 per cent of the Democratic vote and Johnson 49 per cent. When McCarthy first presented himself he was expected to get 12 per cent at best, with a landslide for Johnson. Hamilton thought Johnson had a pretty shrewd idea of the likely result when he saw him yesterday. Johnson said the pound looked pretty shaky and if the pound went the dollar would go too. He said (surprisingly) that he often thought of what Churchill would do in present circumstances if he were alive and operating in the U.S. Did Denis know? Churchill, of course, would not have had a clue over a financial problem, and would not have been much better over Vietnam, where the problem is political, not military. Denis also saw Woods, the Chairman of the World Bank, who was pessimistic and said our situation would have been difficult if world trade were going well, but it is actually slipping and looks like continuing to do so.

On domestic affairs, Denis said he had had to lunch last week Peter Shore, Barbara Castle and Tony Crosland, none of whom seemed to have any idea of our critical situation. Even worse, Drogheda told me it was Tony Crosland who persuaded Roy Jenkins that the use of the Regulator was not necessary!

Brian Walden to lunch yesterday. He doesn't look much but is easily the most intelligent of the Labour M.P.s I know. He says the P.L.P.* still thinks Harold must know best and they will not believe how unpopular they are until they actually lose the coming by-elections. According to Walden they are bound to lose Acton,

* Parliamentary Labour Party.

Meriden, Dudley and Nelson-and-Colne, but can hardly lose Sheffield (Brightside).* They will also take a thrashing in the local elections in May. They may easily lose control of fifteen London boroughs, of which they hold twenty-three out of thirty-two. They only hold four provincial towns of any size, of which they are likely to lose two, and Labour representation over large tracts of the countryside is likely to be extinguished. If the pound crashes, Wilson will have to go, but no one is establishing a successor. However, Walden promised to start active probing. He said there is no one on either side of the House big enough to be an effective P.M. in a crisis. But clearly the next P.M. will have to be found in the P.L.P. and might well prove to be Healey, though he did not think Healey would last long.

Thursday, March 14th, 1968

Everyone at the Bank gloomier than they were even yesterday. It appears that the rush for gold is quite out of hand. Within a short while, possibly tonight, the U.S. will probably stop buying or selling gold. There will then be no fixed rate for the dollar, or for sterling. It is just possible that by borrowing more money, which it will be unable to repay, the Government may get by for a few days. Quite a lot of this money so borrowed has gone already. But the gold rush this afternoon is reaching such astronomic proportions that the U.S. will probably be forced to do something by 11 a.m. tomorrow at latest. This would bring down the pound anyway. The optimists at the Bank talk of an exchange rate not far below two dollars: the pessimists argue that one dollar per pound is more likely. The price of food would rise fairly soon and unemployment could well reach three million. The nearer the crisis comes the more people argue that there is no figure on either side of the House of Commons who could be regarded as an appropriate P.M. for such a critical period.

Friday, March 15th, 1968

There was a dramatic Privy Council meeting at 1 a.m. this morning at

* Labour lost all five of these by-elections in what had been regarded as safe Labour seats: Dudley, Meriden and Acton on March 28th, Sheffield (Brightside) on June 13th and Nelson-on-Colne on June 27th.

183

which a Bank Holiday was proclaimed, so the banks are only open for routine business and the Stock Exchange and the gold market are closed. The Governors of the Central Banks have flown to Washington for a meeting tomorrow and a communiqué is expected on Sunday night. I went round to see Maurice Parsons this morning to get a line on things. He said the market was closed by request of President Johnson, urged indirectly by the Bank of England, who operate the gold pool. The Americans will have to decide three things. (1) Whether to go on selling gold at $35 an ounce; they have said they will, down to their last bar – I don't believe they will do anything so foolish. Or (2) whether to mark up the price to $60 or more; on balance the Bank thinks this would be the least damaging course for the rest of the world, though it would give an immense bonanza to Russia and South Africa, while the hoarders from France on down would reap a rich harvest – a most undeserving group. Or (3) whether to sell gold at $35 to selected Central Banks but let gold in the free market find its own level; it is thought this would prove only a temporary measure as some Central Banks (notably the French) cannot be trusted not to buy at $35 and sell at the free-market price. Knowing the weakness of governments, it is likely that the third course will be adopted. Parsons clearly thought it likely that the world's economy would collapse on Monday. If it does, it will be because of the weakness and incompetence of the Governments of Britain and the U.S. He said the Budget is a realistic one, but then the Budget has ceased to be really relevant. It is too late, and, in any case, we do not now control events. I think the real crisis is now on and can only end in the collapse of the pound and of this Government.

Apparently George Brown was not told of the midnight Privy Council meeting and so did not attend the Cabinet meeting. He may have resigned, but this is now of no importance.* Reed's agent in Paris rang up to say that gold this afternoon in Paris is changing hands at $45 an ounce.

Monday, March 18th, 1968

We really have had a very stirring few days. The Central Bankers

* George Brown did resign from the Cabinet on this issue.

met in Washington and did, indeed, announce the adoption of a two-tier system for gold sales. They also announced further support for the pound. As a result the dollar–pound exchange rate recovered from $2.37, or so, to $2.40, and the free market in gold is now about $39. I called on Maurice Parsons in the afternoon to see if I could learn anything. I gathered the new loan was of money already spent by us. He had seen the Budget and thought it was about right – if the prices and incomes part was really made to stick. The Bank of England governors are living from day to day and if you ask about the prospects over a period of months, you might as well ask about them over a period of centuries.

Dick Marsh came to lunch. He was very friendly and did not see any way out of the present impasse. He said if Wilson stood today for the leadership of the Parliamentary Party he would win by a large majority. He said twice during lunch that he doubted if the new Prices and Incomes policy would get through the House. He was very insistent – and that is why he brought the matter up twice – that in that event there must be no General Election, as that would leave the country without a government for two months. There is the further point that a General Election would presumably produce a Conservative majority at the present time, but it would be a Parliament without much authority and with large minorities of Scottish and Welsh Nationalists, and possibly some sort of Poujadist* members from English constituencies. I said to him, as I have said to Denis Healey, Brian Walden, and others, that the immediately necessary next step is for the P.L.P., or at any rate, a powerful group in the Cabinet, to choose Wilson's successor. When that has been done other forces can be mobilized behind the new man. But this cannot be done by newspapers or anyone outside the House of Commons.

Wednesday, March 20th, 1968

The Budget yesterday was better than expected. Extra taxation reached a very large figure. To be critical, too much was taken from the business sector and so will come out of what should be savings,

---

* After Pierre Poujade, a French provincial shopkeeper, who founded in 1953 a right-wing, authoritarian movement aimed at encouraging small tradesmen to refuse to pay their taxes until the French Government introduced certain fiscal and other reforms.

and too little from the public, but in terms of practical politics, this is all that could have been expected. If events continue out of control – as I expect – the Budget will be seen to have been irrelevant.

Thursday, March 21st, 1968

At the Bank as usual. There was nothing new at Court but afterwards I had some talk with Maurice Allen. A week ago the odds in favour of a crash were a hundred to one: now he would put them at ten to one. It is likely that the shock everyone had last weekend and the loan we have received will stave off trouble for some few months. He regarded the Treasury forecast, released with the Budget, as wildly optimistic. There are so many unknowns in the situation that it is impossible to say what will happen when. The two weakest areas of Government policy are Government expenditure, about which nothing was said in the Budget speech, and wage increases. These are to be limited to $3\frac{1}{2}$ per cent plus anything to be had from productivity agreements. This means that $3\frac{1}{2}$ per cent will not be the ceiling, but the floor. Other points of danger are that holders of sterling – even the most loyal ones (presumably Australia or New Zealand) – are edging out of sterling. America's position is weak, Wilson is doing badly, so really anything might happen. The fact that Bobby Kennedy is challenging Johnson will necessarily weaken Johnson, and the three by-electionsthe Labour Party are to lose next week will weaken Wilson. Meanwhile, a number of people, for mainly personal reasons, will be seeking to undermine Wilson and his policies – de Gaulle, Frank Cousins, George Brown, Scanlon (the new President of the Amalgamated Engineering Union), and doubtless others.

Tuesday, March 26th, 1968

David Bruce, the American Ambassador, to lunch. He is just off to the U.S. for a fortnight, glad to get out of this country, which he finds very depressing. Last time he came to lunch he thought our financial debacle might be delayed till June. Now, with the Budget, he thinks the Government can carry on for a few months. He sees clearly that nothing short of a financial crash can bring Wilson down, but for the present sees him as an increasingly discredited figure, clinging to office in the hope that something might turn up. He wrote George Brown a letter of condolence on his resignation. He likes George, but regards him as a disastrous Foreign Secretary.

Monday, April 1st, 1968

Had lunch with Kenneth Keith on Thursday. His people think we shall only move into equilibrium in our balance of payments in the third quarter of next year. By contrast, the *Sunday Times* yesterday offered the opinion that we should have a surplus of £350 million in our balance of payments in the first half of next year. Kenneth Keith had been approached some time ago by George Brown who demanded, not directorships, but the control of some company as executive chairman. He was very put out when told there was nothing doing.

I did a broadcast yesterday with Robin Day – half an hour at 2.15. I was pretty evasive, but did say it was hard to see how the Labour Party could make a fresh start or the country get a fresh infusion of leadership without a new face at No. 10. This has been taken up in a big way by all the newspapers this morning. Cudlipp says this is a new departure, snapping our last links with the Labour Party. He sees a new situation arising in which there is open warfare between Parliament and the press. He thinks this was coming anyway, but we had meant to delay it. None of the newspapers is critical of what I said – only Manny Shinwell, who says that if there is any attempt to unseat Wilson, whether sponsored by the newspapers or not, he will resign from the Labour Party. I have no idea what he thinks he is achieving by this announcement.

Sunday, April 7th, 1968

The most important news since I wrote last has been the assassination of Martin Luther King at Memphis and the consequent rioting all over the United States, notably in Washington. The Negro problem was going to be a nightmare this summer anyway, but this murder makes a desperate situation even more so. Part of the attraction of the riots is the looting, which seems to be almost unrestrained. I always thought that when rioting breaks out, looters must be shot. Otherwise the situation will get entirely out of hand. Johnson has made all the right gestures but it is exceedingly difficult to see any end to the tension, let along the violence which seems to be in some way part of the American way of life.

Wilson announced his Cabinet changes on Friday night. The trades union representation is increased with a couple of nonentities as under-secretaries; the left-wing seems to be fortified to counter balance the emergence of Jenkins, Healey and Crosland, but mostly it is just a shuffle. Shore, who has been a total failure, is relieved of Prices and Incomes which are made over to an enlarged Ministry of Labour in the charge of Barbara Castle. Gunter moves to Fuel and Power and Marsh to Transport; Gordon Walker goes, but the other two conspicuous failures – Greenwood and Ross – remain. The idea, in so far as there is one, is that Barbara will be able to get more agreement out of the unions than Gunter because she is left-wing. I don't think the unions care what her political ideas are and will resent having to deal with a woman. On television Barbara is obviously delighted with herself – quite unaware that on her devolves the responsibility of keeping this country out of a financial abyss. The newspapers take the changes too seriously, clearly reflecting too closely the briefing given them by the P.M.

On Wednesday at the Committee of Treasury, the Governor revealed that the loss of reserves, given officially as £20 million, was in fact £400 million, $250 million in three days. The previous month the official figure was £8 million up – which was very different from the real figure, which I gathered (but was not told clearly) was £100 million down.

Last Sunday Desmond Donnelly had a piece in the *News of the World* in which there was a paragraph to the effect that a senior Cabinet minister very well in with the Downing St set had said to Donnelly that the Government is going to stick it out and, if it comes to that, pull the whole temple down on top of themselves. One doesn't have to take Donnelly's pronouncements too seriously, but I thought it might have been said by Crossman in an indiscreet moment. However, I asked Grimond when he came to lunch on Friday and he said the statement was made by Peter Shore at dinner at Nuffield College and that he made it clear to those listening that he was quoting the P.M. – or, at any rate, reflecting his view. Leslie O'Brien says the P.M. is much less ebullient these days – as well he may be. Jenkins told O'Brien that the Washington weekend was the worst of his life!

Easter Sunday, April 14th, 1968

When I had some talk with Maurice Allen on Thursday, he showed me some of the secret figures. I am not much good at these, which tend to be compiled on different bases at different times, but they were clearly disastrous. The total deficit for the first quarter was well over £500 million. Allen thought £250 million for the whole year would prove an optimistic forecast. Meanwhile the spending spree seems to be continuing. Reed's on Tuesday said the demand for corrugated cases was showing no sign of flagging, up to Monday the 8th. At Harrods on Thursday they had sold out of most sizes of Easter egg by midday. Withdrawals from building societies are at a record level; the Stock Exchange index goes on up and up.

Wednesday, April 17th, 1968

Committee of Treasury and lunch at the Bank. The intake of dollars since Washington has been good, about $100 million a week, but our real reserves are so low that two bad Fridays could clear us out. While the immediate outlook is better the longer term indications are very adverse. The Governor said he had been urging the Chancellor to take all available drawings from the I.M.F. as these funds would not be available to us if there had to be another devaluation. This sounded to me like another debt to be incurred that we shall be unable to repay.

Thursday, April 18th, 1968

A short, rather dull Court, but a long talk with Maurice Allen afterwards. The present position is that we are about $4,300 million worse off than we were at this time last year. The loss of reserves has been heavy and continuous except for a short period around the time of devaluation. We have lost reserves this month, but at a slower rate than last month or the month before. Any hesitation about borrowing money that we shall be unable to repay has been surmounted and the generosity of our creditors is not due to our prestige or our credibility, but only to our power to blackmail. Various serious strikes are in prospect, notably in the steel and engineering industries, any one of which might renew the attack on the pound. Ministers are not informed of the true situation owing to their inability to keep their mouths shut, and many optimistic statements may well be believed by the speakers.

Monday, April 22nd, 1968

Iain Macleod to lunch. He wanted to know how I saw things, as I had been right all along! I told him substantially what the Bank had told me. Evidently a crash was coming and equally evidently nothing could be done about Wilson until it came. Our conversation was coloured by the fact that Enoch Powell had made a violently racialist speech at Birmingham on Saturday and had been dismissed from the Shadow Cabinet. If he had kept to his theme of stopping the flow of immigrants he would have been all right, but he spoke of the black man taking over this country and much other wild talk – warmly supported by the *Express* this morning. Macleod thinks the prompt dismissal by Heath will enhance Heath's standing in this country. I rather think that this revelation of the nastier aspects of right-wing Conservatism will do no good. Confidence in the Tories, already at a low ebb, may well sink.

Macleod agrees with me that our Parliamentary institutions are threatened and that we are heading for a right-wing dictatorship. He is distressed that at this moment there is nothing to be done. He thinks Denis Healey the ablest of the Labour Ministers; Roy Jenkins is too keen on popularity. He thinks a coalition quite a possibility but only after a crash. He regards Callaghan as entirely devalued. In the plight they are in, the Labour Party might look for a neutral figure as their new leader. What about Michael Stewart? I really cannot believe this is possible – I hope not anyway!

Wednesday, April 24th, 1968

There is no hard news. Two remarks made at the Committee of Treasury may illustrate the prevailing mood. (1) Unemployment is still low, 2.3 per cent, but for two months, seasonably adjusted, has shown a small rise. Apparently Roy is 'scared' (O'Brien's word). One would have thought he would be pleased that his policy is beginning to bite. (2) O'Brien said, 'We are just holding on – afraid almost to breathe unless we bring something down on us.'

Friday, April 26th, 1968

At Court yesterday there was no particular news, but afterwards I had some talk with Maurice Allen. Discussions are going on between the Governor and Jenkins on the loss to our reserves in April. The figure will be over $100 million but Jenkins is determined to announce a plus of £20 million and overnight borrowing is being arranged to give this figure plausibility at the end of the month. The Governor wants the Government to withdraw its entitlement from the I.M.F. as this would not be available if the pound goes down. Jenkins has so far refused, 'as it would be damaging to his prestige'. This would seem to imply that O'Brien is thinking of the next devaluation while Jenkins is not. Maurice Allen does not now expect a crash before June but sees even less than before how a crash can be avoided, though the dollar may go before the pound.

I had lunch yesterday with Harry Walston. Harry had dinner with George Brown recently. He had been summoned to 10 Downing St, where Wilson, in a two and a half hour talk, downing three glasses of brandy to one of George's, said they had both been perhaps over-hasty and what about a return to office? Not now, of course, but perhaps in the autumn. I would take this to be a manoeuvre by Wilson to keep George quiet until his influence has entirely evaporated. But it is surprising how often ministers fall for this ploy. George apparently refused offers from the *News of the World* and the *Sunday Express* (one of them for £25,000), but these came after he had agreed to write three pieces for the *Sunday Times* for a far more modest amount. He is now to work for Courtaulds along with Douglas Jay, David Eccles and Rab Butler! However, they are directors and he is to be a 'consultant'.

Wednesday, May 1st, 1968

The Committee of Treasury as usual. The Governor, who used to be rather irrationally cheerful, now seems to be sunk in gloom. We are to announce an increase in our reserves of £21 million in April. The real figure is a loss of £80 million.

At an Anglo–Danish dinner last night Ruth sat next Reggie Maudling, who told her that one-third of the Tory M.P.s in the House would now prefer Enoch Powell to Ted Heath as leader of their party. Not far away at the dinner was —— [a senior civil servant] who looked, she said, completely exhausted.

Wednesday, May 8th, 1968

At the Committee of Treasury: the Governor gloomy as usual these days. Things are sometimes better, sometimes worse, but our reserves slip away all the time.

Thursday, May 9th, 1968

Some two or three weeks ago I said to Hugh Cudlipp I thought the time had come to step out and launch an all-out attack on Wilson and that the Labour defeats in the local elections would provide the peg on which to hang the attack. Hugh thought the matter over and agreed. So tomorrow there will be a piece signed by me on the front page of the *Mirror* and quoted in full in the *Sun* and the *Glasgow Record*. Since suggesting the attack, opinion has moved fairly fast and it appeared that we should be overtaken by events if we put this off – even to Monday. Obviously I shall get a lot of abuse from the politicians. Shall I get any worthwhile support? It necessitates resigning from the Bank Court and I am sending a letter by hand this evening to that effect.

Saturday, May 11th, 1968

The big blast went off yesterday* and had a greater impact than I expected. This was due to my references to 'lies about our reserves'. The pound had a bad day and I am blamed. As I know the Governor has been very worried about last month's published figure, I feel I am on safe ground. In view of the probable collapse of the pound in the fairly near future, I had to say something on our finances. The *Express* yesterday made no mention at all of my piece. This was childish and they had to catch up in the *Standard* and in the *Express* today.

* The piece was entitled ENOUGH IS ENOUGH, and suggested that Britain needed a new Prime Minister and the Labour Party a new leader. It claimed, in part, that Britain was 'threatened with the greatest financial crisis in our history. It is not to be removed by lies about our reserves but only by a fresh start under a new leader.'

The newspapers are pretty hostile, notably the *Guardian*, and so are the politicians. Crossman launched an attack on me yesterday, but it was very poor stuff. Wilson looks pretty bedraggled on T.V., as well he may. The local government elections went far worse than anyone expected. Labour's hold on twenty-three London boroughs was reduced to four and they lost many provincial towns including Sheffield and Norwich – and there were not all that number to lose. There is to be a further piece by me in the *Sunday Mirror* tomorrow, but from then on we shall have to play it by ear.

Woodrow Wyatt rang up yesterday and said my piece would increase support for Wilson for a few days, but the hard facts of the elections are bound to sink in. He said he met Jenkins yesterday morning, who was in a bit of a tizzy. He said he was being urged by Barbara Castle to repudiate my plea for a new P.M. Woodrow Wyatt said why should he repudiate anything: I had not named him. In fact Jenkins has said nothing. Michael Stewart is said to be standing in the wings awaiting a call. He might indeed get one as he is the sort of nullity everyone might agree on. In any event, the range of selection is narrow and uninviting.

Monday, May 13th, 1968

Stacks of letters this morning – mostly hostile, but an encouraging letter from Robens and a word of praise on the telephone from Garfield Weston.

Had some talk with Denis Hamilton at the N.P.A. He said Rees-Mogg had recently been in Washington meeting all and sundry, including the I.M.F. people and the B.I.S.* people and he was assured by those who should know that the U.S. will protect the pound at least until July. The test will come in the autumn. Labour Party chiefs tell their friends they will have Wilson out by October, but how do we get there?

Tuesday, May 14th, 1968

There was to be a meeting of the Coal Board to meet (at their suggestion) nine M.P.s who are members of the N.U.M.† and two

* Bank of International Settlements.
† National Union of Mineworkers.

peers. I was met at the door of Hobart House by the publicity man of the Coal Board who told me the M.P.s would walk out if I attended. In spite of this, Robens would prefer me to come, which I did. The M.P.s, a sorry-looking lot, then walked out. As a result I had a long talk with Alf, who is in good form and delighted with my piece. He told me Leslie O'Brien rang him up on Friday and asked if he was going to resign from the Bank. Robens said he had not thought of doing so; did O'Brien want him to? If he did, R. was quite prepared to go. O'Brien, in a panic, said quite the contrary; he was extremely anxious R. should remain on the Court.

Wednesday, May 15th, 1968

The papers in London were all stopped owing to a one-day strike by the engineers. This is purely political and aimed at the Government. In Manchester and Glasgow all was normal.

The mining M.P.s put down a motion saying I should be dismissed from the Coal Board. This morning it had 155 signatures. Alf says they feel frustrated and that this is a way of letting off steam. I doubt whether I can be dismissed, but I should certainly not be dismayed if the Government were so foolish as to try.

Friday, May 17th, 1968

Louis Franck to lunch yesterday – a nice man and immensely able. He says large sums are pouring out of the country to Australia. Banks have been asked not to do this but private individuals can transfer any sums they like. I asked if the total would amount to £1 million a week. He said it was more than that. This is fully legal. Franck says the Continental Central Banks will help us no more, though the Americans might. He assumes the collapse of sterling by September.

At dinner last night with Joe Hyman. He is full of energy and ambition but has no political sense. He tried to draw parallels between Cromwell, Magna Carta and Wilson, and thinks the inevitable future P.M. is Crossman.

Wednesday, May 22nd, 1968

The news since last Friday has mostly been growing chaos in France.*

* For some years in France each academic year had opened in an atmosphere of discontent and protest, with some political basis, but mainly on account of inadequacies

The General is to broadcast on Friday evening and is to have a referendum next month. In the meantime it seems that he has lost prestige which, at his age, will prove irrecoverable. The main lesson so far is that de Gaulle and his ministers were completely out of touch with opinion in the country and the general strike sparked off by the students was indeed very badly handled in the early stages, but was clearly totally unexpected.

In the House last night the Prices and Incomes Bill passed with a majority of thirty-five.* The highlights of the debate were an outstandingly poor speech by Barbara Castle and an outstandingly good one by George Brown. With so much opposition it is doubtful if it can be made to work.

Friday, May 24th, 1968

Hugh was at a drinks party at No. 11 last night: Crossman very friendly; Wilson polite; Mary Wilson very hostile. He had no talk with Jenkins who was always being drawn away, but he seemed quite friendly. Wilson looked tired, with dark rings under his eyes as never before. Hugh is to lunch on Monday with Ray Gunter, suspected, apparently by Wilson, as the man to wield the dagger when the time comes.

Monday, May 27th, 1968

The news this last month has been of the riots in France. Yesterday was quiet but they are due to start up again this evening. They were sparked off by students at the Sorbonne, but since then more than half the workmen in the country have joined in and gone on strike. De Gaulle (1) refused to postpone his state visit to Romania, (2)

---

of premises and staffing. On May 3rd a feud between the administration of the Nanterre campus of the University of Paris and some students led by left-wing groups spread to the Sorbonne. The result was intermittent demonstrations, strikes and street-fighting which lasted for almost the whole month of May, and led to a partial general strike. President de Gaulle was on a visit to Romania and Georges Pompidou, the Prime Minister, was in Afghanistan. De Gaulle's first intervention on his return to Paris on May 24th was somewhat ill-advised and added fuel to the flames by its repetition of well-worn policies. After rumours of resignation, the President announced a general election, and on June 12th all demonstrations were forbidden until after this had taken place.

* This Act renewed and extended the 1967 legislation. The normal Government majority in the House was seventy.

refused to return early, though the situation had turned very nasty, then (3) finally had to return a day early but (4) would make no announcement until his scheduled broadcast on Friday, which (5) by Friday was mistimed and had no relevance to the crisis. There is to be a referendum in the middle of June to decide whether or no de Gaulle is to stay. But his mystique and his authority have gone. Meanwhile French unions are demanding huge increases in wages, shorter hours, the lot. The French Government is in no state to reject the claims which can only lead to rampant inflation. It is hard to see how she can play her part as a member of the Common Market under these conditions, and at some stage will be lucky to avoid civil war.

Naturally this has relevance to the prospects here. Successful student riots on television can only lead to imitation. At one time I thought our problems could be solved in due course by a new P.M. and a better team. Now one wonders where it will end. Though widely regarded as a pessimist, I now think the tunnel we are entering longer and darker than I had supposed.

Later

Hugh had lunch with Ray Gunter to talk about the Cabinet and all that. Gunter is very hostile to Wilson and friendly to us – he deplored the financial part of my piece, though he praised the part about continual changes of ministers. He says the sequence of events in the recent Cabinet changes was this: Wilson wanted to put Barbara Castle into the D.E.A. as a set-off to Jenkins, who vetoed this. So Barbara went to Labour and Gunter was to go to Transport, but Barbara vetoed this. So Gunter goes to Fuel and Power and Marsh to Transport. Gunter said it would take a man ten years to be effective at Fuel and Power. He didn't want the job and knows he cannot do it. He regards Barbara's appointment as disastrous. He said Wilson is not in danger until the pound goes down, when his position is immediately in question. He thought the most likely successor was Jenkins, though he personally does not trust him. Denis Healey would be better but with him as P.M. the whole of the left wing would walk out. He did not mention Benn or Short as possible successors and evidently did not take his own chances seriously – nor those of Stewart.

Wilson is obsessed with the 'Press Plot' and can think of nothing else. There is, of course, no plot – nor could there be. Wilson for some reason suspects Gunter of being the leader of the Jenkins–Healey plot. This is very improbable on the face of it and is actually quite untrue.

Tuesday, May 28th, 1968

The situation in Paris is certainly no better and the only certain outcome of the whole crisis is a big dose of inflation for France.

Wednesday, May 29th, 1968

Went to a Gala Concert last night to celebrate the twentieth anniversary of the State of Israel, the main attraction being Rubinstein at the piano. However, at the reception I bumped into (1) Arnold Goodman, mildly friendly, (2) Tommy Balogh, cut me dead, (3) Denis Healey, could not have been more friendly, (4) Dick Crossman, who took one look and fled, and (5) Michael Stewart, who was prepared to be friendly, but we were separated.

Today at lunch with Michael and Pam Berry. Talk about this and that, ending with an argument about our financial state. Apparently Michael and Pam had had the most categorical assurances from Jenkins and Crosland that all is more than well. It is difficult to make much sense of this. The Bank cannot be all that wrong, so presumably anyway these two ministers are putting a brave face on things, hoping that something will turn up.

Saturday, June 8th, 1968

The gap in my diary has been due to my totally unexpected dismissal from the board of I.P.C. While Ruth and I were having a quiet supper in my suite at the office, further along the corridor the directors were having dinner together prior to dismissing me. Anyway, next morning Chandler, the Secretary of I.P.C., called on me at 8.15 a.m. and handed me a letter signed by all the directors to say I was to resign that same morning. When I reached the office, I was interviewed by Cudlipp, Frank Rogers and Don Ryder, and told to resign and to resign my directorship of Reed's. I said they could indeed dismiss me, but I would not resign. As for Reed's, I had told Ryder and

Cudlipp I intended to resign at the end of the year and I had no intention of doing so sooner. They then withdrew to consult the other directors, and I heard no more until 3 p.m., when I got a letter saying I was dismissed. So I rang up B.B.C. News and I.T.N.* and told them I had been dismissed and wished to appear on the six o'clock news. I was in the yard later when a man came up and asked if I was Cecil King and if I had been dismissed. I said I was, and I had been dismissed. They were apparently afraid that my telephone message had been a hoax. Anyway, I.T.N. then interrupted a showing of one of the Epsom races to put out the fact that I had gone – and this was how the *Mirror* staff, including the editor, learnt that I was out. I did appear on both news services and in '24 Hours', and explained what had happened. Meanwhile I have been asked by Granada to do a programme or two on my life, like that done by Reith with Muggeridge. I have written two pieces on politics and economics for the *Financial Times* for next week, I have been asked to contribute to *The Times* when I feel like it; half a dozen book publishers want my memoirs, and I have turned down various television programmes. It seems I shall be in the public eye for quite a while yet.

It is not clear to me why my colleagues were in such a hurry, nor why they chose this moment, nor why they behaved in a way that could only be severely criticized. Obviously Cudlipp wanted my job: he and Birk were the prime movers in the matter. The reason given was my increasing preoccupation with politics. I thought the idea might be to turn the paper back to supporting Wilson, but Cudlipp volunteered the information to me that he intends to be no more friendly to Wilson than we have been in the recent past. The I.P.C. accounts published on May 31st were bad and a further £450,000 of losses had been added that same week. But if I was to take the burden of poor figures, presumably I would be carefully preserved as chairman. My piece, 'Enough is Enough', on May 10th, must have counted for something, at any rate with Birk. But even in this matter Cudlipp had approved the idea and the timing some two or three weeks earlier, and on the evening of the 10th I happened to be entertaining to dinner the various newspaper editors and Cudlipp, on his

* Independent Television News.

own initiative, had asked each editor whether he approved the line taken – and the answer was yes.

Yesterday I had de Courcel to lunch – a very different de Courcel. His English had deteriorated; he looked almost dishevelled, and he had clearly had some of the stuffing knocked out of him by recent events in Paris, and his two days there. He was very frank: the French Government had been taken completely by surprise by the riots, so had the Communist Party. The trouble started with the students at Nanterre, which is on the outskirts of Paris. Most of the students there are middle class as you almost have to have a car to get there. The students are led by small Trotskyite and anarchist groups who are ultimately financed and inspired by the Chinese. After the rioting by students in Rome, the Italian police found the affair had been led by a group living in a small farmhouse in Tuscany. It appeared from the local telephone records that they had been in touch with Paris and London – particularly London. The idea of these Far Left groups is not so much disruption of the existing set-up as the outflanking of the Communist Party. If this can be done the leadership of world Communism will pass from the Russians to the Chinese.

De Courcel was saying France is too centralized and has been, at least since Napoleon. The universities are badly organized and any reform has been vetoed by the dons. The situation is in some respects quite farcical: there are 168,000 students in Paris; half the professors of the University of Lille and one-third of the professors of the University of Strasbourg live in Paris! But though the students have legitimate grievances, it appears that the predominant demand is not for reform of the existing structure but its replacement by something else. The students seem as unable as the rest to say what else. De Courcel thought the strikes and the demands of the Communists were not all that menacing, but he thought the attitude of the students was alarming and would be with us for a long time. Both he – and even more Blankenhorn – assumed the Gaullists would win the election at the end of this month, though it is likely the Communists would gain seats as they did in Italy. De Courcel assumed that de Gaulle would go at the end of the year if things look reasonably peaceful then – after all, his recent policy had been a failure.

His second broadcast to France pulled everything together when it looked very bad, but his first broadcast was a disaster.

Wednesday, June 19th, 1968

Am in Dublin for a few days' rest. It is surprising how many people in the street recognize me from the English television.

Last week I had Malcolm Muggeridge to lunch and I met Alfred Evensen at his hotel. Muggeridge was more pessimistic than usual: feels we are facing the breakdown of law and order which he thinks necessarily follows a breakdown of the moral order. This means a long period of violence and anarchy, which might have disastrous results in highly complex modern societies. He had known Hugh Cudlipp for a great many years and likes him, but thinks him a weak man, quite incapable of holding his job as chairman of I.P.C., from which Muggeridge expects him to be ousted within a year.

Tuesday, June 25th, 1968

Lunch today with —— [a senior civil servant], whom I like more and more. We talked partly of French politics, which he thinks more volatile than ours – fair enough, as they were on the verge of civil war a few weeks ago, and are even now about to return the Gaullists with a clear majority.* From that to the cause of student unrest, which he ascribed to a revolt against the quality of modern life and its increasing regimentation, shortly to be carried a stage further by the computer. From that to telepathy, E.S.P.† and all that. He was urging me to take the whole subject up in a biggish way. I said the trouble is not money; it is to find a starting-point. He suggested getting in touch with Isaiah Berlin or Asa Briggs, both of whom have colleges that might be prepared to take up the subject. I said surely we have to start by finding a way in – without that, money and academic support are hardly likely to be forthcoming. So we parted, determined to keep the subject active in our minds.

Of external news there is little enough. The pound sinks lower and lower; the export figures for cars are much better, but I don't hear that exports generally are nearly good enough. Alf Robens came

* The French general election, which required two ballots, was held on June 23rd and June 30th. The final result gave the Gaullists and affiliates a majority of 219.
† Extra-sensory perception.

to tea on Sunday – I thought very pessimistic. He sees no chance of shifting Wilson even after a financial crash. He will be kept in office by the left wing of the Parliamentary Labour Party, come what may. We had some talk of setting up a group who might hammer out a programme which could be a help in a time of crisis. No names were mentioned. His suggestion for the first item on any policy statement by this Council for National Regeneration (a possible title) is that we believe in a mixed economy! This might have meant something forty years ago, but hardly now.

Tuesday, July 2nd, 1968

The only important event in the political world in the past week has been Ray Gunter's resignation from the Government. His resignation letter is couched in contemptuous terms: 'I do not wish to remain a member of *your* Government.' His place at Fuel and Power is to be taken by Mason, a colourless nonentity. This resignation clearly weakens the Government, but as *The Times* points out this morning, each resignation leaves a weaker Cabinet even more dependent on Wilson.

Lunch with Esmond [Rothermere] yesterday. He is the youngest-looking seventy I have ever seen, very active in his way, but seems to know very little of what is going on in the world. He had heard no whisper of a reason for my departure from I.P.C.

Lunch today with Vic Feather more or less at his request. He had no opinion of Mason; says he is a man of no reputation either in his constituency or in his union (the N.U.M.). He regards Barbara Castle as ready to go to any lengths to get herself publicity or acclaim. The Prices and Incomes policy is for those too weak to protest. The seamstresses at Fords who ignored the negotiating machinery and demanded an extra fivepence an hour are to get an extra sevenpence and the inquiry into the whole matter doesn't even start till Thursday! The only result of the Royal Commission on Trades Unions is the proposal to set up a Commission on Industrial Relations of which Woodcock expects to be the head. Feather assumes he will succeed Woodcock (at the T.U.C.) – but to a bed of nails. Scanlon and his left-wing friends have taken over the A.E.U.;* Cousins is letting

* Amalgamated Engineering Union.

Communists into the T.G.W.U.* so there will be a big lurch to the left by the unions. Cooper and the General and Municipal Workers' Union are ineffective; Cannon, the ablest of the trades union leaders, is likely to leave the E.T.U. and go into industry. He has been so flattered and liked that he is now entirely ineffective.

Feather said Greenwood wants to be Secretary of the Labour Party because he knows he cannot hold his seat at Rossendale; George Brown is not standing again as he could not hold Belper. Feather said George realized at Christmas he had no political future and asked Feather to find him a real job, not an income. Feather made inquiries in three quarters and found that Kearton would give him a job at Courtaulds to produce something between £5,000 and £7,500. It actually sounds more like an income than a job. Within one month of George being told a job awaited him, he had resigned.

Paul Hamlyn looked in this afternoon to my office at Reed's. He was in a very emotional state, but evidently regards me with affection, and wants to see me from time to time. He said very little about my dismissal but said that if he hadn't signed the document he would himself have had to go. It sounded as if a majority of the board wanted a new chairman, but were so scared of confronting me or giving me any opportunity of fighting back that they decided the first I should hear of their plans would be my dismissal. If this is really all there was to it, it must be the most badly bungled affair in all recent commercial history.

Wednesday, July 3rd, 1968

Barbara Ward to lunch. We had much talk of a desultory kind about student riots, American politics and all that. But she did produce one amusing story. Recently Wilson (known to her friends as Wislon, because he just Wisles On) had lunch at *The Economist*. Having consumed half a bottle of brandy at lunch, he asked to be taken to the Gents. When Crowther took him there, he asked him to come inside. While he did what was necessary, he asked Crowther if he would accept a peerage. Crowther asked who else was in the list; Wilson said he had forgotten. He had of course done nothing of the sort,

* Transport and General Workers' Union.

but did not want to admit that Crowther's peerage was a sct-off to Balogh's.

Thursday, July 11th, 1968

Lunch with George Bolton, chairman of the Bank of London and South America – a man of great ability and, in spite of his sixty-nine years, a man also of great enthusiasms. Specific items of news he gave me were that when I resigned from the Bank, Wilson's first choice was Kearton, but he was steered off this by O'Brien.

Bolton had, a few days ago, seen Field-Marshal Sir Geoffrey Baker and Admiral of the Fleet Sir Varyl Begg, the heads respectively of the Army and Navy, who said the trouble with Healey is that on occasions he is intolerably arrogant. Marshal of the Royal Air Force Sir Charles Elworthy, the chairman of the Chiefs of Staff, told Bolton recently that not long ago the four chiefs of staff decided to resign in protest over the handling of defence matters by the Government, but were persuaded not to do so by —— [a senior civil servant], who pointed out that no good purpose would be served.

The new credit foreshadowed from Basle and hailed by the newspapers as a great success, Bolton regards with alarm. Our liabilities are about £3,500 million and the credit is for £800 million to allow us to give some of our creditors a partial gold guarantee. From the British point of view it means substituting a gold guarantee for a sterling one – thoroughly bad business, and there is only money to cover 25 per cent of our liabilities; there is bound to be fierce dissension over who gets what.

Friday, July 12th, 1968

Lunch today with Douglas Houghton, a shrewd little man and no friend of Wilson. He says that if Wilson goes, the present favourites would be Jenkins or Callaghan. He does not think the Tories would consider a coalition but have no idea what a nightmare they would take over if they were to win a General Election. He said Denis Healey does not like the House of Commons and the House does not like him. Of course if there were a crash and people became frightened, then the picture would change and Healey might seem more acceptable. He seemed to think that the time when Wilson's removal

203

would make much difference had gone. The country was moving to the right and looking more to Enoch Powell than to any Labour Party chief.

Monday, July 15th, 1968

Lunch with Ted Heath at his flat in the Albany. He looked handsome, well, and confident; was very friendly, but had nothing to impart. He thought the Labour Party would keep Wilson in office, come what may, and that Wilson would cling on on those terms. The foreign bankers are certainly restive but they are so frightened of the results of allowing sterling to collapse that they will probably continue to support it. He made light of his own troubles with his party, but did realize that he would inherit one hell of a mess whenever he did reach 10 Downing St. He also mentioned in passing that Denis Healey is intolerably arrogant. He had been this when they were both (and Roy Jenkins) at Balliol.

His flat is a luxurious one with many good prints of soldiers in various uniforms and he had acquired some excellently modelled white porcelain horses depicting various manœuvres of the horses in the Spanish Riding School in Vienna.

Thursday, July 18th, 1968

Lunch at the Chamber of Shipping on Tuesday. A small gathering of the top people with me as the only guest. We talked of every kind of thing, but the only hard fact that emerged was their fear of the Russian mercantile marine which is being built up to a size far greater than is needed for Russia's own requirements. In a few years' time they would be in a position to put us out of the carrying trade except for our share of cargoes to and from this country.

George Woodcock, a recent guest, had made a very bad impression, maintaining in the teeth of the evidence (particularly that from the seamen's union) that there was no serious Communist element in the trades union movement.

Lunch today with Jean Monnet as his guest – alone at the Hyde Park Hotel. He thought the trouble with the students springs from the fact that once relations between states had begun to improve, it then became necessary to think about better relationships between

man and man. We must try – as the Communists had tried un-
successfully – to establish a relationship in which no man's superiority or inferiority is to be accepted by himself or anyone else.
Monnet's own grandfather had been a workman and it took fifty
years, and two generations, to come from the proletariat to the *haute
bourgeoisie*; this is too long he said; the younger people will no longer
accept such a time lag.

Personally I don't think the quality of life is to be improved in essen-
tials by better education and in any case one of the most important
parts of education is to be brought up in an educated environment.

Thursday, July 25th, 1968

The morning of the 23rd was my swan song after being ejected from
I.P.C. I had pondered a long time over what to say and decided to
say it without notes. It is easier in this way to be forceful and to
put one's views over. Very briefly I told the shareholders, of whom
there were about seven hundred, that the fall in profits was mostly
for reasons out of our control, but part was within; that I had made
certain provisions for the management of the corporation after my
retirement and these were not altogether successful; and finally told
them exactly what had happened on May 29th. The meeting was
clearly on my side and I had a wonderful press. My speech read
well, as well as sounding good at the time.

Last night we went to a party given by Hugh Fraser at Campden
Hill Square. Everyone was exceedingly friendly and thanks to my
departure from I.P.C. I seem to be positively popular. I suppose
some of them see in me a possible useful recruit to the Tory Party.

The news this morning is of Harry Nicholas's selection as the new
Secretary of the Labour Party instead of Len Williams who has gone
to Mauritius as Governor-General. Wilson was known to be backing
Tony Greenwood and it was thought the job was his. But George
Brown and Jim Callaghan organized the opposition and got their
man in by fourteen votes to twelve.

The interesting thing is that the Labour Party is in an awful mess
and obviously needs the best man they can find. Instead the choice is
between Tony Greenwood who is useless – but a toady of Wilson's –
and Harry Nicholas who is only useless.

Thursday, August 1st, 1968

No particular domestic news these days. I had lunch with Eric Roll on Tuesday. We chatted about the Bank, where he has taken my place on the Court. He – and Warburg's – are more optimistic on the future, but it is hard to see why. The proposals made at Basle and one month's slightly better trade figures do not justify the mood of optimism that is sweeping the newspapers, if not the country.

Friday, August 9th, 1968

Lunch yesterday with David and Sybil Eccles at Chute.

David Eccles is now chairman of the British Museum to which he devotes much of his time. He always seems to me immensely able and I never can understand why he hasn't gone further. His fellow Conservatives always disliked him, calling him 'Smarty-Boots', but I could never make out why. He made a fortune in the financial world and since then must have made a mint of money out of the various things he has collected: Staffordshire plaques, first editions of D. H. Lawrence, books on Venezuelan history, pictures, etc. etc. He has wonderfully sound judgment and taste.

Saturday, August 17th, 1968

The most important item has been the choice of Nixon as the Republican candidate for the presidency. It is appalling that this third-rate man should be disinterred from the 1960 election and run again. As one of the American papers said: it was the greatest act of resurrection since the raising of Lazarus. At the moment it looks as if he will be running against Humphrey who is said to have deteriorated sadly in the last four years. No wonder the young people are disillusioned when their country is in a mess and they are presented with a choice between two obviously inadequate candidates.

Thursday, August 22nd, 1968

The big news has been the occupation of Czechoslovakia by Russian troops supported by East German, Polish, Hungarian and Bulgarian contingents.* It had seemed as if the Czech–Russian differences had

* During the night of August 20th–21st, Czechoslovakia was invaded by Soviet and other Warsaw Pact forces, in response to what was said to be an appeal for help from Czechoslovak officials. In fact, the invasion reflected Soviet concern over the apparently growing liberalization of Czechoslovak society and the Czechoslovak economy.

been smoothed out, but evidently Dubček overplayed his hand – or perhaps his hand was forced by his supporters. Anyway, now he is in Russian custody. The Russians are thought to be having difficulty in forming a puppet government as no announcement on the subject has been made. It is presumed that this move comes after strong differences of opinion in the Kremlin in which the hawks won. The result is certain to be quite deplorable all round. It will undoubtedly influence the American election in a conservative direction. This is bound to help Nixon and may encourage Johnson to stand again after all. French foreign policy is in ruins; the Germans will become more nationalist; the pound is weak again. It is impossible for me to see any good for anyone coming out of this episode. It looks as if the Russians, and with them the Poles and the East Germans, said if they allowed Czech liberalism to establish itself, the infection would spread and become uncontrollable in their own countries. Surely a move like this must come from weakness and fear. We have just been considering the effects of the Pope's Encyclical on birth control which has had a very hostile reception. The loss of authority by the Pope is no help and now the Russians have lost whatever claim they had to moral authority.

Had lunch yesterday with Geoffrey Rippon, always friendly. He seems to me to be a man of massive ability: an invaluable anchorman to have around. He thought Reggie would be a better leader and Alec Home the best of the lot. I said Home was a failure – hopeless on television. He said, but he was decisive, you could get an opinion out of him, which was far more than you could get out of Macmillan. Rippon also said that once you are in politics you might as well stay in, but he couldn't see why a young man of ability should enter politics – which, of course, is why the calibre of politicians is so low.

Wednesday, August 28th, 1968

Gave lunch to Iain Macleod. He was very friendly but increasingly crippled with his arthritis. What is interesting about all these politicians is that they have no foresight or imagination. He is off to the Outer Hebrides for his holidays, thinks our finances are in a mess; but no remarks came out that gripped my attention. He was sorry Ted Heath polls so badly (30 per cent), but is particularly puzzled by the large number of 'don't knows' when people are asked what they think of him as Conservative leader. He is alarmed by Enoch Powell and all that and deplores the rising tide of racialism in this country.

In America we are in the middle of the Democratic Party Convention at Chicago. Nixon did a wonderfully professional job at Miami, but the Democrats are in a state of total disarray. Humphrey, in supporting Johnson, seems to have lost his way and his soul: Senator McCarthy has appeared as a likeable amateur but his slim chances have been wrecked by the Russians in Prague. Johnson is being bloody-minded: rather than admit any mistakes or support anyone who would criticize him, he will hand the election to Nixon – in part because he is the most likely man to continue his policy in Vietnam. The Democrats are so desperate that there is even talk of their drafting Teddy Kennedy who is an inexperienced thirty-six.

Friday, August 30th, 1968

So Humphrey is the Democratic nominee after a desperate last-minute effort to draft Teddy Kennedy. It is clear that Bobby Kennedy would have got the job if he had not been assassinated. The police in Chicago disgraced both themselves and Mayor Daley. The Democratic Party is badly split and it looks like a walk-over for Nixon.

Meanwhile the Russians in Czechoslovakia are behaving worse and worse. They look like turning the country into a slave state though how this can serve Russia's long-term interests is hard to see.

Paid a call yesterday on Rebecca West at Ibstone. She is now seventy-six and showing her age, but still one of the half-dozen outstanding women of her day in this country. Yesterday she was full of subversive, Communist influences in *The Times*! There are many valid criticisms that can be made of *The Times*, but the idea of Denis Hamilton taking his orders from the Kremlin is pure farce.

Sunday, September 1st, 1968

Lunched yesterday with Mike at Lockeridge to meet Roy Jenkins – at his suggestion and arranged more than a month ago. Roy was his usual self: charming, intelligent, relaxed, optimistic. He particularly wanted to tell me that when he received my letter of resignation from the Bank on May 9th he was very tired and did nothing about it that evening. He had been up all the previous night and though he read the letter before going to bed, he did not think it necessary to inform Wilson. When the piece appeared in the *Mirror* next day and Wilson heard that Roy had had my letter of resignation the previous evening, he thought Roy had deliberately kept the news of my resignation from him. In fact he suspected the whole episode might well be a Jenkins–King plot!

Roy had no specific news but expressed a few opinions. He said the two outstanding ministers were Denis Healey and Dick Marsh – to whom he would presumably add himself. He thought O'Brien rather variable but stood up for his opinions. He thought the Bank was too lavish and opined that the next Governor would be either Gordon Richardson or John Stevens. He recalled that I had said in January that there should be a Jew on the Court – hence the appointment of Eric Roll. Roy said he had considered appointing Sigmund Warburg. Would that have been a better idea? I said undoubtedly – if he would have accepted the appointment. He said Sigmund would have accepted.

Thursday, September 5th, 1968

Had Noel Annan to lunch yesterday – very intelligent, very friendly, entirely indecisive. He gave up the provostship of King's because he found Cambridge 'so boring', and is now Provost of University College, London, where he feels he is more in the centre of things. Recently he had been on a deputation of vice-chancellors to see Aubrey Jones. Aubrey Jones and his staff, according to Noel, hardly bothered to conceal their well-justified contempt for the vice-chancellors! He thinks Aubrey's influence can only be for the good as universities are badly run by scholars, who know nothing of administration and recently, in spite of the large increase in students, the ratio of staff to students has *increased* – thus showing a decline in productivity (if that is the word). He thinks the public schools – at any rate the minor ones – will be taken over one by one.

He passed on rather an amusing crack about Jennie Lee 'the poor man's duchess'. He said she just wants to be remembered as the Fairy Godmother of the arts. The fact that the country cannot afford her benefactions, which will have to be pruned in due course, does not bother her.

Today I lunched with Kenneth Keith at Hill, Samuel. He had no specific information, but it was clear he and his like are making a great deal of money. If they were doing badly we should hear much more of the critical times in which we live. He said his profits last year were 40 per cent up on the previous year and this year are 40 per cent up on last.

Saturday, September 7th, 1968

Had a hilarious lunch with Gordon Richardson, whom I like very much. Four other members of his board at Schroder Wagg were present, including Lord Ogilvy, whom I had not met before – perhaps abler but not as nice as his brother Angus. Gordon was perfectly clear that the last year had been a disastrous one for the country while large numbers of people had made a lot of money. He agreed that the Government had had a relatively easy time in spite of its failure, just because so many important people were making so much money. I sold my I.P.C. shares at the beginning of June and have seen everything I bought go soaring up. And I see no obvious reason why this should stop, apart from temporary setbacks.

Friday, September 13th, 1968

Had Aubrey Jones to lunch yesterday. He is not a big man, let alone a great man, but he is highly intelligent and charming. He had dined with Barbara Castle the night before and she told him that in the ladies at the T.U.C. Conference she had been approached by trades union wives who strongly urged on her to refer the price of ice-cream in cinemas to the P.I.B.!* When they sent their children to the cinema the kids spent four times as much on ice-cream as the cost of their seats. To such levels of triviality are our trades union personalities reduced!

I suppose Aubrey's main preoccupation was with his own future. He was appointed for five years, of which eighteen months are still to go. The Government is tending to diminish the importance and influence of the job. Should he soldier on or resign? I said, 'Soldier on.' If he resigns, he will be replaced by some party hack and I cannot see that that would be in the country's interest. I gathered that

* Prices and Incomes Board.

that was what he intended to do anyway. He was pessimistic about the future, foreseeing no end to the present course of inflation.

Tuesday, September 17th, 1968

Roy Jenkins and his wife to dine last night, *à quatre*. He is immensely charming, intelligent and friendly and his wife is as good in her way as he in his. He had little news to impart and we didn't embark on the country's financial plight. He thinks Labour will probably – though not certainly – lose the next election. He thinks Enoch Powell may cause such dissension in the Tory ranks that Labour will be let in. I said I thought violence is bound to reach these shores and when it does it will change the face of British politics – and in the direction of Enoch Powell. Roy thought we had done well to avoid violence so far and seemed to think it would only take a very mild form here.

About Jim Callaghan, Roy said he is good in Cabinet and in Cabinet subcommittees, and a splendid speaker. It is remarkable how good he is on such a poor intellectual equipment. Roy thinks Dick Crossman has mellowed, thanks to his wife, his children and his farm. It has been supposed that Les Cannon of the E.T.U. is looking for a job in industry, which he would probably get. But Roy saw him last week and his conversation suggested that he intends to stay in the trades union movement. But, as Roy pointed out, he is the only trades union leader who could aspire to a big job in industry.

Thursday, October 3rd, 1968

We dined last night with Paul Crosfield on Highgate Hill. Present among the guests were Lord Stamp (medical research), Kenneth Robinson (Minister of Health) and Duncan Sandys. I was anxious to meet Duncan Sandys, but he is at times so right-wing I did not want to take the initiative. Robinson was just back from the Party Conference in Blackpool. He had stayed there for as short a period as he thought he could get away with. I asked him what Wilson would say on Friday, his second Conference speech. 'Oh!' he said, 'it will be the usual – known in the movement as his "Come to Jesus" speech!' Robinson was in crashing form but Sandys, to my surprise, seems to have given up. What with the emergence of Enoch Powell, I thought he might to some extent be pursuing a similar, though more cautious course. But not so. He talked of giving up politics and devoting his time and energy to getting us into the Common Market. He seemed older than his sixty years and I think clearly nothing can be expected from that quarter.

Friday, October 11th, 1968

To the Bank to call on the Governor, whom I had not seen since early May. He could not have been more friendly and the same applied to the messengers I met on my way to the Governor's office. O'Brien is not a big man, but he is a very nice man, putting everything he has into his job. The only time he showed any personal feeling was when he alluded to press reports that the architect of the Basle agreement was Harold Lever.

He said he felt like someone climbing the North Wall of the Eiger. Progress was slow but upwards and he had more confidence in the ropes than he had had earlier in the year. I suggested that it was impossible to get our balance of payments right: £500 million surplus per annum for ten years was surely a pipe-dream, hardly that. With this he did not agree, and we discoursed on the effects of a revaluation of the mark, the weakness of the franc, the deficit in the dollar balance of payments, and so on. In the end – unpressed by me – he said he had to be optimistic or throw his hand in. I think this is fair. You cannot expect a cold realistic view of the prospects from someone so deeply involved. He mentioned in passing that the deficit this year would be 'more than £500 million', and when I suggested a surplus of £200 million for next year, he acquiesced but I thought clearly did not expect so much. All in all, I would get the impression that he does not really think we shall triumph over all our financial difficulties. Things are looking slightly better at the moment but will be upset by the engineers whether they strike or are bought off. But he has to carry on and this is only possible by looking steadily on the bright side.

He spoke with affection of Callaghan and regretted his departure from the Treasury. Jenkins was at first very suspicious but is now much less so. O'Brien does his best to serve this Government and these ministers but finds it difficult to cope with the hostility and suspicion of most of the politicians with whom he has to deal.

Monday, October 21st, 1968

Lunch with Alf Robens and Hartley Shawcross. This had been arranged months ago, but Hartley was to be away and this was the first available date. We met to discuss the future and to decide what, if anything, could be done. Hartley had obviously given the matter no thought and in a crisis would play no part.

Both Hartley and Robens thought the best move for the future would be a coalition: five Labour, five or six Conservatives, and five outsiders. Alf suggested an outside P.M. Hartley made the point that in a serious financial crisis there would not be time for a General Election. In any case I pointed out that the measures to be taken – cuts in Government expenditure, tightening up the administration of the welfare services, a freeze on wages – are steps so unpopular that they would have to be taken by a government not looking for votes. We are to meet again.

Thursday, October 24th, 1968

Willy Whitelaw to lunch on Tuesday and a dinner party at Claridge's last night. Whitelaw is a very nice man with very good instinctive judgment. He thinks Ted Heath is coming on. His trouble is lack of self-confidence but at the Party Conference he made the best speech of his career and perhaps the prime ministership is all that is needed to see him in full command. I said I thought a coalition would be the best answer for the Tories if it was feasible when the time came. He said this had been examined and contacts had been established. He said Ted was quite determined to bring outsiders into his Cabinet and was using some of them in preparing plans. Their names were being withheld as some of them had positions under the present Government. Whitelaw talks more sense to me than any of the other Tory leaders but even so is too optimistic and too narrowly concerned with the reaction of the House, too little concerned with what goes on in the world at large.

Ruth was at a meeting of the Conservative Arts Committee yesterday. The M.P.s present assumed a Conservative government in the near future and spoke of Heath's decision to have a small Cabinet of ten overlords. I have not heard this spoken of anywhere else.

On the Sunday evening, dinner at Claridge's. The German Ambassador spoke of the disintegration of Europe brought about by de Gaulle. He said because of France's geographical position it was quite impossible to expel her from the Common Market and substitute the U.K. His other point was that it is not the generals who are taking over in Russia. They have seen war and are relatively cautious. Nor is it Kosygin and Brezhnev. The trouble is being caused by the younger men in the central government. They have never been out of Russia, are fed the sort of information they want to hear, and are inspired by a mixture of Stalinism and old-fashioned Russian imperialism.

Richard Marsh was there, so fed up with his office (Transport) and his colleagues as to be on the point of throwing his hand in. I told him he was winning golden opinions from the world outside and hope his exasperation will subside.

Parker, the Lord Chief Justice, was also there. He surprised me by saying that the Conservatives have no one in politics on their side fit to be Lord Chancellor, Attorney-General, or Solicitor-General. The House of Commons is full of men who are in politics for the £3,000 a year and such people are not adequate for high legal office.

Monday, October 28th, 1968

Ray Gunter to lunch: a nice little man, a square peg in a square hole at the Ministry of Labour but difficult to place elsewhere. His departure from the Government was mainly because Wilson was convinced Gunter was plotting against him – a suspicion with no foundation. He had little specific news. He had seen George Brown a number of times in the last fortnight. George is convinced he will return to the Cabinet soon.

Gunter was amusing about trying to teach Crossman the facts of life: that the British working man does not want to see equal wages for women; does not like family allowances; has little sympathy for the lower-paid worker. I asked him if he thought the Labour movement and the trades union movement were drifting apart (he said he was afraid of this at an earlier meeting). He said this was already happening and at the local level in some areas had already happened. He dismissed any idea of an engineers' strike; said the Government would compel the employers to buy it off. This would be very inflationary as the engineers' wages usually led the way for wages in other industries.

Wednesday, November 6th, 1968

Basil Davidson to tea on Sunday, just back from Angola and Mozambique – at least those areas occupied by nationalist guerrillas. He says the pressure on Rhodesia to come to terms with H.M.G. comes from Vorster and the South African Government. Vorster wants to build up an economic empire covering the whole area south of the Zambezi. For this to be a success he does not want hostile nationalist states on his borders with continuing guerrilla warfare;* South Africa hasn't the manpower to sustain such a position over such a vast area. Any terms Smith (or Vorster) would possibly accept would be regarded by the Labour Party in this country as a sell-out, leading to even greater apathy on the part of the party activists. It may well be that all the show of negotiation now proceeding is just to convince Vorster and opinion in this country that they tried hard.

Jo Grimond yesterday was friendly as ever, charming as ever, as realistic in his thinking as ever, but had no solution to offer or action to suggest. We were lunching at his very attractive house on Kew Green. He said he thought support for the Scottish Nationalists and the Welsh ditto was decreasing, mainly because of lack of leadership. The improved showing of the Labour Party he thought might be due to the unconvincing performance of the Conservatives at their Party Conference. We talked about Enoch Powell, whom he is disposed to write off, as his politics are such a ragbag of ideas appealing to quite different sections of the community: race relations that appeal to the proletariat in the Midlands; defence of the House of Lords, which can only appeal to a small group of upper-class traditionalists; and so on. Jo thought the quality of administration – central and local – had gone down in the last five years. An M.P. used to be able to get an intelligent letter from a minister about some constituency problem within a week. Now eight months go by sometimes and you get a letter that does not make sense.

* For some years in Angola and Mozambique the Portuguese Government had been attempting to suppress black African insurgents and 'liberation' organizations.

Lunch with Harry Walston today with more of interest than usual. When I saw him last in August he was just off to South Africa to deliver an address on academic freedom to the Witwatersrand University. While there he called on Vorster and had an unsatisfactory talk on apartheid but at the end got on to Rhodesia which led to another talk, and I gathered another South Africa visit – at any rate, several interviews. Smith is very short of foreign currency: whereas in the early days Rhodesia was all right unless the South African Government actively intervened to make things difficult, now it is the other way round – Smith is in trouble unless Vorster actively intervenes to help. Vorster told Harry that if we would drop our idea of appeals to the Privy Council, he would make Smith agree to the rest and guarantee that the agreed terms were adhered to. But – a fact which is obscured in the papers here – there are three parties to any agreement: ourselves and Smith and Kaunda. If things are made impossible for Kaunda, his position may be destroyed. I asked whether Wilson really wanted an agreement or wanted to give the impression of trying hard. Harry said indeed he did want an agreement and some of the Government's optimism is because they think an agreement with Smith imminent and that this will mean an improvement in our balance of payments of £50 million, plus an order for arms from South Africa of £200 million.

George Thomson has gone out to Rhodesia and is there now. Before leaving he dined with Harry. During the evening he said half in jest that if he secured an agreement he would not be surprised if he were dismissed from office as a menace to the left wing. Thomson also said Michael Stewart is indignant at having another Cabinet minister in the office! Harry, when in South Africa, cabled to Wilson what he was doing and got a cable back that any negotiations should go through the Embassy in Pretoria, which Vorster refused to use. Since his return Wilson has not seen Harry though Vorster told him that, but for their chance meeting, there would have been no negotiations and no *Fearless* meeting.*

* Talks were held between Harold Wilson and Ian Smith on board H.M.S. *Fearless* at Gibraltar on October 9th–13th. They were no more successful than previous negotiations.

Nixon is to be the new President: that he is better than Wallace or a deadlock is about all you can say of him.*

Thursday, November 14th, 1968

At lunch yesterday we got on to the subject of censorship, because David Smith of W. H. Smith was the other guest and booksellers are in an impossible position, having no idea what may be sold and what not. I argued that there will have to be a censorship board; you cannot have everyone in print, on T.V. and on the stage tearing society to bits. The old cry was 'Liberty, not Licence'. Now we have licence and the only way back is a curtailment of liberty. I argued that the same is true of the trades union movement. It has grossly misused its powers which would have to be curbed. The others present seemed to think the whole trend of our permissive society must just be allowed to jog on.

Lunch today with Mosley in his sitting-room at the Ritz. I had previously met him briefly at a press conference he gave in connection with the recent publication of his book. He is much gentler in his manner than I expected and his handwriting is small and suggests sensitivity more than anything else. He is at pains now in interviews to convince everybody that he was never anti-Jewish, never pro-German, and never favoured violence at his meetings. Surely he protests too much. I am not clear what he is aiming at now. He is seventy-one but pointed out at lunch that Adenauer came to power at seventy-four and continued to be important till he was ninety-one. He had been seeing something of Enoch Powell. Though he lives in France I think he is still hoping to play some political part here. He thinks an economic breakdown here is inevitable and that then we must all be ready – but ready to do what?

Wednesday, November 20th, 1968

Dinner last night with the Eccleses. The Belgian Ambassador was foretelling the devaluation of the franc. The Eccles's daughter was there, aged thirty-one. Unlike her complacent father, she was appalled by the future and spoke to Ruth about the importance of further stocking her mind as a safeguard against possible imprisonment

* Polling day in the United States presidential elections was November 5th.

in the future! Eccles was lyrical about Arnold Goodman and his skill in getting money for the arts out of Jennie Lee. Eccles thought if Goodman can do it, why not me, and had had good success on the same lines for the British Museum. Jennie Lee apparently can get money out of Wilson, by-passing all normal official channels. Though unattractive to look at, Goodman has apparently a very beguiling voice. I am not susceptible to voices and so don't know.

Lunch today with Blankenhorn, the German Ambassador. There is a big financial crisis on, beginning on Thursday, as today, Wednesday, the foreign exchange market is closed and Jenkins has flown to Bonn. There is huge speculation against the franc and the pound and in favour of the mark. The French want a revaluation of the mark, but the Germans don't see why they should. Under pressure they have offered to adjust their import and export regulations to make importing easier and exporting harder by about 7 per cent together. Willi Brandt spoke to Blankenhorn on the telephone yesterday and said he didn't see why they should do more. Blankenhorn thought that if driven to it, the British Government would devalue again, blaming it all on the Germans and French. Whatever the outcome of this, the last few days mark a further deterioration in the world's monetary system.

Blankenhorn went on to talk about Russia and all that. He said his Government had been very badly shaken by events in Czechoslovakia. They seem to have no real knowledge of the Russian intentions but believe Kosygin and Brezhnev are little more than figureheads while real power is held by younger men lower down. For the first time for a long time the generals have some real political power. The Germans believe the increase in the Russian Navy in the Mediterranean is not really in connection with the Arab–Israeli clash, but that they mean to have permanent naval strength there, ultimately acquiring a naval port in Albania or Yugoslavia. They have a very powerful submarine force in the Indian Ocean that could easily cut off the supply of oil from the Middle East to Europe. Blankenhorn thought that the Russians, deeply impressed by the certainty of eventual trouble with the Chinese, might try to absorb Western Europe so as to be sure of their rear. This might be done over the years by agreement, but the Russians prefer force to negotiation and appear to have a, quite illogical, inferiority complex regarding Germany.

He thought any move by us at the present time to join the Common Market was out and the recent conference at the Hague quite futile. He also said in passing that the Germans expect our deficit for next year to be £200 million.

Tuesday, November 26th, 1968

Lunch today with de Courcel whom I had not seen since June. Much had happened, particularly in the last week. He said there were still almost no relations between the French Government and the British Government and that the Foreign Office was still very definitely anti-French. Over the financial events of the last week, he said that in the end the French were faced with the alternatives of a big devaluation or none, and had opted for the latter. Neither he nor anyone else thinks this is the end of the matter and we must get the foreign exchange arrangements on to a more flexible and workable basis. The French were no longer arguing for the return to a June gold standard, but to some system linked to gold. It seems clear that both Jenkins at Bonn and Wilson to Blankenhorn tried to bully the Germans into revaluing the mark. They assessed the cards in their hands quite wrongly and merely made fools of themselves.

De Courcel said the Americans and the Russians were co-operating in ending the Vietnam war. Talks might go on for two years but the war is over. The Russians have been very keen on a rapprochement with the Americans: over an anti-missile missile system, over Vietnam, and over the Middle East.

Wednesday, December 4th, 1968

Enoch Powell had a long interview on 'Panorama' on Monday night. Has much more idea of what it is all about than his colleagues. Basically a nice man with kind eyes, but has horrifying flashes of what looks like mental instability. What impressed me, and what I did not know of before, was his love of the Army and particularly of the discipline of the Army, especially when he was a private. He may be the herald of a new Fascist regime -- but we have certainly not heard the last of Enoch Powell.

Maurice Allen on Friday was almost cheerful, and does not expect financial trouble till March or so. He said the Bonn meeting was the worst organized of all time. It was still not clear at the Bank who summoned it. They thought Fowler, but it might have been the Germans' own idea. The Americans, with ourselves, the Dutch and the French completely misjudged the German position and thought the Germans only had to be shouted at to give in and revalue. But Strauss is a far stronger personality than those seeking to bully him and Kiesinger has an election coming in September and had no intention of antagonizing his farmers now. When the Americans realized this, they swung right round and supported the French idea of no devaluation of the franc. Their reasoning was that the alternatives by then were a big devaluation or none. The former would put the skids under the pound and gravely weaken the dollar. Ortoli, the French Finance Minister, was in constant touch with Paris and at one stage had apparently agreed to a 10 per cent devaluation.

Thursday, December 5th, 1968

—— [a senior civil servant] to lunch today. He says Crossman has not been satisfied to be head of two departments but has tried to merge them, though they have really nothing in common. Staff are being redistributed between the Adelphi and the Elephant and Castle and the net result is bound to be a loss of efficiency. Crossman does not stick at things and is quite likely to churn things up and then ask for a change, leaving someone else to pick up the bits. —— was very discreet, but did say that Wilson paid far too much attention to the small change of politics, and said he thought some of the ministerial changes were merely frivolous. He said he thought that somehow the standard of living in this country would have to be reduced before the balance of payments could be got right.

Friday, December 6th, 1968

Lunch with Aubrey Jones. He was very spry but evidently thinks this time the balloon is really going up. His most interesting point was about Heren, *The Times*'s Washington man, who is having a rest in this country after a strenuous presidential election. While here, he is talking to all sorts of people with a view to some pieces in *The Times* at the end of his holiday. He told Aubrey Jones the most striking state of mind he has found has been the contrast between those over fifty and those under thirty. The former see no reason why things should not continue for the next twenty years as they have been for the last twenty. Those under thirty think our political institutions have now failed and are discussing what is to take their place.

Remark by Dora Gaitskell to Xenia Field: 'Harold Wilson is not nearly so clever as we thought, but he is nicer.'

Wednesday, December 11th, 1968

Was at *The Times* yesterday talking to Denis Hamilton; then attended a cocktail party at Vickers. Denis said he had lunch with Wilson about ten days ago: Wilson impenetrably complacent, full of stories of his cleverness. In reply to questions he said there was no point in legislation on trades unions, it would only fill the police courts; Government cuts in expenditure would cause even more dissensions in the Cabinet than Rhodesia.

The Times on Monday had an excellent leader suggesting a coalition. I knew nothing of it until I read it in the paper, but it has been widely attributed to me – even in Switzerland, so Denis Hamilton said; he had just returned from there. Both Oliver Poole and Wills of Rediffusion came up to me to ask if I had written it. It has caused quite a stir and I appeared yesterday on radio and television, which gave further currency to my own views and those of *The Times* leader. However, what was my amazement this morning to see my choicest epithets spread over the front page of the *Daily Mirror*. This is presumably an olive branch, though one I do not intend grasping.

The main interest of yesterday's meeting was a talk to Enoch Powell, who was at the Vickers party with a very nice wife I had not met before. I find it hard to believe he has much of a future. He is insignificant looking and comes over better on T.V. than in real life. Ruth says he may be like an actor off-stage, who is often not at all noticeable, and maybe Enoch really comes alive with a platform, a theme and an audience. This may well be, but a politician is on view all the time and though oratory may demand an occasion, authority requires a personality that is commanding or at least significant all the time.

Whitbread, the brewer, was at the Vickers party and came up to me to deplore the lack of integrity in the Government. He said that the Jockey Club was run by people who often were not very bright, but their integrity had to be unquestioned.

Thursday, December 12th, 1968

Lunch with John Stevens, whom I had not seen for some months. He had come from a rather lively meeting of the Court provoked by Robens who apparently was saying that he didn't see why directors of the Bank should be kept in the dark while all those gathered at Basle were given the true figures of our reserves: even the representative of Luxemburg knew more than our Cabinet! The Governor is away and Parsons deprecated a discussion on such an important matter in his absence.

Friday, December 13th, 1968

The papers are all very optimistic this morning because of the trade figures, which are better. The *Financial Times* takes off into the realms of pure fantasy. It is a strange aspect of our affairs that newspapers like the *Financial Times*, essentially hostile to a Labour Government, go out of their way to emphasize the cheerful points of Government propaganda. The monthly trade figures are 'seasonably adjusted' and omit purchases of American aircraft and so are virtually meaningless. But even so, bad figures are shrugged off and good ones – or at any rate better ones – wildly over-emphasized. In any case, if you forget our financial troubles, the high and rising crime wave, increasing numbers of strikes, student unrest, growing international tension and the rest combine to create a situation which is not just going to come right.

Lunch with David Bruce who kept me till nearly three and saw me to the front door of the Embassy in Grosvenor Square. He said he does not know the total of our short-term debts. He puts the figure at £3,500 million, but it may be more. He says the Germans have not more than $500 million for supporting any currency and the Americans have no further funds for this purpose. He regards the collapse of the franc as inevitable, to be followed (or even preceded) by the collapse of the pound. He thinks the whole system of swaps between Central Banks a bad idea and that it has got them into a frightful tangle.

He said Nixon had tried to get David Rockefeller for Finance and Jackson (Washington senator) for Defence, but neither would accept. He did not think much of the new Defence Secretary (Melvyn Laird): and the new Secretary of State (William Rogers) is a pleasing fellow who knows nothing about foreign affairs. Nelson Rockefeller wanted to be in Nixon's Cabinet, but was not offered a post. If Nixon does well he will be re-elected in 1972; if not, the front runners in these early days are Teddy Kennedy and Muskie for the Democrats.

Asked about the Middle East, he said the Russians do not want war; the Arabs do. Faisal is the most sensible of the Arab rulers; Hussein means well but his position is weak and growing weaker. The Israelis are arrogant and intransigent and are in no way under the influence of the American Government.

I said some Scandinavians think the next Russian move will be against them, a move of some sort to scoop the Scandinavian countries – anyway Norway, Sweden and Finland – into the Russian orbit. He said he thought this was of a piece with the Berliners who thought the next move would be against them and the Central Europeans (unnamed) who thought of themselves as the next target. However, he was puzzled by the fact that the big concentration of Russian naval vessels (mostly submarines) was north of Norway. There is a chart in the American admiral's office in Grosvenor Square which shows day by day where each vessel of the Russian Navy is. There has been a build-up in the Mediterranean and in the Indian Ocean, but the big concentration is in the Arctic and has been there for some considerable time, for reasons unknown to Bruce.

Monday, December 16th, 1968

Dick Marsh to lunch. He was in very good heart but was not very informative. He knows nothing of our financial affairs and clearly does not inquire. He didn't see how a coalition could be established – under whom? Clearly not Wilson and clearly not Heath. Anyway, if the Tories know they are going to win the next election, why should they share the spoils of office? I said there will be no spoils, only odium, and I should have thought they might want to share the odium, and the Labour Party might want to save something from the wreck. Returning to the leadership, I said what about Callaghan or Healey – or Marsh? He was amused by any suggestion of himself, and said indeed that Healey could have become a formidable figure in the Labour Party but hasn't bothered – perhaps, like Maudling, is too lazy. In Cabinet he makes no attempt to hide his contempt for Wilson and limits his efforts to protecting the armed forces from the sillier vagaries of his colleagues. Marsh was disturbed by the low poll of Wilson and Heath and did not rate his own chances of re-election all that high, but seemed pretty complacent.

He had a story about the purchase by Transport Holdings of Lunn–Poly Tours. A British merchant bank was after it; so was American Express, and Transport Holdings wanted to make a bid. Marsh established with Diamond that this lay within his authority and then summoned the civil servant who dealt with the matter. He had some difficulty in getting this man (on £6,500 p.a.) to confirm that the matter did lie within the competence of the minister and then gave instructions, as time was very short, that the deal was to go through. Next day he was surprised when this civil servant circulated widely in Whitehall a memo in two foolscap pages indicating that this transaction was done entirely on the initiative of the Minister, pointing out several times how he had stressed to the Minister that these transactions were normally cleared with the Treasury, and in fact washing his hands of the whole business. Marsh treated the whole matter as a joke, which is more than I should have done.

We had a joke about Bob Mellish who was in Housing and Local Government when it was transferred from Crossman to Greenwood. Marsh asked how he liked the change and he said if Crossman was angry, he kicked you in the balls; if Greenwood is, he hits you over the head with his handbag.

Thursday, December 19th, 1968

Lunch yesterday with Beeching; dinner with Esmond Rothermere; and a long letter from Douglas Houghton. Beeching in good health, very frustrated. He does not see what can be done now and derides those who think there will be a crash, a quick pick-up, and we're away. There is bound to be a period of chaos. Esmond held forth on the importance of Kenneth Keith as Wilson's adviser on City affairs. This is the first I have heard of it, and it is almost bound to be wrong. Rupert Murdoch* was the other guest – improved since I saw him last. I have no idea why he wants the *News of the World*, though apparently it will give him greater standing in Australia. Neither Murdoch nor Esmond seemed well-informed. I came to the conclusion Esmond resembles Wilson in this; he wants the status and prestige of a major newspaper proprietor but has no ambition to do the job. Wilson enjoys the flattery and patronage of being P.M., but takes no interest in the work.

Douglas Houghton sent me a long letter in his own hand explaining why a coalition is not on. But his basic assumption is that the economy is now moving into smoother water. The coalition assumption is that the ship of state is not moving into smoother water but is about to hit the rocks. I have sent him a short letter to that effect.

Saturday, December 21st, 1968

Took some trouble over a piece for the *Financial Times* – agreed with them beforehand – on the views held at the Bank of England. The first draft was 'lost'; the second praised but not printed. I offered, after a lapse of a few weeks, to do the same thing for *The Times* at the end of this month. This Rees-Mogg has put off till February. It is astonishing to me that these papers are frightened of printing the views of the Bank of England (without attribution of course) though it is the official adviser to the Government.

Monday, December 23rd, 1968

We had a warm invitation to Ted Heath's carol service at Broadstairs. We went two or three years ago; it is an intimate family affair for Ted. I was surprised to be asked again this year and still more surprised to get a second letter thanking me for accepting. At Broadstairs he could not have been more friendly to us both.

* Rupert Murdoch, the Australian newspaper proprietor, was making strenuous efforts to acquire the *News of the World*. He succeeded early in 1969, and later in 1969 took over the *Sun* from I.P.C.

The other guests were a mixed lot – Toby Low (now Lord Aldington), Cowdrey, the Kent cricketer, the Tory M.P. for Withington (I did not catch his name), and one or two others. Ted was in very good heart though he has taken a bad bashing in the last year from a disloyal lot of colleagues and from the opinion polls. He seemed more confident, though his place on the opinion polls is lower than ever. There was no political talk. Ted always puzzles me. He is a nice man and an honest one. He is capable and works extremely hard, but fails to get across to the public at all. He has no understanding of politics or public opinion but then that is true of most politicians these days. Partly he suffers from the poor record of the administration from 1951–64 and from the very low esteem into which all politicians have fallen. But in addition he seems to convey a lack of self-confidence which his friends hope will vanish when he gets to 10 Downing St. But a deeply felt lack of self-confidence is perhaps not eradicable at all when a man has reached the early fifties.

Sunday, December 29th, 1968

There has been no news over the holiday except for the American circumnavigation of the moon. The whole thing went like clockwork with no hitch of any kind. The photographs of the moon from the spaceship and of the Earth very far out were shown on T.V. but were very unimpressive. It is a staggering technological achievement but one of astonishing irrelevancy. The world is more and more a confused and bewildered place, but circumnavigation of the moon is no contribution to the solution of our problems. It has cost the United States a vast sum of money which, one would have thought, could more profitably have been employed nearer home.

It has been pathetic reading *Business Week*'s attempts to find something good to say of Nixon's Cabinet. Several of them are second or third choices which itself does not augur well for a new administration. What has astonished me is that he obviously got the presidency first before thinking of who should run the country for him. He then had ten weeks or so to work out the biggest administrative job in the Western world – without any personal experience of administration.

Tuesday, December 31st, 1968

Mrs Healey was saying to Ruth the other day how wonderful it is that the members of the Cabinet have found a new unity. R. thinks the confidence being breathed around by ministers is a planned confidence trick. If the trouble is loss of confidence, let us all say how confident and united we are and things will come right of their own accord! How else do you account for the total lack of agreement between the optimism of ministers and the near-despair of anyone else who has any inside knowledge?

1969

The eighteen months which ended in June 1970 saw not one, but two, landings on the moon – in July and November 1969 – and one dramatically abortive attempt at landing in April 1970. They were also a period of continuing and considerable international turbulence, and, for Britain, of political frustration.

In response to increasing domestic pressures President Nixon began to withdraw United States forces from Vietnam, but, in spite of peace talks in Paris, there was no indication that the war would ever reach a conclusion acceptable to the West. In Nigeria the civil war finally ended with the collapse of Biafra early in 1970, but the problems of relief and rehabilitation remained. In the Middle East recurrent breaches of the cease-fire between Israel and the Arab States were accompanied by an escalation of guerrilla operations by Arab organizations. There were ominous signs that Ulster would become a major trouble spot, as the conflict between Protestants and Catholics developed. In France, however, after defeat in a referendum on constitutional reform, General de Gaulle left the political scene, and was replaced by M. Pompidou; the veto on negotiations on Britain's entry into the European Economic Community was lifted, and it was promised that these negotiations would start by the end of the first half of 1970.

Internally, although stringent economic policies were reflected in improved trade figures, the Labour Government continued to suffer from public discontent. The five-year term of office of the Government extended until April 1971, but in practice British governments usually chose favourable moments for elections, well in advance of the final deadline. However, the Prime Minister could draw little comfort from the polls and other indications during 1969, for all suggested that the Conservative Party had a commanding lead. Relations with the trades unions deteriorated over a trades union reform Bill, which the Government had promised but eventually had to abandon; student unrest continued, though on a reduced scale; there appeared to be no likelihood of major relief from economic stringency. The 1969–70 defence White Paper noted, however, that this was the first year since 1962 when British forces had not been actively engaged in colonial or former colonial territories, though British forces were still located in Hong Kong, Malaysia, Singapore, the Persian Gulf and the Caribbean. The White Paper suggested that by 1972–73 British defence expenditure would be reduced to about 5 per cent of the gross national product; the Conservative opposition feared that this would be insufficient and stated that a Conservative government would maintain a military presence east of Suez.

Eventually, after gleaning some encouragement from substantial gains in local elections in April and May 1970, the Prime Minister decided upon a General Election on June 18th, some nine months before one was legally necessary. The Conservative Party was returned to power, and nearly five years of Labour government in Britain ended.

Monday, January 6th, 1969

Lunch with Peter Carrington at the Australia and New Zealand Bank, and had some talk with Sir Colin Anderson of P. & O., whom I had not met before. He said some kind things about my pieces in *The Times** and, following on that, I said I had at one time thought of writing a book on the baleful effects of charm on British public life – beginning with Anthony Eden.

Saturday, January 11th, 1969

Have been in Kuwait three days listening to all and sundry – notably the Foreign Minister and his deputy. I thought that as Kuwait is geographically so far from Israel we would encounter a less emotional point of view. But this is not so, largely because of the numbers of Palestinian refugees here. The authorities are obviously deeply concerned about the possibility of present hostilities escalating into war – perhaps a world war. They suffer from a deep sense of injustice, but their proposals seem quite unlikely to help.

One put forward quite seriously at the Ministry of Foreign Affairs this morning was that Palestine be constituted as an independent state with absolute equality for all its citizens and incorporating all the returned Arab refugees. This would have a numerical superiority of Arabs and could not conceivably be accepted by the Israelis. They did admit the possibility of accepting a separate Israeli state, but did not lay much emphasis on that. They made great play with the fact that American and Western support of the Jews left the Egyptians with no alternative but to seek the help of the Russians who have now infiltrated the Arab world in a big way. This is evidently very unwelcome in Kuwait and doubtless elsewhere.

The idea that a beginning on the whole problem might be made by resettling the Palestine refugees on Arab land in Sinai and Iraq is

* Several articles by Cecil King on such subjects as prayer, death, sex, had been published in *The Times*.

dismissed as quite unacceptable: the refugees would rather wait for the possibility of a return to Palestine, however remote that possibility.

One idea which was new to me was that the principal terrorist organization, Al Fatah, has as its policy the provocation of the Israelis to occupy Jordan and perhaps Damascus. The Israelis would then be so overstretched that their destruction would be easier. The general impression is that there is likely to be an escalation of guerrilla warfare leading even to a sort of modified Vietnam. Certainly nothing I have heard of in these last three days provides any basis for a peaceful settlement.

Thursday, January 16th, 1969

Bahrain. Have been in Dubai for two days and arrived here last night. I brought along a Koran as a gift for the Ruler. It is a Turkish one dated 1813 and quite a nice manuscript. This has produced in return a gold watch with diamonds and a real pearl necklace for Ruth – all very unexpected.

Sunday, January 19th, 1969

Saudi Arabia. Am in Riyadh and last night had an audience with King Faisal – a most impressive figure. He is tall and immensely dignified and carries great weight and authority. I suppose we were with him for forty-five minutes or so. He is clearly obsessed with the Israeli problem and expressed little more than beneficence for the sheikhdoms in the Gulf. With us at the interview was the Minister of Information, an entirely admirable man with high intelligence and great feeling. Previous to him during the morning I had a long talk with the Deputy Minister – younger, cleverer, but not yet so wise. I would give the king and these two ministers very high marks indeed: the king is the most impressive political figure I have ever met.

On the Israeli question all the Arabs to whom I have spoken take the same stand. They say that Palestine should become an independent democratic state; all Palestinian Arabs should return to their homes; all Israelis should return whence they came. When I point out that the Israelis would fight such a plan to the last ditch and the last man, they say that it is the right solution because it is the just solution. Under pressure the Arab states have agreed to recognize an Israeli state but whether they would be able to implement this in the teeth of violent public opinion is another matter. All the Arabs I have spoken to have a huge sense of injustice and the young are more militant than the old. They all seem determined to destroy Israel however long it may take and however many battles they may lose. When I suggest that continued escalation of the war may lead to it getting out of control, and we could have an atomic war on our hands, they say they would rather be wiped out than put up with the present state of affairs.

I have asked several times if it would not be a useful beginning to deal with the refugee problem. There is plenty of empty Arab land and finance could be found for irrigating the necessary area. They say the refugees would settle for nothing less than their old homes. I don't really believe this, but it is quite clear that this is the attitude of Arab public opinion and that any government that started a plan to resettle the refugees would be destroyed overnight.

The present state of unrest in this area is greatly to the advantage of the Russians who are moving in cleverly and in slow stages. I referred to their naval forces in the Mediterranean as evidence of this, but they don't think in naval terms. They say that Egypt is increasingly dependent on Russia; that Syria and Iraq are likely to fall completely under Russian domination. But for the Israeli question this would not have happened. The growth of Communist and Russian influence is very unwelcome to the vast majority of Arabs but they feel it to be forced on them by the support of Israel by the West.

There are no bouquets for British policy in this part of the world. The king last night pointed out that it was the British who created the Israeli problem by their political antics between 1917 and 1947. Whatever may be the responsibility of the Americans now, the original errors were made by us. The Gulf sheikhs are all indignant that our withdrawal from the Gulf was sprung on them and that we are taking no responsibility for the set-up which will succeed on our departure. The king last night was also very severe on our departure from Aden which has left control in the hands of subversive elements.

A Mrs Margaret McKay, a trades union M.P., has been here and had an audience of the king. I have never heard of her and the idea of letting insignificant M.P.s drift around the world, doubtless at public expense, interviewing important and busy statesmen is rather alarming.

King Faisal is a genuinely devout Moslem and I have no doubt that genuine Moslem piety plays a large part in the public life of Saudi Arabia. One major problem of which Faisal is very well aware is how to advance into the twenty-first century on the material plane while retaining the central importance of religion. It is the same problem mentioned by Cardinal Heenan when we dined with him. How can one take advantage of the technical discoveries of the twentieth century and yet retain the strong religious sense which is still to be found in the Catholic Church? At Kuwait our guide professed to be ashamed to have gone on a pilgrimage to Mecca: he had only gone to escort some ladies! This shallow cynicism is not in evidence here and the piety of the Saudis is referred to by the Kuwaitis as their bigotry. Though these purely Arab countries do not allow the sale of alcoholic drinks they put up with a vast amount of smoking which must be distasteful to the Wahabis of these parts.

The blankets in our not very good hotel are pure camel-hair which is fair enough in this country. But they are 'Eskimo' brand, made in Switzerland.

Thursday, January 23rd, 1969

We are in Cairo till Sunday. So far I have met Dr Zayyat who is Government spokesman, Haikal, the very well-known editor of *Al Ahram*, and Sir Harold Beeley, our Ambassador. This is in many ways the centre of the Arab world. Haikal told me this morning that his paper sells 500,000 copies, of which one-third are sold outside Egypt. The people in the streets are quite different from those in Riyadh: more mixed, less religious, less disciplined. But I discern a considerable change since I was here last: I should say better health and more prosperity were evident.

It is clear Nasser is mainly interested in building up Egypt and regards the Israeli war as an expensive irrelevance. He is keener on a settlement than the Saudis, who showed no wish to negotiate.

I doubt whether there is any basis on which the Israelis and the Arabs could meet, and here they are evidently hoping for a settlement to be imposed on both sides by the Great Powers – in effect, Russia and the U.S. Personally I think Russia is doing too well out of the present situation to want to bring it to an end and we now have a weak President in the U.S. who is likely to be obsessed with the problems of Vietnam and the Negroes. Surely over the Middle East he will temporize. However the Russians are the people most keen on opening the Suez Canal as they rate its political importance to them rather high. It is the link between the Baltic and the Black Sea on the one hand and the Pacific bases on the other. This may make them ready to get a settlement in the Middle East, but at present the most likely development is an extension of the fighting and this may escalate beyond control.

Haikal this morning was very definite that Israel could not become a viable economy without active trade with the surrounding states. This will not be available as long as Israel is regarded as an enemy. At the moment Israel is dominated by the East European Jews, but within twenty years or so the majority of the population will be Arabs or Oriental Jews and such a population will more easily be absorbed into the Middle East. British policy in the Middle East since 1917 Haikal described as catastrophic.

Sunday, January 26th, 1969

Since my last entry I have had half an hour with the Egyptian Foreign Minister, Riyad, and have seen some more of the country. Riyad is an intelligent little man, lively and forthcoming. He did not seem to have heard that the Russians are keen on opening the Canal and, on commercial grounds, did not see why they should be. He said all Arab governments are supporting the commandos both with arms and money. They do so willingly but public opinion would force them to do so anyway.

Touring about Cairo and Haluwan one could see progress being made, particularly in industrialization. There are industrial centres in the Delta, and the Aswan High Dam is nearly finished. The tourist trade seems to be dead. Travelling all over the Arab world in the last three weeks I cannot recall seeing one obvious tourist. In view of the way other countries are inundated with Americans and Germans, this is surprising.

We drove out to a refugee settlement in the Western Desert, about halfway between Cairo and Alexandria. The place was really an irrigation project and forty-five thousand farmers had been resettled there from the over-crowded Delta. But after the 1967 war they were landed with fifteen thousand Sinai refugees. These people on principle will do no work as to do so would imply acceptance of resettlement. They sit in the sand, plan revenge, and dream of the return home. Certainly the very humble people I spoke to would resist resettlement with any means at their disposal.

Saturday, February 8th, 1969

Not a very eventful fortnight since our return. The authority of the Government declines with trouble in Ulster,* with the trades unions, and with students. The pound has been strong but so has gold, and gilt-edged are at an all-time low and still going down. The House of Commons is debating the reform of the House of Lords in the coming week. The proposals are silly and serve no purpose, but presumably will be adopted.

The *Telegraph* colour supplement has been trying for months to arrange a dinner to discuss the state of the nation. At last it came off on Thursday. Donald Stokes (Chairman of British Leyland Motors) was put in the chair. I had never met him before and so was interested. He has a pleasant personality and is, I believe, a good salesman, but that is all. Any suggestion that he is a 'great industrialist' or whatever is obvious nonsense. Bill Deedes (on the staff of the *Telegraph*) was there. The idea of him being a minister, as he was, is quite preposterous. Bagrit seemed to have no information but was quite sensible; [Lord] Gladwyn talked about the Common Market;

---

* The sectarian conflict between the majority of Protestants and the (large) minority of Catholics in Northern Ireland was continuing. In April 1969 Miss Bernadette Devlin, a 21-year-old student standing as an independent candidate, defeated her Ulster Unionist opponent in a by-election for the House of Commons in London. By the end of April, British troops were in Ulster to guard key public utility installations, and the Ulster Premier had resigned. Major Chichester-Clark, who succeeded, was committed to a modest programme of reform, which would permit greater equality and opportunity for Catholics in Ulster. This programme proved totally insufficient and ineffective, and violence continued to escalate.

Beeching talked most and was far and away the best, followed by Kenneth Keith. Kenneth has good judgment and does know what is going on. Stokes was wildly optimistic; the others pessimistic to very pessimistic.

Tuesday, February 11th, 1969

Denis Healey to lunch, in crashing form. I had said to him, I suppose three years ago, that Wilson was a failure and that it was up to him or Roy Jenkins to be the new P.M. He was very unreceptive at that time but has been warming to the idea since. Today he almost admitted that he would have to make a bid. He said he thought a financial crash this year was likely and that some Government thought had been given to the emergency measures that would be required. He implied that a State of Emergency would be declared and various measures introduced by Order in Council. These would have to be accepted by the House of Commons and he did not believe there would be a Labour majority for them in the House. At this point Denis doubted Heath's capacity for leadership and thought he might well stick out for a General Election, which he well might lose. He did not think Wilson would be any longer acceptable as P.M. and this would be Denis's chance. He did not deny that there might very possibly be a general strike, but thought the possibility of the intervention of the military quite negligible.

Denis derided Jim Callaghan's pretensions, pointing out that he is trying to establish a position by making concessions. Heath, he thought little of, as his promises to return to Singapore and the Persian Gulf and to scrap the Prices and Incomes policy were both politically expedient on only the shortest view.

Denis commented very severely on the British press. He gives a talk on his Defence White Paper once or twice a year. The London newspapers have defence correspondents who seem to know nothing of their subject; the Continental papers publish far more British news than we publish Continental news, and seem to know what they are talking about on defence. The London correspondents of the American papers have to cover all aspects of life in this country but are far better informed on defence than our men are – they never ask foolish questions.

On Monday I met a Dutch editor in the street. He was here to take part in the B.B.C. 'Europa' programme. I had known him as our guest when we had a conference of Czech, Polish, Dutch and British editors. I didn't catch his name or his paper. Early in the American presidential campaign he had been in the United States and had had some talk with Kissinger who was then supporting Rockefeller as the Republican candidate. This Dutchman asked why. Kissinger said because it would be such a disaster if Nixon became President. He is now Nixon's principal adviser on foreign affairs!

Wednesday, February 12th, 1969

Lunch with Ted Heath or rather, this time, his with me. He arrived late, having been detained by some ceremony and rather gave me the impression of being displeased at having to lunch with me. However, he warmed up and by the end was almost communicative. I told him I didn't think a return to the Persian Gulf was now feasible. This is what I was told both by our officials there ('They were told to tell you that') and by the rulers. He and Alec Home had dined with Faisal at his Embassy recently and had got nothing out of him except 'Allah will decide'. I suspect that, for whatever reason, Faisal was not talking. He asked me who I thought the ablest industrialists and we ran over all the obvious names, but I pointed out that we were desperately short of administrative talent in industry, the civil service, and the Government. So, he said, taking able men out of industry would be robbing Peter to pay Paul? I said to a large extent this was so.

He spoke of his intention of shutting down the P.I.B. and Woodcock's C.I.R.;* he continues to think that wages can be kept in control by monetary means. He recently dined with trades union chiefs: Woodcock was incoherent and negative; Cannon and Scanlon were both ready to accept the enforceability of labour contracts but only if they were effectively operated in the cases of all unions. I said I thought a general strike was certain in due course, but Heath did not agree. On our economic plight he knew that our indebtedness

---

* Commission on Industrial Relations, chaired by George Woodcock, retiring Secretary of the Trades Union Congress. Its function was to advise both sides of industry on methods of improving industrial relations and negotiating machinery.

was more than the £3,000 million he had quoted publicly. I think he expects a financial crisis in March if brought on by the franc; later in the year if it is due only to our own troubles. I think he thinks this will lead to a General Election and his own appearance in office. I could detect no alarm and no sense of emergency.

At one point he asked what names I proposed to submit to the Queen for my Businessman's Government. I protested that the B.M.G. had never been my idea but Robens's, and the episode passed over, but it was not entirely a joke nor entirely friendly.

Friday, February 14th, 1969

The complacency and optimism of the newspapers is quite extraordinary. Both *The Times* and the *Financial Times* lead their papers on the trade figures with no conspicuous cautionary notes. The *Daily Mail* dissects the figures very realistically but puts on the front page a leader which swallows them holus-bolus. It is quite impossible for the ordinary citizen to have any idea of the mess we are in; and neither the Conservative Party nor the right-wing newspapers do anything to help.

Monday, February 17th, 1969

Had lunch with William Whitelaw. I like him very much and find him far more realistic to talk to than any other politician I know. He agreed that parliamentary government is dying all over Europe, and opined that the House of Commons just cannot go on like this. He thought well of Crossman's plans for specialized committees of the House of Commons. However, Crossman had not the patience to see through this development, which is now being abandoned. Whitelaw would like to see this idea developed with hearings before the T.V. cameras at which both ministers and civil servants would be grilled. What did I think? I said I thought the suggestion good but that it was now too late. It would be a severe test for ministers, most of whom would not emerge very well. Whitelaw thought this might well make prime ministers more careful in their selection of ministers.

We talked about Enoch Powell; Whitelaw in no way minimizes his importance but doesn't see how he can emerge as a successful political leader. Some of his ideas are popular; some are sound; some

241

are neither. Some other political figure might profit by Enoch's success and climb on his shoulders, but who? He thought in circumstances of great crisis an emergency coalition might be possible, but it would cause a great uproar in the Tory Party, whose members still regard office as a prize which they have no wish to share with others. I asked who would be acceptable as a coalition P.M.? He said his party would refuse to have any dealings with Wilson, but would favour Callaghan. Healey has gone out of his way to antagonize the Tories and would not be acceptable in easily foreseeable circumstances. He agreed that a fight with the unions was inevitable and that it would be more difficult for a Tory government than for a coalition to conduct. Whitelaw did not mention other Tories, but the newspapers have been saying that Rippon is gaining importance within the Tory ranks.

Wednesday, February 26th, 1969

On February 4th de Gaulle at a private conversation before lunch suggested bilateral talks to Soames. They were alone and no record was made by the General. One was made by Soames, was not initialled by the French, and its accuracy – but not its good faith – has been questioned by the French then and since. The Government seems to have suspected a trap and Wilson – at Bonn – told Kiesinger of the talks before the French had been told that that was his intention. The matter leaked in a vague way in the *Figaro* and this was used by the British Government as a reason for publishing their version of the whole matter. The result is the worst diplomatic row in peacetime for many a long year. Relations between the French and the British Governments are now almost non-existent. The Government's argument is that it was impossible to negotiate with the French behind the backs of our other European friends – they had to be told. The French say that de Gaulle was suggesting preliminary talks to see if any basis for negotiation existed. If negotiations were thought worth embarking on, then of course the other members of the E.E.C. would be kept in the picture. De Gaulle spoke to Soames in a rather grandiose way but does not seem to have gone any further than he has before: that the accession of Britain, Ireland and the others to the Common Market would alter its character and before this could be achieved we must all decide what we have in mind for the future of the Common Market, whose agricultural policy is not working satisfactorily, to name only one point. In reply to a question by Soames he said in due course NATO* would have to give way to another defence system not dominated by the Americans.

After watching the British spokesman on television, reading the papers and listening to the French Ambassador this afternoon, it seems to me that what really happened is more or less as follows. (1) Soames has taken his mission too seriously. Our financial difficulties are such that we could not anyway join the Common Market for three years. Yet Soames has been pressing on, to the boredom of those in Whitehall. The lunch took place at Soames's request. (2) The Foreign Office is violently anti-French – or at least anti de Gaulle – and it may have been the Foreign Office which feared a trap. (3) It looks as if Wilson thought he had de Gaulle by the short hairs and decided to humiliate him. If this was the idea, it has disastrously misfired. (4) What infuriated the French more than anything else was that the British official statement, though based on Soames's notes, did not follow them but rewrote them in an anti-French sense. This means that any improvement in Anglo–French relations will have to await a new government here – and by then the world may be a very different place.

Saturday, March 1st, 1969

An hour yesterday with Blankenhorn. His theme was the intolerable attitude of the French, and in particular of General de Gaulle. He was assuming a right of veto over any event on the continent of Europe. The Germans have been increasingly exasperated. Over the 'Soames affair', Blankenhorn said he had done his best in an interview with Heath to get him to play the whole matter down. If the Tories were to argue that the Germans should not have been told of the talks, then the repercussions in Germany would have been bad, just at a time when Anglo–German relations were improving. Blankenhorn thought the timing of the General's move was chosen to have a disruptive effect, though it is true he had been saying much the same things as far back as Adenauer's time. The talks were at

* North Atlantic Treaty Organization.

Soames's request and it was at that point that we got ourselves into a false position.

Wednesday, March 5th, 1969

Douglas Houghton, Chairman of the P.L.P., to lunch – a very nice, shrewd, intelligent little man. I wouldn't say of real ministerial calibre but well above the average of contemporary ministers. The talking-point was the debate last night on the Government's White Paper, *In Place of Strife*. Though this is to be the Government's policy paper on industrial relations, it was only put before the Cabinet in proof – so Houghton says and he should know. He himself abstained in the debate, so did all the Tories, so the Labour Party disarray was obvious. In the end sixty voted against the Government and forty abstained. Houghton's position seemed to be that industrial relations were not too bad and anyway the Government's proposed legislation could not be made to work. He seemed to me optimistic, as do all politicians, but did say we could get no further with Wilson – we need a strong man. I asked whom he had in mind? The answer seemed to be no one, but that the hour would find the man. It sometimes does, but by no means always. I said his best man seemed to be Denis Healey, but I gather he is his own worst enemy in the House. Houghton spoke of him as a 'dark horse', discounted Callaghan's chances, and seemed to imply that under appropriate circumstances Denis would be his man.

Thursday, March 13th, 1969

Lunch for Richard Marsh yesterday; Jo Grimond today. The complacency of ministers continues to surprise me. Marsh does not have to tell me what is in the back of his mind but we have been friendly for a number of years and I have been helpful to him, so I would expect to get his general impressions. According to Marsh, nothing is likely to happen until the General Election. Ted Heath is so wet that the Labour Party may well win. It is true people do not like the Labour Party or the Tory Party either, but there are effectively only two parties and the British public is stuck with them. The Communists don't amount to anything here, there is no risk of a military coup in this country, so we just soldier on. The idea seemed to be that any safety valves have been so effectively wired down that the British people can be compelled to put up with misgovernment for ever. Financial crisis? No real danger as the foreigner cannot afford to let us go down. As with nearly all M.P.s, the whole situation is viewed from within the House – no revolt is visible among M.P.s and you can safely ignore the voters.

Grimond today quoted the chairman of the Bank of Ireland who opined that the major danger confronting all of us is runaway inflation, which dwarfs all other problems into insignificance. Jo thinks Parliament is incapable of reforming itself and ministers have no wish to restore the House to its proper role of watch-dog for the people against the Executive. He thinks the problems piling up – social, financial, constitutional – are so enormous as to be insoluble as far as he can see. He is particularly depressed by the way the quality of the civil service administration has been deteriorating, particularly in the last two years. The morale seems to have gone out of the service. Government is by a succession of gimmicks – no real effort is made to tackle problems and see them through. The old maxim, quoted to me the other day by Blankenhorn, 'Gouverner, c'est prévoir', has been entirely lost sight of.

Sunday, March 16th, 1969

Lunch on Friday for Aubrey Jones. He is incensed against Ted Heath who has described him at a private dinner to back-bench Tory M.P.s as a 'ministerial failure'. He also knows Heath plans to shut down the P.I.B. Aubrey's appointment runs to next March and he doesn't want to wait to be sacked, but he agreed that much will happen before March. He hadn't any striking news, though he doesn't share the buoyant optimism of ministers. He had seen Roy Jenkins recently who showed no signs of strain or anxiety.

Tuesday, March 18th, 1969

Lunch with Eric Roll to meet Sir Denis Greenhill, the new head of the Foreign Office. Owing to a misunderstanding about the venue for the lunch I arrived late. However, all went fairly well. I thought Greenhill might have been trying to take me down a peg: recalling how I had shocked the Washington Press Club many years ago; how my remarks about Jinnah in my book* all but led to the burning down of the British High Commission office in Pakistan; and so on. He may, however, not have meant it that way. He is an improvement on Gore-Booth, who was a pleasant lightweight. This man carries more guns, but is very cautious and seemed to go out of his way to support the Government's decisions. He spoke most highly of Freeman; praised Wilson's initiative in going to Nigeria. When I said Beeley was a good man in Cairo and it was a pity he was being retired at sixty, he said an excellent man was going in his place. This may be so, but the diplomatic service is not blessed with so much surplus talent it can afford to let Beeley go. One of their duds could be retired early.

The Times has an absurd piece today from Washington saying that Freeman will be a smash hit and that Michael Stewart is regarded by the Americans as the most underrated man in London. This may indeed be the opinion of Nixon but merely shows (over Stewart) that he has a preference for dim little men.

Wednesday, March 26th, 1969

I have not written in this diary for a week. Today's instalment was Reggie Maudling. He could not have been more friendly. He was quite definite that a Conservative Government that won the next election would have a honeymoon period of at most six months; it would be faced with the same problems that it was confronted by in 1963–4, only these problems are now aggravated, to which it has no solution. If after the failure of the Labour Government the Tories were to fail too, that would indeed be the end of Parliamentary government. He did not seem to have any knowledge of our financial affairs. He regards Jenkins as a failure with no particular future. He likes Denis Healey but says he is unbelievably arrogant in the House. He is afraid of the vagaries of Enoch Powell who, he said, seems to have the support of the *Telegraph* and the *Express*. On the whole Reggie and Whitelaw seem to me to have the best idea of what it is all about, but in Reggie's hands nothing much would happen.

Last Thursday I had lunch with Oswald Mosley. He thinks the drift towards the revolution that he tried to take charge of during the

* *Strictly Personal* (London: Weidenfeld & Nicolson, 1969), p. 166.

'thirties has resumed. He maintains that everything points to the decay of our society. No one any longer really believes in it, least of all the young. I think he sees himself in charge at last. This seems to me quite fantastic, but there is so little leadership of any kind these days that even the Enoch Powells and the Oswald Mosleys are not entirely incredible. He spoke of de Gaulle as a great personality but only a second-rate statesman.

Tuesday, April 1st, 1969

Lunch with John Stevens, recently back from Paris and Washington. He says the important people round Nixon are Laird (Defence) and his assistant Packard, Rogers (State), and Burns. Kissinger pretends to more influence than he has. Nixon's grand strategy is an agreement with the Russians. His argument is that an agreement with the Russians would kill three birds with one stone: Vietnam, the Middle East and disarmament. His flattery of de Gaulle is because he thinks de Gaulle may help him in the Middle East and with the Russians. I don't think de Gaulle can help at all and flattery will only make him more intransigent. I doubt whether a far-reaching agreement with the Russians is available. In diplomacy limited objectives are more likely to be reached.

Stevens was at a Washington party where most of the guests were Americans. Freeman, newly arrived as Ambassador, seemed very shy, buried himself in a corner with Clark, former P.R.O. at No. 10, and finally left without saying goodbye. His appointment is still being widely and strongly criticized.

Stevens thinks the American boom will continue at least for the rest of this year. This will lead to such trouble for their balance of payments next year that they are bound to resort to tariffs and a measure of isolationism. This will lead to world-wide trade depression and this Stevens now regards as inevitable – with all the social and political consequences that will ensue here and elsewhere.

In the meanwhile the financial front has been surprisingly quiet here. This Stevens attributes to a variety of causes: (1) the import deposit scheme; (2) the dollar guarantee given at Basle, which means that the holder of sterling can have a dollar guarantee and $8\frac{1}{2}$ per cent; (3) this is the easier half of the year. The underlying situation continues to deteriorate. He puts our short-term debt at £4,000 million. He quoted Maurice Allen as saying that at least £500 million must be taken out of the economy by the Budget, but this will not be approached. The present prospect is for a £200 million deficit for this year and a larger one for next year. Our indebtedness to the U.S. is so huge that when we need to borrow more to pay our deficit in the autumn, the Americans may well oblige – to help out the dollar, which is increasingly suspect.

Thursday, April 3rd, 1969

Lunch at the Bank – the first time since I resigned. At his suggestion I first had forty minutes with O'Brien. The situation since the Bonn meeting last November has gone better than expected. The dollar guarantee and high interest rates are important factors but there seems a greater tendency to think rather better of our condition than existed abroad at the end of last year. The Germans, the Italians and the French – even the Swiss – have been losing dollars, while we have been gaining them. It is not clear why this should be so. The prospect of a £500 million surplus seems a mirage as distant as ever.

I said I gathered a deficit was assumed now. O'Brien said we might break even, or have a £200 million deficit. The possibilities at the moment were in that range. The outlook for 1970 was worse. O'Brien said the Germans were acting to check inflationary tendencies in their economy. This would harden the mark and make revaluation in the autumn more likely. He assumed the franc would go some time this year. The American boom was unlikely to be checked this year and drastic steps to improve the balance of payments might be necessary next year. This could have a very serious impact on our exports.

I said though our finances might be in better shape, our industrial affairs were going badly; that Plowden's expression has been 'anarchical'. I didn't see how this could be righted without a showdown which would be very damaging to our economy. O'Brien said ministers felt they had tried everything except massive unemployment. I wondered whether this (mass unemployment) would bring the powerful unions to heel, and in any case it would have all sorts of unforeseeable social, political and economic effects. I said there had been talk of an authoritarian regime of the Right in all sorts of un-expected quarters. O'Brien did not seem to have heard these. His attitude remains optimistic – because, as he said last time, if he saw things as I do, he would have to resign. As it is, he sees things in terms of the Bank and hopes, like ministers, like Micawber, that something will turn up.

Saturday, April 12th, 1969

Dinner last night with the Robenses; lunch yesterday with Mike. Mike had been talking to Chalfont who was very critical of Lee, the British Commissioner on Anguilla.* Mike had said surely he should have been removed by Caradon on his first visit. As it is, he is to be removed on Caradon's second visit.

When Mike was in Rome recently he was told by his contacts that the present Pope was the worst in living memory. He certainly delivered two quite hysterical speeches over Easter.

Robens told us he had been approached by an emissary from Transport House who said that if the Labour Party is to win the next election they must get rid of Wilson. A small group was being formed with this objective. Would Robens join them? Very wisely he said he is not joining any group.

Friday, April 18th, 1969

The Budget speech was on Tuesday. The requirement of the Budget was to encourage industrial investment and, above everything else,

---

* Anguilla, a small Caribbean island, was the centre of an extraordinary international incident. Originally part of the British territories of St Kitts and Nevis, Anguilla seceded from the Federation in 1967 and its self-appointed President, Ronald Webster, demanded complete independence. On March 12th, 1969, a junior British minister visited the island and was 'forced off' at gun-point'. The Government, fearing that certain United States elements would attempt to take control of the island and use it as a gambling centre, and apparently in the belief that an arms factory was operating, landed 250 troops and 35 Metropolitan policemen from three Royal Navy frigates on the island. There was no resistance. It seems likely that any shots heard by the Minister, or any weapons seen by him, were part of a salute, and it is certain that no arms factory existed. After some months the situation became calmer, partly because of the exemplary behaviour of the British troops and policemen, and partly because of improved relations between Anthony Lee, the new British Commissioner, and Mr Webster. At the time, however, Britain's latest attempt at gunboat diplomacy encountered a great deal of ridicule.

abstract money from the pockets of the consuming public. So what happens? The increase in Corporation Tax and S.E.T. means that industry has less money for investment, and higher old age pensions and income tax concessions for the lowest group of tax-payers means some hundreds of millions of pounds transferred into the pockets of the consuming public. This is popular on the Labour back benches and may be designed to help along the legislation for controlling the trades unions, which in any case has been so watered down as to be virtually meaningless – perhaps under the very real threat of Callaghan's resignation. To make time for the trades union legislation, the House of Lords reform Bill has been scrapped. It was a silly Bill but its death will not help the prestige of the Government in the House.

Denis Hamilton and *The Times* people think this is an electioneering Budget: that the P.M., foreseeing disaster, is going to leave the crash to the Tories, afterwards explaining that everything went smoothly while he was in office. This idea is that there would be a General Election in the autumn, which the Tories would win, and the crash is due for then anyway. This does not sound to me at all like Wilson, since (1) he does not look ahead so far, and (2) I think he will hang on to the last hour.

Lunch today for Stonehouse, Postmaster-General. I had not really met him before. He is a very good-looking and sensible man of forty-four and has been Postmaster-General since July. Among the titbits of gossip was that our intelligence services advised the Government that the occupation of Anguilla would be resisted with armed force – hence the paratroopers! Stonehouse is appalled by the low quality of ministerial administration and the equally low quality of civil service administration. He says the civil service is actuated (1) by a terror of publicity, (2) by ditto of responsibility and (3) by an overriding determination to protect their position in the professional hierarchy at all costs. He asked why I thought things had gone wrong with Labour and I said Wilson from the beginning had no administrators to help him, with which he agreed. He also agreed that Labour was likely to be massacred at the next election. He thought Wilson would cling on to the last, 'hoping', as Stonehouse said, 'for something to turn up'.

Monday, April 21st, 1969

Paris. I started off the day with forty-five minutes with Pompidou, whom I had met twice before, at Lancaster House at dinner and with the Lazareffs at lunch over here. Pompidou is an impressive man – more impressive than any of our politicians. My visit was allowed on the understanding that in anything I write I do not mention I have seen him. He clearly sees himself as the next president of France. If the referendum on Sunday goes against de Gaulle, he will be president by June. If, as is more likely, de Gaulle wins a derisory majority on a low poll, the whole matter will remain in suspense awaiting the confrontation with the unions deferred from March.

As a political leader, the complaint against Pompidou is that he has no passionate convictions; moreover, that Gaullism has no philosophy. This is true, but one has to settle for what one can get, and by current international standards Pompidou would make a good president. Giscard d'Estaing has put forward a claim to attention by urging Frenchmen to vote against de Gaulle. I asked Pompidou if he thought Giscard would make a convincing candidate for the presidency. He said, 'Not until 1985 or so.' I said, 'That would be after your retirement from office,' and he laughed.

Next came a long lunch with Soames alone. He was very friendly and said how the visit of the French editors to London which I arranged four years ago or so is still frequently mentioned. He thought, as do most well-informed people, that de Gaulle will get his 'Yes' on Sunday by a narrow majority on a low poll.[*] If the referendum goes against him, Pompidou will be president by June.

Soames brought up 'l'affaire Soames'. He said his lunch with de Gaulle had been the result of much hard work, and was arranged through the medium of five of de Gaulle's entourage with whom Soames is friendly. He is convinced that de Gaulle was serious and intended to initiate negotiations on the conditions under which England, Ireland, Norway and Denmark could join a renovated Common Market. He thinks he handled the matter well and that H.M.G. should have responded by saying they were ready to go ahead, but only after an agreed statement (saying that talks were taking place) had been circulated to the other Common Market

* See p. 255.

countries, to the EFTA* countries, and to the United States. De Gaulle might not have agreed to this, but if he didn't, the talks would not have started; if he did, we were out in the clear. He did not criticize anybody by name but said the whole matter had been handled most clumsily at the London end. He thinks he could, after a suitable lapse of time, raise the matter with de Gaulle again – even with the present Government. I very much doubt this.

Soames did not mention any Labour ministers but expressed the opinion that members of the Conservative Shadow Cabinet now were not a patch on those in 1950, when he came into serious politics. He may have a point here, but not nearly such a strong one as he imagines. He said Rueff (financial adviser to de Gaulle) had told him that we were now at the same stage as we were in 1928 – very high interest rates and inflation – and that in due course we should proceed to a new version of 1929 and 1930. Of this there is increasing talk in London.

In the afternoon I had an hour with Peter David Weill, a director and perhaps owner of the French Lazard's. He is an experienced, wise, shrewd old man: a cautious banker with much experience and good judgment. He thought the French price level was too high for the current rate of exchange and that France could not afford to lose reserves at the present rate for long. He thought a devaluation of 15 per cent would be fully sufficient. He thought French financial policy from 1958–63 had been sound but that since then it had been irresponsible, and in consequence France was now dissipating the reserves that had been accumulated by 1963.

Asked if he thought we were heading for a world depression, he said a lot depended on England. If England could at this late hour put her affairs in order, the rest of the world might be able to do so too. But if England failed, it would make things very difficult for the other countries. I asked if he thought we were in for another 1929 crash and he said so many factors had changed since then that a repetition would not be possible. Though the relative positions and strengths of England, France and Germany have changed, America is still the dominant economic power, so I don't think things have changed all that much. It has been assumed that the mark would be

* European Free Trade Area.

revalued after the elections in September. Weill didn't think this was at all certain. Why should they revalue to help us and other countries out of the mess they had got themselves into?

The referendum on Sunday is to decide three things: (1) whether to reform the Senate (which can only hold up legislation for thirty-six hours!); (2) whether to introduce a measure of decentralization and regionalization; and (3) whether the interim president on the death or resignation of a president in office shall be the prime minister and not the president of the Senate. This is the important provision, as it would enable the temporary president, with his control of television, to mount a strong campaign for election to the presidency. Being P.M. he would be an active politician, which the president of the Senate is not. All these measures could be brought about by normal legislation through the Chamber in which de Gaulle has an overwhelming majority. So why a referendum? It is generally supposed that de Gaulle knows everyone attributes the electoral landslide last June to Pompidou and this referendum is for de Gaulle to show that he doesn't need Pompidou; he can win a popular victory on his own.

Tuesday, April 22nd, 1969

From the English newspapers it appears that matters in Ulster have taken a very nasty turn. When Healey had lunch with me some weeks or months ago he said he thought Ulster was more likely to bring down Wilson than economics and finance. It may develop into an impossible situation particularly with the Prime Ministers both in London and Belfast lacking authority or prestige of any kind.

Thursday, April 24th, 1969

Lunch yesterday with Beuve-Méry, editor of *Le Monde*; later half an hour with Prouvost, proprietor of *Le Figaro*; and dinner at Orsay with the Mosleys. Beuve-Méry had very little news, and we subsequently learnt from Prouvost that the staff, who own the paper, have decided to retire him at sixty-five – to his indignation. This is still a secret. It seems quite mad as Beuve-Méry has built the paper up from nothing to be the outstanding serious paper of the world.

Ruth thinks Paris very different from our last visit. There is less

253

glitter, sparkle and self-confidence, but more general prosperity. Paris is cleaner and the people more orderly and subdued.

The Mosleys have a charming little house at Orsay. Its name is the 'Temple of Glory' because it was built for General Moreau at a time when he was a rival of General Bonaparte. Lady Mosley is a very nice woman and she and R. got on immediately and well. The impression left on R. by Mosley is how sensitive he is. But like Enoch Powell and others in the past, he has a curious look in his eyes which comes and goes. R. thinks he has moments or periods when he is a compelling influence on others, of which he is afterwards unaware. So that when he protests that his movement was not a bullying, Jew-baiting one, he sincerely believes this and does not realize the character or misdeeds of some of his followers under his influence. His wife does not think he sees any political future for himself and regards Orsay as his permanent, final home. He makes it quite clear that he foresees a major economic setback ahead of us – even more far-reaching than the depression of the early 'thirties. If there were such a crisis it would necessarily end in some sort of authoritarian regime of the Right.

Monday, April 28th, 1969

Lunch with Norman Collins and Bob Renwick (their lunch). Though I used to meet them over A.T.V., their interest to me is their importance in the inner workings of the Tory Party. They are very worried by the complete lack of success Ted Heath has in getting across. Harold Wilson's latest rating is down to 30 per cent satisfied. Poor Ted is not very different. Renwick, who knows him much better than I do, says Enoch Powell could never lead a party. It is impossible to establish any relationship with him – even more difficult than it is with Ted Heath. They say Ted Heath thinks of himself as already P.M. and therefore speeds around to keep himself informed. Of all the available material Renwick thinks Alec Home the best, but he is so deplorable on T.V. it is hard to see how he could be resuscitated. Renwick is in favour of a coalition but says most of the Tory leaders take the line that they see no reason to share the prizes with anyone.

When I arrived in Paris it was assumed that de Gaulle would

scrape through on a low poll. However, he has lost and resigned at noon today.* It is thought most likely that Pompidou will be elected in his place, but this is not certain as he will not be supported by the Left – not even the Left of the Gaullists.

Wednesday, April 30th, 1969

Lunch yesterday for Vic Feather whom I had not seen since his appointment as Acting Secretary of the T.U.C. I have known him well for years, as the *Mirror* paid him a £500-a-year retainer, and he was a useful source of trades union opinion. I think greater responsibility has brought him on. He is not a big man but is warm, shrewd and experienced. He sees the Budget as an electioneering one. His interpretation is that Wilson thinks he will lose an election in the autumn but that the Tories will not have more than a sixty majority. Wilson thinks he can make mincemeat of Heath in the House and so will return to office in four years' time and will have another eight years in office before retiring. He said – and others have said the same – that Wilson is in a buoyant, self-confident mood; he thinks that he is the only man to handle the problems before us, and points out that with the departure of de Gaulle he has been in office longer than any other head of government in Europe.

I asked why the Government is pressing ahead with legislation to curb the trades unions. The measures proposed are unpopular and at the same time weak and likely to be wholly ineffective. Feather said part of the motive may be pressure from the foreign bankers but the main motive is Wilson's conviction that this is a vote-catcher! At a meeting between the T.U.C. on one side and Wilson and Barbara Castle on the other, Wilson produced figures from a public opinion poll showing that 72 per cent wanted legislation to curb unofficial strikes. Feather retaliated by saying if they were going to discuss public opinion polls why not begin on those dealing with the standing of the Government? The latest show Wilson scoring 30 per cent, and 63 per cent of the electorate wanting a General Election. He said at this Wilson went white and 'Barbara's jaw nearly hit the table'. The subject of public opinion polls was dropped!

* The result of the referendum on de Gaulle's complex set of proposals for constitutional reform was: 'No', 11·9 million (52·3 per cent); 'Yes', 10·5 million (46·8 per cent).

I asked him about Callaghan's standing in the party. He has been making a bid for trades union support and I wondered how he was doing. Vic said his attempts to take the leadership were too obvious and that he has now written himself off. It is only a few months ago that Douglas Houghton said if Wilson dropped dead he would be the successor. I asked Vic the same question. If Wilson dropped dead, who would succeed him? Vic said it would certainly not be Callaghan. He thought M.P.s would make for some grey, colourless figure – Peart or Michael Stewart. I said a society in which casual labourers on building sites got more money than university lecturers or hospital doctors was not stable. Surely there would have to be some system of job evaluation that established some relationship between the importance of the job and the pay. If everything was up for grabs, life would become impossible for everyone. He seemed to think a national wages board was not an impossible idea.

Lunch with Hugh Fraser at White's. He was most friendly and communicative, though he had not much news. Guy de Rothschild had dined with him a fortnight ago and he also said the franc would go some time this year. In the Budget it was announced the old age pensions would go up in the winter by 10s. per week but it was not revealed what increase in the stamp will be necessary to supply the wherewithal. This, according to Fraser, was because this provision was inserted at the last moment on the Prime Minister's orders and the method of meeting the cost has not yet been worked out. On the present state of the opinion polls the Tories, after an election, would have a majority of four hundred – and, according to Fraser, one of their first moves would be the removal of Ted from the leadership, probably in favour of Enoch Powell. Fraser says Enoch is indeed a lone wolf in the House, but why not? He is not looking for his future to existing M.P.s but to the movement of opinion in the country. Fraser felt strongly that the Tories should have done something about Ulster during their thirteen years in office but Macmillan was all for letting sleeping dogs lie. Now, as he said, the sleeping dog looks like being a very noisy dog indeed. Feather yesterday assumed the Government would have to take over the administration of Ulster. He spoke as if he had heard this. If this proves to be true Her Majesty's Government is in hideous trouble. It apparently has not even enough troops! He also said, as Dick Marsh did not long ago, that both front benches are pretty weak, containing no really first-class leadership material.

Thursday, May 1st, 1969

Humphrey Reeve, the handwriting expert, to lunch. During the afternoon I showed him letters from my various political contacts for his comments on the signatures and handwriting generally. The only one that showed any leadership potential was Christopher Soames! Rippon – 'clever boy'; Jenkins – 'more than half feminine'; Crossman – 'intelligent activist, courageous, erratic'; Crosland – 'putting on an act'; Whitelaw – 'independent, honest, good judgment; needs to know he is appreciated'; Callaghan – 'loose-knit with no brains'. His most interesting comment was on Wilson pointing out that his Harold is much surer than his Wilson. The Wilson used to be broken up into two parts but more recently into three. Both Macmillan and Heath were secretive and gave themselves away to no one.

Thursday, May 8th, 1969

An hour with Rees-Mogg at *The Times*. My visit came after a statement in the evening papers that Douglas Houghton had stated at a Parliamentary Labour Party meeting that the Government could not get its trades union legislation through. It is only a few days ago that Mellish, the new Chief Whip, said that this very feeble legislation was a matter of confidence and that if it was defeated there would have to be an election. I imagine that there will be no election but much eating of words and the feeble *In Place of Strife* will be still further diluted.

All this comes in the middle of the local government elections* and, following the departure of de Gaulle, with a serious financial crisis. Finally to cap all, Crossman announced on Monday an increase in the charges under the National Health for false teeth and spectacles. The money involved, about £1,700,000, is minor, but the timing unbelievably bad, as Health Service charges are such an emotional subject in the Labour Party. Apparently it was to have

* After these elections, held between May 5th and 10th, Labour was left in control of only 28 of the 342 borough councils in England and Wales. They fared slightly better in Scotland.

been announced in the Budget, but it was an unpopular item and Jenkins would not have it in his Budget speech.

The financial crisis takes the form of world-wide buying of marks. The franc has been at its lowest support price. The pound has been hit, though not so hard as previously, but its weakness shows up in the forward pound which is at a heavy discount. The Euro-dollar interest rate is now over 9 per cent, and is above the Rate here, which has led to the withdrawal of funds. The papers this morning speak of a possible closing of the European currency markets to-morrow. On any view, the world's system of exchange rates cannot stand much more of this.

Tuesday, May 13th, 1969

Today I had lunch with Louis Franck at Samuel Montagu. He told me that last year he was asked to get up a dinner for Nixon which he did – at his home in the country. At the last moment Nixon asked if he could bring two friends. Franck had never heard their names before and rang up his friends in New York to find out who they were. He was appalled to find that one had been to gaol and the other was going there. He did not feel he could refuse to entertain these men, but when later Nixon asked himself to lunch in the City with these friends, Franck refused to have them. When Nixon asked why, Franck told him quite frankly! Franck said Kennedy (the Treasury Secretary) is a very ordinary provincial banker – and no more. The argument in favour of Nelson Rockefeller was that anyone in America would be glad to serve under him, but this by no means applies to Nixon.

Friday, May 16th, 1969

Lunch with Arnold Weinstock – older and more experienced, as shows in his face and manner. He thought our problem in industry was not strikes but the fact that though the men didn't strike they didn't work. In industry he agreed that the women were subsidizing the men. He believed in equal pay for equal work, but the men's wages should be brought down to that of the women. On the whole our efficiency in light industry is better than that in heavy industry because light industry depends on women employees while heavy industry depends on men. He thought men take jobs because it is the done thing while women work because they want the money.

Of the political figures he has high hopes of Ted Heath and Iain Macleod; does not take Enoch Powell seriously, but has the greatest confidence in Alf Robens of everyone in the political world.

Thursday, May 22nd, 1969

Iain Macleod to lunch yesterday, even more bent than I remember. He is the Shadow Chancellor, and quite determined to abolish S.E.T. when he gets office. In its place he plans to have not a pay-roll tax but a value-added tax. We talked about Wilson's performance on T.V. the night before. Professor McKenzie of the L.S.E.* was quite a good interrogator, firm but polite. Wilson was not impressive, evidently bitterly resentful of the press, but otherwise complacent. All the Government's good work would soon bear fruit! This reminded Macleod of Perry Worsthorne's piece in the *Sunday Telegraph* last Sunday. He said Wilson goes on behaving as if he were in command of the ship – issuing orders and so forth – but no one has told him the crew has deserted and there is no one at the other end of the speaking tube. *Newsweek* this week says rigor mortis has set in but the patient, Wilson, has not yet been informed. Macleod feels something is bound to give and the Labour Party will have to throw out Wilson or go to the country. It is hard to see how they will do it but surely this state of affairs cannot continue. I think Macleod was in general unduly optimistic about the future. The outlook gets worse and these politicians catch up with the situation as it was two years ago.

Macleod felt that the situation is now so bad we need a catalyst. Is there no venerated national figure outside politics who could bring our affairs to a head? We talked about Mountbatten and he left me, suggesting that Mountbatten or someone – or several prestigious figures – should write a brief letter to *The Times* that would at least compel a change in the Labour Party leadership. The trouble is that there is no one in the country at this moment who has any authority at all, though presumably if the situation gets much worse the public will be ready to listen to anyone.

* London School of Economics.

Friday, May 23rd, 1969

Dinner last night at the Dartmouths. The only interesting piece was that Charles Clore told Ruth that though he had quite a lot of money he had never found happiness. R. said how happy she was and Clore said he could see that was true but he had never previously met any-one who was prepared to say – and obviously truthfully – that they were happy.

Monday, June 2nd, 1969

Have been preoccupied by all the hoo-ha over my book.* On Wednesday I was a guest at the dinner in honour of Annenberg, the new American Ambassador. I went expecting nothing but even so was appalled. In the United States he is a man of no reputation. He publishes the *Philadelphia Enquirer* but in all my trips to America no one ever mentioned his name, let alone suggested I should call on him. His sister's publication, *Seventeen*, is very good of its kind but hardly a qualification for an ambassadorship. He is a man of no presence; made a violent attack on American students. This was a purely social occasion and there is nothing we can do about American students anyway. In fact he is a totally unsuitable appointment who got off to a bad start.

On Thursday I addressed the Bow Group on the failure of the Wilson Government. Though these are supposed to be the young, intelligent, progressive wing of the Tory Party, there was nothing about them to suggest anything of the kind. There is no sense of urgency or crisis about any of them. If politically conscious Tories still think we live in Edwardian times, how can one expect ordinary citizens to be more than intuitively uneasy, which they are?

Friday, June 6th, 1969

Lunch yesterday with Barbara Ward. She had only just flown over from Chicago and her news was all American and Papal. On the latter, she thought the Pope was scared; if only he realized the im-portance of holiness: Heenan's strength was he had a spark of this at his centre. But what are you to make of a Pope who is unaware of the significance of holiness! All this from Barbara, one of the twelve lay

* *Strictly Personal* had many hostile reviews and gave rise to much controversy.

advisers to the Vatican, formerly President of the League of Catholic Women!

Barbara was very severe on Nixon and his entourage: Rogers 'knows nothing of foreign affairs'; Kissinger, 'narrow German who has missed two approaches by the Russians, one on disarmament and one on the Middle East, on which they are becoming seriously alarmed'; Kennedy (of the Treasury), 'sound provincial bank manager'. Nixon himself she regards as a hollow man: a 'suit with nothing inside it'. His wife goes around saying she will allow neither of her daughters to marry politicians.

She said McCarthy's stand against Johnson was not inspired by courage or principle. It was an act of revenge against Johnson who had promised him the vice-presidency in 1964 but had not delivered. This was also why he did not support Humphrey who had got the position in 1964 instead of himself.

She thought the general turmoil in American society was due to a realization by the young that affluence was not enough. As yet they do not know what they want, but 'economic growth' will not serve as an ideal towards which to strive.

Monday, June 9th, 1969

Lunch with the Denis Healeys at Admiralty House. It was a very pleasant occasion as we all like each other. I had a long but rather indeterminate conversation with Denis who was poised between two Cabinet meetings on the proposed trades union legislation. He said Callaghan's tactics were based on the assumption that Labour would lose the next election and that Wilson would now be anathema to the trades union movement, who would welcome Jim as the Leader of the Parliamentary Party after the defeat. Denis, or at any rate his wife, harbours a hope that Wilson may pull it off and win the next election. Denis feels he himself is gaining support in the P.L.P. and that events are moving his way. I don't think he really wants the premiership: I think he feels he is doing a good job at Defence and is content to remain there. He is not far-sighted, takes the financial outlook fairly complacently. He is nice; he is tough; he would be a far better P.M. than Wilson.

I asked him what his Government was really up to. The Budget seemed to be an electioneering one. Could this be true? He said in the early spring Wilson thought the situation would improve and stay good long enough for him to have an election – and win – later in the year. Hence, I suppose, the Budget. Wilson also thought legislation to curb the unions would be popular and a good plank in the election platform. It was doubtful if the legislation would work, but this did not matter as the election would be over before the snags appeared. They are now wasting vast amounts of time trying to find a formula that will not bring the Government down, and yet will not seem to be too evident a surrender to the unions. Denis did not seem to think there was any practical way of curbing the unions. He also said he thought Jack Jones (of the Transport Workers) was in close touch with Reg Birch of the Engineers.

Denis was in Washington earlier in the year and formed a very favourable opinion of Kissinger. He said the only policy in Vietnam is to pull out. He thinks Laird at Defence is a very able local politician but knows little about defence and is not as good as Clifford, whom Denis liked more than McNamara.

He thought the withdrawal of 25,000 American troops from Vietnam (out of over 500,000) announced this morning, was an inadequate gesture that would be quite ineffective at home or in Hanoi.

Wednesday, June 11th, 1969

Harry Walston to dine last night. He had an item of news. He had lunch yesterday with Robert Adeane and Angus Ogilvy and they were expatiating on the alarming outlook: 'This is 1929 all over again,' and more in that vein.

Lunch today with Sir Frank Kearton. He has admirers but I can see no signs of great ability. He is a nice chap and an intelligent one, but there it ends. His two principal colleagues seemed nice but no more. Kearton said he started as an admirer of Wilson's and had been very ready to help, but he had been quite disillusioned by Wilson's inability to get anything done.

Wednesday, June 25th, 1969

Have not written in this diary as I have been away in the provinces. The big item of news has been the complete climb-down of Wilson to the T.U.C. over the proposed trades union legislation. Having said that it was a matter of confidence, he found, at the crucial Cabinet meeting, that he and Barbara Castle had only one supporter, Thomas of the Welsh Office. Even Peter Shore deserted him. The importance of this event is not so much the humiliation of Wilson and his Government, but the fact that the Government took on the T.U.C. and was thrashed. Sooner or later the government of the day will have to take on the trades union movement – and win.

The T.U.C. with this victory under their belt will be that much more intransigent. Ted Heath on television last night said he was confident that the trades unions would accept the mandate for reform the Conservative government would have after the next election. Heath said the same thing to me over lunch. It just isn't true. The whole idea of a 'mandate' is a politician's idea and has no meaning to the man in the street. In any case the important unions are not run by their officials, still less by the T.U.C., but by the militant shop-stewards who at the moment are under no control. Incidentally Vic Feather played his hand exceedingly well. It was a deplorable episode but Vic came out of it with greatly enhanced prestige.

I had lunch with Tony Keswick and Hugh Fraser on Monday. They had no particular news. I asked why the Tories had been such a feeble opposition. He said it was because they do not see themselves as an opposition party but as a government-in-exile. I thought this a very good point.

Thursday, July 3rd, 1969

William Whitelaw to lunch today. I always like Whitelaw. His first remarks were about Wilson's humiliation at the hands of the T.U.C. His reaction is the same as mine: this will encourage the hotheads in the trades union movement and make the unions that much harder to deal with when the time comes. I said they will not be brought into line without a general strike. He said he wondered if the emergency powers had been looked at recently. He thought it very likely they had not and would need refurbishing. Whitelaw had no great revelations to impart. He said it would be impossible to recall Alec Home to the leadership and that Alec knows that. He said about Enoch Powell that he has only recently discovered that he is a very

263

good demagogue. He regards himself as an English General de Gaulle waiting at Colombey-les-deux-Eglises for the nation's call.

He asked me what I thought of Ted Heath's recent T.V. interview. I said Ruth liked it but I thought it woolly, too detailed and no sense of urgency or crisis. Whitelaw accepted this and said there is no sense of either at Westminster. I said I doubted whether Ted could weather the storms ahead and the only alternative in sight is Enoch. Had he ever considered himself for the leadership? He said, no – he had always seen himself as serving others. I said I thought he should reflect that if the new Tory Government is a failure, he might be the man. It would all depend on his T.V. impression. If he could get his humanity over, his honesty and his judgment, he would be just what the British people are looking for. He said he was unknown. I said this was an advantage. The other Tory leaders had been around too long and look how quickly Poher got known in France – thanks to T.V.

I was told some time ago that about eighty of the Tory M.P.s would prefer Enoch to Ted as their leader. But in the course of general conversation – not in answer to any question – Whitelaw put the figure at twenty-eight.

Jenkins has made wildly optimistic statements about our economic condition and Wilson goes about as if his surrender to the T.U.C. was a personal triumph. Whitelaw said that from all he can see, this is not just a cynical act. They have somehow convinced themselves that this is true. He believes Wilson still imagines he will win the next election.

Friday, July 11th, 1969

A hilarious lunch with Blankenhorn. He was full of bits and pieces. (1) The aggressors in the Russian–Chinese clashes are the Russians.* The German intelligence does not know what the idea is but they may be working up to an operation to destroy the Chinese nuclear capacity. (2) Negotiations to join the Common Market will begin in January. It should take two years to complete the negotiations and

* Sino-Soviet hostility in the Far East reached a new peak in March, when Chinese troops were reported to have crossed the border on the Ussuri River and been driven back by Soviet border guards. Diplomatic offensives, propaganda exchanges, allegations of various kinds and frontier incidents continued throughout the year.

then a five-year transition period. With this timetable we become full members in January 1977. (3) The German Government will be returned more or less unaltered at the elections in September. He thinks the mark will be revalued. He also thinks, incidentally, the franc will be devalued after the pressure for wage increases in September. (4) No German government under foreseeable circumstances would withhold financial assistance from the U.K. We are too important a part of the world economy. (5) Germany does not want the hegemony of Europe and Strauss does not want the hegemony of Germany. He wants to remain in charge of the German economy. (6) He assumes Ted Heath will take office and within two years will be a manifest failure.

He told me Annenberg had been to see him on the routine ambassador's visit. He told Blankenhorn he was very interested in golf and they talked about that; then he revealed his real interest – gambling. Where could he gamble? So Blankenhorn gave him the names of places where he could gamble in Germany. Apparently Annenberg is a grossly unattractive man who knows nothing of foreign affairs and revealed no particular wish to learn about them.

Tuesday, July 15th, 1969

Lunch for —— [a senior civil servant]. I had met him at dinner at the Royal Institution in February, but otherwise had had no conversation with him for six months or more. He was exceedingly friendly; commented on my appearance of good health, but himself looked dried up and worn out. He greeted me at the outset by asking what mischief I was up to. I said I merely sought to keep well-informed. As for the rest I was an old man in retirement. His comment: 'Rubbish.' In the past he has urged me to do more about E.S.P. – and he was on again about it today. He thinks the subject more important than politics which he regards as very ephemeral. What about more systematic study of the subject?

We talked a lot about Enoch Powell, whom he completely discounts. He sees the drift of British, even world, politics to the Right and thinks this may get out of hand but doesn't see how Enoch can come into it. He has no following in the House and unless he can secure the support of the House of Commons he must be looking for a military dictatorship which we have not had since Cromwell and did not like then. —— said he had been brought up with a great respect for the House of Commons and looked to the House to rise to the occasion when the time came. I said the prestige of the House with his fellow citizens is so low it could hardly fall. Like so many of those at the centre, they don't see how things can go on like this – nor how they can alter!

He thought the House of Commons had done a wonderful job over the last three hundred years. I replied, 'But look at the last fifty!' He asked if I thought politics responded to Gresham's Law – bad currency driving out the good. I said democracy depended on everyone speaking in good faith, then the best measures may win. But in politics you now have so many men who are prepared to advocate anything if they think it will be popular, and against this competition the honest man has not got a chance. The bad currency has driven out the good.

These senior civil servants are so discreet it is hard to interpret what they say, but he put in no defence of this Government at any point. Nor did he demur when I said this Government had lost its authority and it would take a period of exceptionally good leadership to get it back.

Thursday, July 17th, 1969

Douglas Houghton to lunch, in excellent form. He was in no way alarmed by our financial affairs: the other countries would have to keep us afloat whatever happened. Our problem had been to have full employment and a surplus on our balance of payments. We had not learnt how to have both at the same time and some other countries were having the same difficulty, notably Holland. His main theme was Wilson's inability to look ahead. Years ago Jenkins announced we were pulling out of Concorde; but he hadn't read the contract – we couldn't. Wilson had plunged into reform of the House of Lords and the whole business had got so bogged down it had to be abandoned. Then there was the trades union legislation. The Bill was hardly worth having anyway, but it was important for the Government not to be defeated by the T.U.C. Here again Wilson had not looked far enough ahead.

266

The most startling thing Houghton said was that Ted Heath is the trustee for our constitution. People were disillusioned by Wilson. If Heath failed there would be an irresistible demand for something else. I said that that was where Enoch Powell came in. He said this was so and he had heard Rab Butler only recently say that under such circumstances Enoch was the heir-apparent.

Tuesday, July 22nd, 1969

Lunch with Paul Hamlyn at his invitation. He wanted to tell me that he planned to leave I.P.C., a move which caused me no surprise. It was announced at the annual general meeting that Aubrey Jones would join the board as deputy chairman in May when his contract expires with the P.I.B. I said to Paul that this read as if he had been pressed on the board by the Institutions.* Hugh Cudlipp might think of Aubrey as a congenial fellow Welshman, but Aubrey was not that sort of man. Both he and his wife are very ambitious. Aubrey will be aiming for the chairmanship with all the political influence involved. Paul said the board had not been consulted and had had the news broken to them in instalments. He thought Hugh's idea was that Aubrey should do the chores of chairmanship while Hugh flitted around the world.

The big news for weeks and months past has been the landing on the moon. The astronauts are now on the way home and face re-entry as the last hazard. It is an immense technological achievement. In all the American space missions only three men have been killed and that was on the ground before leaving. The foresight involved has been miraculous. The men's courage has been admirable. They have been in an unknown world and in great danger for a week, and have never faltered. But having said all that, it is hard to see what of real value has been achieved. The Americans are beset with problems: their big cities, the Negroes, Vietnam, inflation, the armament race and the rest. The moon is not urgent and not a purely American problem, and in any case the biggest problem facing all of us is a spiritual and moral one, not a political or technological one at all; I regard the moon as an escape.

* Financial organizations – in particular, insurance companies and pension funds – which are responsible for massive investment funds.

When the Pope does not know what to do about his Church, he goes to Bogota or Geneva; Wilson to Lagos; Nixon to Bucharest; the American people to the moon.

There is much talk of visiting Mars, which is just possible, and the nearer stars, which is not. There is even talk of colonizing the moon – with absolutely no atmosphere!

Wednesday, July 23rd, 1969

Spent forty minutes with Enoch Powell at 33 South Eaton Place this morning. He is having lunch with me towards the end of August, but that seemed rather far away, so I asked to see him sooner. He has a nice small house – nice atmosphere. He was very polite; said my calling on him was a great compliment! He was a bit mystified by my request to see him and thought I might have something to discuss with him as a matter of urgency. However, when that was explained, he became friendly and communicative. He sees no great change in the next twelve to fifteen months: if anything labour relations will ease and politics will become more normal. He assumes a Tory victory in the election when it comes. I think he thinks his chance may come at some date after that. He explained that he is not the sort of man to lay a plot which will reach a climax at a given point of time. He preaches what he believes in and hopes events will prove him right. He would like to be leader of the country but his primary motive is to advocate causes in which he believes. He does not anticipate any financial crisis. He thinks the answer to all our financial problems is to float the pound. When I tried to argue that those most experienced in this field did not agree, my objections were brushed aside as mere conservatism and self-interest on the part of my friends at the Bank of England. He thinks that if the supply of money is restricted really seriously then there would be no money for wage increases except at the expense of others. In his experience trades union leaders are very sensitive to any moves that lead to unemployment, even unemployment among non-members of their union.

On television one could see him as a future Führer. To talk to, this is not so and I think there is an irrational element (of which he may be unaware) which only emerges on occasion. Obviously, he

268

does not have to reveal all to me, but at no time did he speak in a way which would lend one to suppose that he thought Parliament was a very threatened institution or that he saw himself in charge of a dictatorial government of any kind.

Lunch with Grainger, scientific member of the Coal Board. He was employed by the Atomic Energy Commission and I wanted to talk to him about nuclear energy and all that. He said the disagreement between the Coal Board and the Central Electricity Generating Board is partly personal. Their respective chairmen are not on speaking terms and this is Robens's fault.

It is extraordinary that a Labour Government should be so anti-coal and willing to swallow any propaganda for atomic energy. Grainger says the reason was to show that the Labour Party is indeed in its element in the latter part of the twentieth century. The costs of atomic energy have been estimated wrongly and in every case optimistically. The optimism could well have been detected. Furthermore in the costing of atomic power the proceeds of the plutonium have been credited at a price, though it is unlikely to be sold for twenty years. What with optimistic estimates of building costs and of fuel costs, and fudged accounts, the result is to show up coal in a bad light. But even if atomic power came up to every hope, there would still be the mining industry and the miners. They would be almost as expensive to keep in idleness as in producing coal and if they produce coal it has to be burnt.

Grainger thinks that once a green light had been given to atomic power, then all the powers of the Establishment combined to prevent a change back. To change now would cause so many red faces, so many lost professional reputations, so many redundancies, that it has become impossible.

Thursday, July 24th, 1969

Thinking over what Enoch said yesterday, perhaps I haven't made it clear to what extent he is a believer in good old laissez-faire. Currencies, gold and everything else are to be a free market at whatever price they would fetch; labour would be in the same category. I said this would mean a very low rate of exchange for the pound because of capital movements, and our imported food would accordingly be very dear. No, says Enoch, whatever happened to the pound our food would cost no more; on the labour front the strong unions would not use their power to secure unfair advantages for their members at the cost of a higher general level of unemployment, or lower wages in some other sector. All this seems as irrational as the views of Michael Foot and his friends. Caught in a cleft stick you dream up a panacea that will solve all our difficulties. All that is actually achieved is to give the ignorant public the false impression that there really is an easy way out of all our difficulties.

Wednesday, August 6th, 1969

Today I had a long lunch with Alfred Robens which was productive. Jenkins the other day made a speech taking credit for the Labour Government and for its liberal measures on homosexuality, divorce, abortion and so on. This has gone down very badly with the rather puritanical Labour voter in the provinces. He thinks Wilson was right when he said early on that the Labour Party is a crusade or it is nothing. Under him it has been no crusade and is now nothing.

Alf had had some talk with Aubrey Jones after it was announced that Aubrey is going to I.P.C. as deputy chairman. Aubrey specifically mentioned to Alf that the attraction of the job was that it would give him more scope and, with it, political influence.

Alf thought Wilson could have had his way on the trades union legislation if he had stood firm and threatened the P.L.P. with a General Election. The issue will have to be fought out sometime and the unions will be that much harder to tackle, having this victory behind them. In any case the attitude of the unions is calculated to destroy our economy in due course whether by a conflict or by inflation. Either might lead to a revolutionary situation and to dictatorship, which is why Alf is so keen on a coalition (or National Government) as the only way to head off such a catastrophe.

It is a pointer to our diminished influence in the world that Kiesinger, the German Chancellor, is in Washington. Wilson has been trying to get an invitation from Nixon but has not yet been offered a firm date.

I said to Alf that it looked as if Denis Healey had missed the bus: he was waiting for the big battalions to be on his side, and now it is too late. Alf said he thought Healey, Jenkins and Callaghan had all had their eye on 10 Downing St, but had failed from lack of courage.

Saturday, August 9th, 1969

What was my surprise last night when a $12\frac{1}{2}$ per cent devaluation of the franc was announced. I think it was clear the Bank knew nothing about it at lunchtime. The level of devaluation may be designed not to wreck the pound but may prove to be too much for it and not big enough to stabilize the franc. Strauss immediately came out with a statement saying this proved how right the German Government was in not revaluing the mark.

There was one major point mentioned by Maurice Allen at lunch yesterday. I said something about our short-term liabilities being £4,000 million. Maurice said they were actually £5,000 million, on top of which we had given a dollar guarantee on a further £1,250 million of sterling funds.

His point about the grim outlook for 1970 and 1971 was that Government expenditure had been held down, not cut. Some expenditure could not be postponed much longer: anyway not beyond April next year.

Tuesday, August 12th, 1969

Val Duncan of Rio Tinto–Zinc to lunch. I had only met him twice before and never for any talk. He apologized profusely for being one minute late – and stayed till three o'clock. He is an almost fanatical European and thinks the E.E.C. provides the answer to our problems.

When Duncan attended his first meeting of the Court at the Bank he found they were discussing messengers' wages. So he protested at the Court being involved in such trifles. He also said that if it would strengthen the Governor's hand he was sure the part-time directors would, on an appropriate occasion, be prepared to join the Governor on a deputation to the P.M.! Anyway the outcome of this and some agitation by Alf is that they were told the exact state of the country's indebtedness: information known to few officials and fewer ministers. He spoke most warmly of Parsons and Allen and was horrified to hear the latter was not to be reappointed after February.

Duncan is at present negotiating with the Persian Government for the development of what has been reported to be a copper mine. But apparently it is far more than that – it is a copper belt. He has also recently been to Moscow where the Russians want Rio Tinto-Zinc to help them with the development of their Siberian copper deposits. The Russians made an approach about three years ago and this latest development was in answer to a letter written two and a half years ago!

On domestic politics, Duncan has seen something of Heath, whom he likes. He has advised him that on taking office he will not have much time and that appropriate legislation – e.g. on the trades unions – should be drafted now. If he starts getting legislation drafted after he gets into office it will be too late. There are retired Parliamentary draftsmen who could do this work. He assumes that a general strike – or its equivalent – will be encountered and thinks that the Government should very carefully pick the timing and the issue and stage the whole thing. He has a high opinion of the ability of Les Cannon and thinks he should be given any inducement to take over the leadership of the trades union movement. He does not think there is anyone else with anything like the same personality and capacity.

Monday, August 18th, 1969

Maurice Parsons to lunch. He had little hard news but one picks up an atmosphere and point of view. The Bank of England only heard of the franc devaluation from the tape. They were in touch with New York at once and the Americans were very annoyed at having no prior knowledge.

In a general way Maurice continues to think we are drifting to a major catastrophe. He has been in correspondence with Enoch Powell about floating the pound and regards his opinions as quite childish.

Friday, August 29th, 1969

De Courcel to lunch: very friendly and quite communicative. He made one interesting point: that when Nixon was in Paris in the spring he asked de Gaulle how he got out of Algeria, as he might be able to use the same methods to get the U.S. out of Vietnam. I got the impression that de Gaulle was ignominiously thrown out of

Algeria and it was only much later that his P.R. boys discovered that he had meant to leave all along.

Wednesday, September 10th, 1969

Lunch with —— [a senior civil servant]. His most interesting point was that when Thorneycroft resigned as Chancellor it was largely at the instigation of Enoch Powell who, for some days before their departure, seemed unbalanced to the point of insanity.* This point was brought up because I said Enoch was a perfectly ordinary balanced person to talk to but on T.V. there were moments when his eyes took on a fanatical glare.

On Friday I went to Twyford to take part in the B.B.C. programme 'Any Questions', and at the preceding dinner had some talk with Quintin Hogg whom I have known slightly for a long time. Like other M.P.s he speaks as if politics were where they were in 1907: office is a prize and they were all lying rather low as the prize would drop into their laps if they did not do anything foolish. I said they might find things difficult if with a large, rather right-wing majority they had to tackle the trades unions. He thought a large majority would break up into factions and so transform the present party system. He showed no signs of apprehension at the prospect of having to deal with the manifold problems that confront us.

The economic outlook is a bit better, mainly because of a continuing boom in world trade and a huge American deficit. Roy Jenkins has made a speech of almost lyrical optimism.

The main news of the last few weeks has been the deteriorating situation in Ulster and particularly in Belfast. I know nothing beyond what I read in the papers, but it is obvious that the Government here was taken completely by surprise and has no idea of the intractability of Irish politics. The general in command in Northern Ireland, Freeland, looks on television a nice chap but weak, if not wet. Chichester-Clark, the Ulster P.M., looks nice, but out of his

---

* Peter Thorneycroft was Chancellor of the Exchequer in the Macmillan Conservative Government of 1958. In January of that year, he insisted that, in view of the country's stringent economic circumstances, expenditures on the civil service and the armed forces should be held at the same level as the year before. Reductions of about £150 million in estimated expenditures were required, but economies of only about £100 million could be found. Thorneycroft resigned on the point of principle, accompanied by Nigel Birch, then Economic Secretary to the Treasury, and Enoch Powell, then Financial Secretary.

depth. The Governor of Northern Ireland, an ex-colonial civil servant called Grey, has put in no appearance of any kind.

It rather looks as if the administration of Northern Ireland will be conducted more and more from Whitehall. Overdue reforms will be introduced and efforts will be made, with these reforms, to restore the status quo. I don't think this is possible and doubt whether, now trouble has flared up, there is any satisfactory answer. Meanwhile I gather we are getting a stinking press in the world's newspapers and on T.V.

Tuesday, September 16th, 1969

Enoch Powell to lunch, the second time I have had serious talk with him. On this occasion I came away with one main impression: the contrast between his very reasonable and rational conversation and his apparently fanatical personality. I said I thought if there were a referendum today on the public choice of P.M., he would win, though not with a clear majority. He said he agreed but what was the use of that? I said it looked as if Heath would soon be P.M.: that he would be a failure and Enoch would then be in the centre of the stage. He said failure did not necessarily mean a change: look at Wilson who has been a failure for three and a half years. I said the Tories are more ruthless with their failures – with which view he agreed.

His main idea is for the Government to withdraw from as much as possible and to reduce Government expenditure by cutting commitments. He thinks that by floating the pound our economic affairs can be left to market forces and that by strict control of money supply trades union demands can be kept within bounds. He thinks the trades union privileges and immunities can be modified by law and the consequence left to the courts. On law and order he thinks we need more police and more prisons – not to be repressive but to make sure that more criminals are caught and that those sentenced to prison actually go there. His latest hobby-horse is the Common Market. He was a Common Market man because he thought there was an overwhelming economic argument in favour of a larger market and larger industrial units. He now thinks that there is much less to this argument than he supposed. He thinks the Six might become more and more inward-looking and the U.K. would be at an advantage to be outside, trading more freely with everyone. He sees no future in a special link with the U.S. The argument that we should have far more opportunity for greatness as a leading power in Europe than as an independent off-shore island does not ring any bell with him.

We talked a bit about Ireland where the situation is deteriorating. He said Tory friends who had been in Ulster thought General Freeland weak. Callaghan last night on T.V. was merely peevish. Powell asked me if an answer would be to detach Fermanagh, Tyrone and southern Down from Stormont and let them go ahead with an overwhelmingly Protestant three and a half counties. I said this might lead to the Protestants pushing the remaining Catholics out of their rump, which would very possibly be followed by similar pressure against the Protestants in the Republic: the sort of thing that has happened in India and Pakistan. In any case southern Ireland would never accept the border wherever it was drawn. At the moment there may well be no answer to the Ulster problem.

He was obviously deeply impressed by de Gaulle and what he called his 'cosmic' sense of humour, so noticeable in Dante and a necessary concomitant of all greatness.

Powell is a touchy character and I rather wondered how the lunch would go. But he could not have been easier or more friendly.

Wednesday, September 17th, 1969

Mosley to dinner at home last night. Very friendly and talkative, mostly about Europe. He is a fanatical European, thinks the whole of our future turns on this one subject. In general he thinks really serious trouble is blowing up in France and Italy and that an eventual world economic crisis is inevitable.

Thursday, October 2nd, 1969

My lunches with Harry Walston and Dick Beeching these last few days produced nothing much, but Hartley Shawcross yesterday was more rewarding. His most intriguing item was that he had seen something of George Brown lately at weekends in the country, where they are neighbours. George told Hartley that he had been pressed three or four times to rejoin the Government. He asked for reassurances that he would rejoin the Cabinet at his former rank, and also on the Common Market. He made no attempt to conceal his hatred of Wilson, failed to get the reassurances he wanted, and decided that a return to office would just not work out. Hartley gathered that a strong reason for accepting was that he thinks even if Labour wins the next election he will lose his seat; if he is in the Cabinet a seat will be found, though otherwise not. In the course of two long conversations, Hartley expressed alarm at the decline in the prestige of Parliamentary democracy, but (like me) could see no signs of a recovery or of an alternative. He apparently does not know Enoch Powell at all.

As we were leaving the dining-room up came Onassis, whom I had not met before. I thought I recognized him lunching with some woman, not Jackie. He is short and was wearing a badly cut blue serge suit. He is very dark and Greek-looking. The main impression is of huge vitality – quick, forceful, domineering – not particularly nice nor particularly intelligent.

We talked about the Takeover Panel, which is taking up a lot of Hartley's time, as he's its chairman, and about [Robert] Maxwell.

Thursday, October 9th, 1969

In Washington yesterday I had lunch with Bolling, a Democrat Representative from Kansas. He is sometimes spoken of as a future Speaker but protested yesterday that when the job falls vacant it will go to someone even more spineless than the present incumbent.

Later in the afternoon I had a long talk with Senator Fulbright, whose stock has rather fallen since I saw him last three years ago. But he is highly intelligent and meets everyone. He was objecting that American policy is in practice dictated by the Israelis in the Middle East and by the Vietnamese in the Far East (he might have added Chiang Kai-shek in Formosa). He said apart from their numerical strength in New York, the Jews have immense power here. The Israeli Government at the moment has far greater control of the American Government than vice versa. So far I have met no one who thinks Russia is likely to attack China, and talks between them are in fact taking place at the present time. Nixon is still given the benefit of some doubts but the honeymoon is all but over and in future he will be judged on his achievements – if any! The main complaint here, as at home, is the complete lack of leadership. This may seem so to Americans but our own plight is much worse.

Friday, October 10th, 1969

Lunch yesterday with David Bruce in Georgetown; dinner for Scott, Minority Leader in the Senate. The lunch was a marvellous occasion. Mrs Alice Longworth normally gets up at 3 p.m. and goes to bed between 3 and 4 a.m. However, Bruce got her to come to this lunch – her first lunch out for years, or so they say. Bruce said she is the best conversationalist in North America, which I can well believe. She is eighty-five, the daughter of Teddy Roosevelt. She appeared in a smart tweed dress with a black floppy hat and blue stockings, and was everything that was promised: cultured, amusing, full of ideas and of reminiscences that go so far back. The remark that impressed me most was when she said the American people need someone to worship – hence their devotion to Eisenhower, who could have died in the White House if it had not been for the constitutional amendment after Roosevelt, limiting the President to two terms. She had a good opinion of Jack Kennedy, spoke more warmly of Bobby than most, and dismissed Teddy as a spoilt boy.

Another guest was Dean Acheson whom I had not met before. He has written an immense book* which is due to come out any day now. He was particularly pleased with a review by Galbraith that said I don't think much of Mr Acheson but this is a superb book. Acheson made the point that all the world's governments of today are weak and that weak governments take short views. Long views are safer and cause less irritation between one country and another. He thought that in politics there were periods when there are a number of able and brilliant men and then long desert patches. He thought that in the late eighteenth and early nineteenth centuries the United States had been brilliantly served but that this period had been followed by one with no one of any talent. Perhaps the volume of human knowledge was now so vast that the brilliance of late eighteenth-century politicians was no longer to be looked for.

* *Present at the Creation* (New York: W. W. Norton, 1969; London: Hamish Hamilton, 1970).

Acheson is to make a speech today supporting the President, to whom he has been opposed, on the grounds that it may be possible in the next few days to destroy Nixon, but what then? You would have for three years a broken man. He could not even resign because to do so would put in Agnew, who is a figure of fun. To quote Rab Butler, he is the best President they have got.

Scott is the Senator from Pennsylvania. I had met him before but he is now the leader of the Republicans in the Senate. He said Nixon is under no illusion that he has to get out of Vietnam – with or without honour.

Saturday, October 11th, 1969

Another busy day yesterday: lunch with Bradlee, executive editor of the *Washington Post*, followed by visits to the State Department, Mrs Graham for tea at the *Washington Post*, and dinner with Anderson, the columnist who has taken over Drew Pearson's column.

Bradlee is a good editor but had no particular news. My next call was on Hillenbrand, the Under-Secretary in charge of European Affairs (including Canada!). A very dull little man who had been Ambassador to Hungary. I said our people were disturbed about the prospect in Italy where the Government was discredited and the political influence of the Vatican was slipping. He pooh-poohed this and said the only source of some mild anxiety in Europe was France. He thought my watered-down views on Britain eccentrically over-pessimistic. He did not strike me as having either information or judgment.

On from him to one Nathan Solomons, Under-Secretary for Economic Affairs, and in charge of American reactions to the Common Market. The American Government is still ready to accept a certain amount of trade discrimination to help forward the idea of a united Europe. This might be modified if the Common Market was enlarged and continued to take a restrictive stand against imports of food. He thought the Continentals would do more about letting us into the Common Market if they felt we were wholehearted. At present they do not feel that either Wilson or the general public are really determined. Solomons is no great statesman but pleasant and intelligent.

Mrs Graham was very friendly. Her son has done his military service and is now a policeman learning about the crime wave the hard way. At lunch on October 9th Bruce said there was more serious crime in Washington than in the whole of the British Isles and it is only now that they are getting round to more police and more judges. The delay in bringing crimes to trial can run to more than a year. This law and order issue is obviously important as it affects everyone in their daily life. Another big problem is inflation. Mrs Graham had recently to give her printers a 20 per cent increase. I think her impression is that measures so far taken to curb inflation are inadequate.

Dinner with Anderson – the very well-informed columnist. He thinks the measures to deal with inflation are too severe and will cause considerable unemployment. He does not, however, anticipate more than a very mild recession. He sees a lot of secret government reports – for instance that at the moment the Viet Cong are doing badly, but the plan to Vietnamize the war won't work as the reports on the quality of the South Vietnamese troops are very unfavourable. But whether the Viet Cong are getting the worst of the fighting or not, the Americans are fed up with the war and determined to pull out.

Anderson said the information available from satellites is fantastically detailed and accurate. Nixon recently said in a speech that there were sixty-seven anti-missile sites round Moscow. Not only was the exact figure known but in fact they knew that some were not occupied. They can record the sound from a submarine's engines, run this through a computer at headquarters and know almost at once the name of the submarine. It is in this way that they know every day where every Soviet naval vessel is. They can pick up radio messages from aeroplanes in central Russia asking permission from the local control tower to land.

Anderson has been widely reported in England for his statements on the Kennedy affair at Chappaquiddick. Unlike other commentators he thinks Teddy has charismatic (his word) political gifts and may well survive his succession of blunders over the drowning of the girl in his car. Apparently Kennedy wants to be president – or so Anderson thinks.

Sunday, October 12th, 1969

Lunch at the Embassy yesterday. Michael Ayrton, the artist, and his wife and ourselves were the only guests. The conversation was mostly about Ayrton and a maze he has built in the Catskill Mountains. Freeman has acquired a certain presence, but is very nervous. The Freemans had recently met Mrs Longworth, who described a smile she bestowed on someone she doesn't like: 'I creased my face in his direction.'

Monday, October 13th, 1969

Forty minutes with Kennedy, the Secretary of the Treasury. He was described by George Bolton as 'just a provincial bank manager', but he is better than that, and to meet, better than Fowler. His theme was that steps had been taken, which seem to be adequate, to deal with inflation here. Unemployment at 4 per cent might go a bit higher before going lower. The whole situation, including the Eurodollar, was under control. Wages were moving strongly up in some sectors, but with increasing unemployment in other sectors the overall increase would be manageable. The balance of trade was worrying: imports, particularly from Japan, were worrying. This would have to be corrected in due course and such correction would inevitably reflect on other nations' surpluses. He told me nothing new but reflected the atmosphere of optimism which I find it impossible to share. Are we not relying on the kind of measures that would have worked in 1929? In other words are we preparing ourselves for the last war?

Lunch with Noyes, editor of the *Washington Star*, a pleasant but stupid man. With him were his brother, a little less stupid, and their woman columnist, Mary McRory, who was much better. She was in full support of the Moratorium, as it is called, the demonstration on Wednesday all over the U.S. to get the Army back from Vietnam. None of them seemed to understand Dean Acheson's point that you can perhaps destroy the President, but then the country has no real government for three years. Noyes did not see that the authority of a government could be destroyed and Mary McRory thought the President in any case could follow public opinion. That the principal people on the second newspaper in the capital should be so obtuse sccms rathcr alarming – but, the Noyes said, there are no outstanding publishers in the U.S. today.

From them to McNamara at the World Bank. I had met him twice before when he was at the Pentagon. He is immensely able and such a nice man with it all. His principal problem, he said, is the movement into the big cities. In developing countries this takes place from the country into the towns; but in the developed countries, anyway the U.S., the movement is from the smaller towns to the larger ones and from the centre of the country to the eastern and western seaboards and the Great Lakes. He is doing his best to make birth control respectable and he finds the attitude of Catholic countries growing rapidly less rigid.

From him to meet Charles Gombault of *France-Soir* who is in the U.S. for a short visit. He thinks the franc will be all right for six months but may not do much better than that as prices are rising so fast. A year ago, Pompidou said when (not if) he is president he would not allow any P.M. to serve him for more than two years, so Chaban-Delmas may not have long to go. To convince the extreme Gaullists that things have hardly changcd, Pompidou has sent a man to Quebec, which infuriates Ottawa; and as part of the same policy he is likely to be very unhelpful about our joining the Common Market. The political and economic future of the country is not clear as no one knows what the trades unions will do nor how successfully the Government will be in dealing with them.

Tuesday, October 14th, 1969

First a visit to Dr Burns, principal economic adviser to the President – intelligent, slow, quite nice. He is an academic type and is an adviser not an operator. Like others, he is optimistic. It seems that the economy is cooling off – all indicators point in that direction. The balance of trade is worrying, but confidencc in thc dollar remains unimpaired. He thought the German mark might have passed its best; in Italy the doubts are political not economic; in France we can only keep our fingers crossed.

I think what emerges in all my various talks is the lowly position occupied in these people's minds by the U.K. The second impression is of diminished confidence, which has been replaced by optimism.

There is more crime in Washington than in the United Kingdom: the principal cause of death between the ages of fifteen and thirty-five in New York is heroin; the young are alienated; foreign commitments in Asia are being liquidated; but even responsible officials look on the bright side and keep smiling.

From Burns to Klein, the President's super P.R.O. He is presumably a Jew but does not look like one. He was called to the telephone so often that we really had no conversation. But he was another of Nixon's top advisers and therefore it was interesting to see what sort of man he is. Though I have no respect for Nixon and regard him as a very inadequate president, he has better people around him than one would suppose from reading the English papers – and better men than one usually finds in Whitehall. The only real dud I met was Hillenbrand, responsible for European affairs at the State Department.

Mollenhoff, a member of the White House staff, last night made one good point about the Teddy Kennedy affair – that the truth can now never be known. Even if it were unearthed and published it would not be believed whatever it was.

Thursday, October 16th, 1969

This morning a long talk to Maurice Parsons whom I had met in the hotel lift. He has been here a week or two and is going on to Washington. He thinks the improved trade figures at home do not mean much and are largely the reflections of the big deficit in American trade. He gave me the impression that the bankers here take inflation much more seriously than the people I have talked to. Under the American Constitution it is difficult for the Government to do anything effective about it, so they very warmly welcome revaluation as it is for them a painless means of devaluing the dollar. The dollar is a world currency and how do you devalue it in any other way? Maurice said that both here and in Britain it is hard to bring home the dangers of inflation, which neither country has experienced in extreme form. Governments ought to know better but it is governments that cause all the trouble.

Lunch today with Mike Cowles, publisher of *Look*, and one of the principal publishers in the U.S.A. He sees everyone of importance and is at least well-informed. He thinks 1970 will show poor financial results, but it is an election year so they will not be allowed to be too bad. He thought any real trouble would wait till 1971, though there are so many unknowns that speculation on 1971 is not very profitable. He said there are a number of facts which would lead to very gloomy conclusions – for instance that if the banks entered their bond holdings at market value in their balance sheets very large numbers of them would be seen to be bankrupt. Nevertheless, he thought the United States would muddle through.

He thought public pressure, evidenced by the so-called Moratorium yesterday, will compel Nixon to get out of Vietnam even more quickly than he intended. There may be a residual force of 100,000 men left there indefinitely, but in the end the Viet Cong will take the whole country. Cowles thought that when the story comes to be written it will be found that there was more graft and corruption than in any previous war. The American Army has lost a lot of prestige and Cowles thinks the generals will counter-attack with a huge public relations campaign saying the Army could have taken Vietnam at any time if it had not been hamstrung by the politicians.

He showed little or no interest in the Middle East or in Europe. He thought Humphrey would stand for the Senate in 1970 and he would certainly be elected and so be available as the Democrat candidate for president in 1972. He had dined with Governor Rockefeller the night before who told him Lindsay would certainly win the mayoral election. This is an unexpected opinion.

Saturday, October 18th, 1969

One and a half hours yesterday with George Ball. He was in great form – a most attractive man. He said he had told George Brown that in foreign affairs Britain since the war had missed every bus except the ones for Cuba! He thought that whatever Nixon's own opinion may be, he will be compelled by popular opinion to bring large numbers of troops home from Vietnam. At some point the Saigon politicians will realize they have no future and will turn up in Europe to live out their lives on the money they have stacked away. Those unable to get away will seek to make their peace with Hanoi. At this point the American position in Vietnam becomes impossible and they will withdraw altogether. He thinks this will happen by the end of 1970. The feeling against the war is so strong that every withdrawal will only lead to a demand for further withdrawals.

On inflation, he thought the American Government is caught on the horns of a dilemma. If they do not take fairly drastic steps inflation will roar ahead, but almost any possible steps will lead to unemployment. And in this country an overall increase in unemployment of 1 per cent will represent a 10 per cent increase among Negroes, particularly the young Negroes in towns. At the moment, with racial tension so high, this will cause really serious racial trouble. Previously no shooting war had been fought without price and income controls. Johnson tried to fight the Vietnam war without them because he knew the war to be too unpopular. It was this that really set off the inflation which is now so difficult to damp down.

Friday, October 24th, 1969

I called this morning on Professor Elliott Janeway at Claridge's – at his request. He is a tall, rather imposing-looking American, more like an editor than a professor. He sat in his shirt-sleeves in a howling gale of wind from an open window, holding forth for an hour. I asked some questions but he showed no wish to hear any opinions I might have.

He spoke with great admiration of Nixon's political flair: how he has been recruiting the support of the conservative, middle-aged, middle-class citizens who dislike both what he called the 'Beards and the Bees' and the Negroes. This should get him the support of California and Illinois, two of the three key states, and ensure him at least a close run for the election of 1972. Next year the Democrats may well gain but this will suit Nixon who will be able to speak of the measures he wanted but was unable to get through a Democrat Congress.

He thought there would be a growing shortage of capital in America, not only for business but for local governments, who need new schools, new houses and an entire new transport system. The Germans had made a mistake in channelling their output into exports and had neglected to re-equip. I said they had done a vast amount of re-equipping over the last twenty-five years – nobody more. He said their steel trade was seriously in need of modernization. I said we had put our output into consumption and our investment at home was at the lowest level of developed countries. This was ignored. He thought inflation would continue here, in America and in Europe, and other people's inflation would save us from serious consequences. The stickiest outlook was that for Italy, France and Germany – for reasons I did not gather. Japan he thought would be all right.

American politics would be dominated by the fact that the elderly would control the voting until 1972; but by 1976, the young would have the majority and by then both policies and personalities would have to change. Janeway spoke of Nixon as a man who was good at making the right gestures – and this with no critical intent. This is the new politics of both Wilson and Nixon: you don't attempt to solve any problem but reckon to keep the voter quiet for the present by the right gesture or the well-turned speech. By this standard, Agnew, with his crude clowning in the Southern States, may actually be an asset to Nixon in shepherding the more ignorant and prejudiced Southern voter.

When asked what the consequences would be if all the world's leading countries indulged in rapid inflation, Janeway gave no answer. He is said to be a respected economist in the U.S. expressing a minority opinion, but I found a lot of what he said today either very short-term thinking or merely unsound. I think he is more concerned with the Stock Market than anything else – and he is sure that is in for a fall.

Afterwards, lunch with Tony Keswick who had abandoned a plan to build a towel factory in Dumfries to replace imports. The Board of Trade did everything possible to discourage him. He is chairman of the Staff Council at the Bank and finds the staff getting increasingly restive. They see the dustmen and the miners getting what they want by unconstitutional action, so why not them too?

Since I left England on October 5th the Labour Party has recovered its position in the polls to within 3 per cent or so of the Conservatives, but the strike situation is clearly worse. The Government reshuffle ended in the sacking of Marsh, the resignation of Reg Prentice, and the giving to Tony Benn of Technology, plus Fuel and

Power, plus a large chunk of the Board of Trade and a part of the D.E.A. Crosland moves from Trade to become a super-minister with nebulous power over Housing, Local Government and Transport. The shuffle will certainly not add to the efficiency of the Government and is hard to explain unless one can assume that Wilson thinks he is an administrator and that these manœuvres help in some way. He has had to scrap, as a separate department, the D.E.A., which he was advised against in the first place. Such little authority as the Government retains is crumbling fast.

Monday, October 27th, 1969

At the B.B.C. yesterday, a discussion with Robin Day. He had seen something of the Tories lately and these are his opinions: (1) Ted cannot get over his inferiority complex; (2) Maudling is bone-lazy and quite useless after lunch; (3) nevertheless he and Hogg are carrying the show in spite of Hogg's increasing liability to lose his temper; (4) Iain Macleod is a cripple; and (5) Enoch Powell is out on a limb. The polls show the Tories only 3½ per cent ahead and unlikely to win any of the five Labour seats being contested this week.*

Wednesday, October 29th, 1969

Lunch yesterday with Alfred Robens; in crashing form and very friendly. Since I saw him last he has had a strike on his hands, mostly in Yorkshire. He had anticipated this and had decided in advance to give way on the money but not on the hours. He thinks this is only the beginning of trouble in the coalfields. The miners have behaved well and see themselves among the least well paid – the dockers have behaved disgracefully and are far more generously rewarded. The new Secretary of the N.U.M., Lawrence Daly, is well aware of this and will act accordingly.

The really disastrous episode when I was in America was when the dustmen staged an unofficial strike. Their union had been negotiating for 15s.; but they demanded, and got, 50s. The lesson will not be lost on any shop-steward. Jack Jones, the new General

---

* By-elections were held on October 30th in five safe Labour seats – Swindon, North Paddington, North Islington, the Gorbals and Newcastle-under-Lyme. Labour held all but one, Swindon, but with very much reduced majorities.

Secretary of the Transport and General Workers' Union, is working with his shop-stewards. His national executive is largely ignored. Whatever the polls may say, Robens says that in the mining villages, where he spends a lot of his time, there is no revival of pro-Labour feeling. This is not their Labour Party and they are not interested. Alf said there has been a great change in the House of Commons in the last ten years. There are now no businessmen and no sincere devoted trades union officials. The trades union members have been given a seat as a supplement to their pension. In return they vote as they are told.

Alf thought Ted is now obsessed with the thoughts of 10 Downing St – at least Alec Home was above that level. He doubts whether Ted will be a success; has no time for Wilson or Powell, but does not see anyone else. I told him I thought that under all the circumstances he would make the best available P.M., but I do not see how we get from here to there. He just laughed! I asked him why Wilson kept Barbara Castle as Minister of Labour, which is no post for a woman anyway. Moreover, her policy has been abandoned and she is persona non grata with the trades unions. He said she had made it clear she would only move to the Home Office or to whatever Dick Crossman now calls himself – Health and Social Security. Neither Callaghan nor Crossman can be moved, so for Barbara it is either Labour or the sack. But to put her on the back benches would leave Wilson with a dangerous rallying point on his Left – so she stays. Robens thought Marsh had been dismissed because Wilson saw in him a potential rival. Anyway Marsh had had no suspicion of the way Wilson's mind was working and thought when summoned to 10 Downing St that if anything he would be offered promotion.

Robens said that owing to mistakes made by the C.E.G.B.* and by the Government over atomic power, the coal industry was now inevitably on its way out. No new pit had been dug for ten years and in spite of a new coal-mining Bill on which Robens had not been consulted he thought the British coal-mining industry was facing a decline which could not now be reversed. No such decision had ever been made but it was the long-term result of a lot of short-term decisions.

* Central Electricity Generating Board.

He asked me if I had seen Freeman when in Washington. I said I had told the *Mirror* people who had arranged my programme that I did not wish to see him. Nevertheless he had asked me to lunch and had been very friendly. I also said the *Washington Star* people told me he was doing well. Some months ago Freeman told Robens that since the day he went to Delhi he had only had three conversations with Wilson. This makes the appointment to Washington even more extraordinary. If Freeman was not a real buddy of Wilson's what was the motive for an otherwise inexplicable appointment?

Alf said Maurice Allen is convinced that the Government's favourable balance of payment figures are faked.

Alf also said that the motor manufacturers are pricing their cars on the supposition that they will lose a month a year in stoppages of one kind or another.

Friday, October 31st, 1969

Lunch yesterday for Jo Grimond. He made a few points of interest. (1) That the election, when it comes, will be a matter of life or death for Wilson and Heath. Defeat is likely to put an end to their leadership. (2) Heath makes a great mistake in the House of putting on his front bench young men who may in time become junior ministers. In Jo's opinion 'old sweats' like Duncan Sandys and Boyd-Carpenter would be much more effective Opposition spokesmen and critics. If Heath takes office he doesn't need to put them in his Government. (3) Seen from his (Jo's) constituency, so much of Government activity seems to be imposing unnecessary overheads. A grocer in Kirkwall has now to pay a training levy: he has had final notices from two quite different training boards, neither of which could under any circumstances be of any help to him. Kirkwall has now got a welfare director on top of three welfare officers. There are also a music adviser, youth officers, etc. etc., who are unnecessary or useless, and only add to the acute shortage of office staff. Though the unemployment rate in the Orkneys is nominally 8 per cent, everyone complains they are desperately short of labour. (4) Jo thought Heath would do well to have around him some figures from outside politics – people who are influential in the business world.

Monday, November 3rd, 1969

Dick Marsh to lunch. In the recent Cabinet changes he was dismissed from the Ministry of Transport and only half-heartedly offered a Ministership of State in his previous department (at least I think it was in his previous department). He had no idea he was in any danger though he had hardly spoken to Wilson for four months. It is nearly a month since he lost his job but he is still obviously badly shaken. Ministers under these circumstances are treated without courtesy or consideration. On the day he is out of office he loses his car, his secretary, his salary and his room. No firm would treat an ex-employee so scurvily. Marsh put his dismissal down to the hostility and intrigues of Barbara Castle – furious with the changes Marsh made in the transport Bill which she had introduced. Marsh said Barbara is much nearer the P.M. than anyone else; the second nearest just now, most unexpectedly, is Denis Healey!

I asked what was the point of putting Fuel and Power, Technology, Trade and the D.E.A. all in one ministry, and under Tony Benn at that. Marsh said this and the arrangement under which Crosland is overlord of Local Government, Housing and Transport (but with no real authority apparently) were dreamt up by Wilson who only took into his confidence two senior civil servants. I cannot believe either of these recommended an agglomeration of responsibilities which no one man could carry. Marsh, in talking about his removal from Transport, pointed out to Wilson that he was about to launch the very complicated ports Bill.* It is long – over a hundred clauses – and both complicated and difficult. In his absence neither under-secretary was capable of piloting the Bill through the House. Wilson's response was to transfer Carmichael, one of the under-secretaries, to an exactly equivalent job in another ministry. So now Mulley, not the brightest of men, has to handle a Bill of which neither he nor his under-secretary knows anything. Wilson said he thought it would be all right as Mulley had three weeks before the second reading! Marsh thought a big department like Transport or Fuel and Power would take a minister two years to get acquainted

---

* The Bill to establish the National Ports Authority to take over all docks and harbours handling more than 5 million tons per year, whether privately owned, owned by local authorities or already nationalized.

289

with. It is only from then on that he would be effective. I doubt whether two years is long enough. However, Marsh did not have two years in either job.

I said there is a suspicion that, regardless of the public interest, Wilson will not keep a minister in a job long enough to make a mark; that constant musical chairs leaves him almost alone as the constant factor, enhancing his prestige and reducing everyone else's. Marsh thought this might very well be true. But he said Heath was no better: that Mrs Thatcher had held seven jobs in Heath's Shadow administration since he became leader – four of them in the last eighteen months.

I tried to cheer Dick up by saying Wilson's approval or otherwise would have no long-term validity: in fact his departure from the Wilson circle might be to his advantage. Politics would not remain in their present groove for ever and he is young enough to play his part in future changes. He was not to be cheered and evidently thinks the present political set-up will be continued unchanged into the distant future. I said either we curb the present inflationary wage awards – or we don't. The former would require autocratic measures. The latter would lead to wild inflation and economic collapse and the same political result. But I could not get Marsh beyond the point that with our present style of Government it is impossible to keep the unions in order. He said that at the time of the seamen's strike the Government was determined to make an issue of it and fight the strike to a finish, but it proved so damaging to the balance of payments that the Government had had to back down. Marsh said he had voted for the confrontation but he now saw he was wrong. Whether the Government was right or wrong to bring on a confrontation at that time, this is the kind of fight no government can afford to lose.

Marsh has been offered a directorship of G.K.N.* which he had to turn down as they are large subscribers to Conservative Party funds. He has also been offered a seat on the board of Rotaflex, a quoted company but much smaller, which he will accept. He is much bothered by the lack of a secretary and of money. His wife, mercifully, can type, but he is doing some journalistic jobs to earn a few

* Guest, Keen and Nettlefolds Group of Companies.

guineas and while doing that he cannot think out the serious speeches he ought to be making. He feels the need for a research assistant but I think the real difficulty is a lack of education, though obviously the lack of facilities for anyone not in office is a factor, too.

Tuesday, November 4th, 1969

Peter Carrington to lunch. I have met him several times before but this was the first sustained conversation. He is not a big man or a forceful or creative one, but he is an excellent human being and as such has good judgment. But his outstanding characteristic, which shines out from him, is his niceness. There is no nicer man anywhere – honest, honourable, reliable. He spoke up most warmly about Whitelaw for whom he has a great admiration (as I have). He thinks Heath is doing better both in the House and on television. He thinks he may prove to be a great P.M. even if a thought too dictatorial. Like others he speaks of Enoch with distaste but without, so it seems to me, an adequate sense of his importance – at least under some circumstances.

Carrington thought the most disastrous single event in Wilson's administration was his acceptance of defeat by the trades unions. The complete chaos caused in the administration by the constant changes of ministers and ministries does not seem to have made any serious impact on these Tory leaders.

Thursday, November 6th, 1969

Geoffrey Rippon to lunch yesterday; Laurence Scott today. Laurence Scott had hardly any news and is in fact largely retired. He said he thought *The Times* was losing nearly £2 million a year and that these losses had meant economies at the *Sunday Times* which were far from popular.

Geoffrey Rippon is now Shadow Minister of Defence. He clearly regards this as promotion from his previous slot, which I think was Housing and Local Government. He said in passing that Johnson said the Americans had 50,000 tons of T.N.T. equivalent for every man, woman and child in the world, while the Russians had only 20,000 tons. This is a souped-up version of what Denis Healey told me. Rippon also said that the British were in a position to destroy with rockets 100 million Russians or Americans and in addition we had bombers which could do further damage. Rippon is a nice man – big, solid, reliable and able. He has no enthusiasm and no foresight that I have ever noticed. I can see him in some heavyweight administrative office but not one where any charisma is required. He, too, tended to belittle Enoch Powell. They all look at his potentiality *now*, which is not the point. His importance will come, if it comes at all, after a crisis of some kind in which the existing leaders of the Conservatives have proved ineffective.

Sunday, November 9th, 1969

The Oswald Mosleys to dine last night – at his suggestion (or, to be exact, hers). He seems to be in touch with various personages on the Continent and here; is certain that a major crash is coming; and is concerned to organize appropriate steps to contain the consequences. He assumes that the Americans will pull out of Europe and considers that there is a grave danger of serious disturbance in Western Europe, organized to provide the Russians with an excuse to intervene. He is still very much the professional soldier at heart and confident he still has a part to play. *Can* this be so?

Monday, November 10th, 1969

Lunch today for William Whitelaw. He started by talking of a lunch at the House of Commons for Annenberg, the American Ambassador, who is uneducated to the point of illiteracy. Whitelaw says Ted Heath was good at the Party Conference,* though the chairman, one Crossman of Watney-Mann, the brewery, was the worst chairman in living memory. Ted was even funny. Wilson's speech at the debate on the opening of Parliament was so bad as to cause a lot of speculation on the reason. Whitelaw now accepts the virtual certainty that the Conservatives will win the election. In the meantime he expects the trades unions to get increasingly out of hand, so that when the Tories do take over their first task will be to overhaul the emergency powers and to look for an occasion to take on the trades unions and put them in their place. He was confident that Wilson

---

* Held in Brighton from October 8th to 11th.

would have got his way over the trades union legislation if he had stood firm and made it a matter of confidence – 'either support me or I dissolve'. Rupert Murdoch apparently had a long talk with him at Chequers over the relevant weekend when Wilson held forth on his determination to show who was Prime Minister – it was the very next day that he caved in!

I asked about Crossman and his pension scheme, at one time thought to be a vote-winner but now suspected of being a vote-loser. The trouble is apparently that Crossman has become bored with the whole thing, as he was over Parliamentary reform when he was Leader of the House.

Tuesday, November 11th, 1969

Dinner last night with Maurice Allen at the Reform Club. He is as charming as ever but I thought he looked older: his approaching enforced retirement perhaps casting its shadow before.

Last time I saw him he said things had improved from the first three calendar months of this year, but that there was no chance of the Chancellor's forecast of a surplus of £300 million for the financial year being realized. Since then a number of unexpected things have happened and now the expectation for the current fiscal year is for a surplus of £350 million. Imports have been unexpectedly low: perhaps the import deposit scheme had more effect than was thought earlier. The level of trade in Germany, France and Italy was maintained at a higher level than was expected and even for this higher level the volume of imports was unexpectedly high: 25 per cent up into Germany, 20 per cent into France. Without any warning and for no obvious reason our exports in the last few months of 'mechanical engineering' (which is machines but not motor-cars) has risen by 9 per cent. Invisibles again, for no very obvious reasons, have been going great guns and finally there have been a number of rather freak capital transactions which add up to a further credit of £200 million. Exports to the United States have stayed level at a high rate, but the real bonus has come from exports to Continental Europe and, to a lesser extent, the sterling area.

None of this affects the long-term outlook which remains as it was – that if Government expenditure remains as high as it is and if wage increases go ahead at the rate they are, then the destruction of the currency is ultimately inevitable. After the collapse of the Government's trades union legislation, demands for more money have become more insistent and unprincipled than ever. So far, little of this has shown up in retail sales, but in time these increases are bound to work through to the retail trade where they will show up in increased volume and rising prices. But it is impossible to say when this will happen. Maurice thinks the present conglomeration of favourable factors so improbable that in time an equal and opposite set of factors is likely to emerge that will cancel out what is happening now.

Wednesday, November 12th, 1969

Aubrey Jones to lunch yesterday. He had no great news as his board is now more or less inoperative. He asked if he should resign and go to I.P.C. as soon as possible or work out his contract to the end of March. I advised him to move as soon as possible. We talked a bit about I.P.C. It is widely believed he was invited there under pressure from the Institutions. This may well be so but it did not appear to be with his knowledge.

Stonehouse to lunch today. He is very good-looking, very inexperienced, and also shy and suspicious. However, we got on quite well. I asked him why the new appointment for Benn, which includes a greater area of responsibility than it is possible for any one man to cover. He said Benn is one of the most persuasive and articulate of all the ministers in committee, has had the idea for some time of becoming a Minister for Industry, and eventually got Wilson to see eye to eye with him. Stonehouse clearly thought the agglomeration of responsibilities far too big. He went on to say he had put forward the idea in a discussion at *The Times* that government should be by men chosen for their ability not for their political complexion. This view had been supported by one Wood, presumably the M.P. son of Lord Halifax. They discovered that you can move the dispatch box to the Bar of the House and then a minister could become answerable to the House without being a member of it. I cannot believe Stonehouse would air such views if they were his alone, and the ideas themselves are encouraging.

Sunday, November 16th, 1969

No particular political news these last few days but some Fleet Street gossip. Lunching with Rupert Murdoch on Thursday and having Robin Gill to dine on Friday and my son Colin on Saturday, this is what I picked up.

Gill left A.T.V. because of the hostility around when he refused to sign a seven-year contract. But he is a very nice man and extremely able so he had no doubt that he would have appropriate offers. I must say I was surprised – as doubtless he was – when he was offered the chairmanship (or anyway the position of chief executive) in Debenham's, Lucas, Davey-Ashmore and I.P.C. He had already resisted the strongest pressure to take over the management of Pergamon. He was not too explicit, but implied that he was in close tough with Rothschild's and Lazard's – perhaps also Schroder Wagg. These merchant banks are alarmed at the mismanagement of I.P.C., and intend to mobilize the Institutions to bring about changes at the top. This is not surprising, but what does surprise me is that Gill – much as I like and admire him – should have the offer of four such large and important companies. It does illustrate the forlorn state of management in British commerce and industry. Gill seemed inclined to let the situation ripen for three to six months before moving. Rupert Murdoch says the *Mirror*'s colour supplement on Wednesdays is losing £80,000 per week. Ruth had some talk on the telephone with Vere Harmsworth who also expatiated on the subject of chaos at I.P.C.

Gill met Roy Jenkins at dinner about ten days ago and said he was utterly relaxed and appeared not to have a care in the world. Gill thought this good public relations, but I should have thought caution a wiser line.

It is reported in the papers that Wilson's visit to Washington is deferred to 1970. In January he announced he was going in March, but no invitation came. Further hints since then have proved unproductive as Nixon knows full well that Wilson only wants to visit Washington to improve his political image here.

Monday, November 17th, 1969

Lunch for —— [a senior civil servant]. He greeted me with the question 'What mischief are you up to?', and ended by saying that the difficulty of lunching with me was that the conversation could go on indefinitely. We talked about Ted Heath, Enoch Powell, the American situation, etc. etc., but he did not tell me anything I did not know. At one point he asked who I thought the customers of Claridge's restaurant were. I said they were mainly tourists. He said was I happy that some people were so much richer than others. I said it had been thus since the beginning of recorded history. He said he was rather pleased about the dustmen whose union had asked for a rise of 15s. per week but who had themselves demanded, and got, 50s. It was an example of the worm turning. I said I thought it was disastrous as the dustmen's increase had led to the firemen's increase, and now the teachers were up in arms in the middle of a contract period. The dustmen had given the green light and there would be no containing fresh wage demands. I said I thought the abandonment of the Government's wages policy was a disaster. The battle would have to be fought again and next time the unions would be even more intransigent. —— did not disagree with any of this – or at any rate did not show any disagreement. He brought up the man Lindsay, just re-elected Mayor of New York. I said he was an attractive personality but said to be a poor administrator. He said administration was a secondary function and surely he could hire someone to do his administration for him – as Enoch might need to do. I said the administrative scene in this country was a flat barren plain with no eminences. He did not disagree with this.

He was very sorry that Edward Boyle had left politics for the vice-chancellorship of Leeds University. I said his colleagues thought his ceiling was to be Minister of Education and, if this were so, what was wrong with a vice-chancellorship? —— said he thought Boyle would make a good chancellor of the exchequer and even prime minister: that his colleagues underestimate him, but that quality will always be recognized in the end. In view of the lack of quality in nearly all our politicians – notably Wilson – I didn't know what to say to this.

Friday, November 21st, 1969

Arnold Weinstock to lunch. I have known him and admired him since he first became managing director of G.E.C. His themes today were: (1) anarchy in industry and (2) anarchy at Winchester where his son is at school. The original Government legislation was for curbs on wage increases with a few sweeteners thrown in. The curbs have been abandoned but the quid pro quo has not.

He says that if a factory is stopped work because of a strike in another factory then the wages of the employees in the first factory must be paid. If there is a strike at Girling's brake factory and Leyland's are stopped then Leyland's employees must be paid. This will force Leyland's to insist that Girling's pay whatever increase is demanded. Wage inflation, as he said, has hitherto been allowed, now it will be compulsory. Incidentally when 300 men at Girling's did go on strike on a Friday, on the Monday 146 of them secured medical certificates and drew £18 per week wage-related benefits. If strikes are to be subsidized in this fashion, it is difficult to see where or when it will all end.

Weinstock is thrilled over a new invention which is about 80 per cent definite. Instead of copper wire they have developed aluminium wire with a very thin copper surface. As electric current is carried on the surface of a wire, this will behave like a copper wire but be much cheaper.

On the trades union leaders, Weinstock said Clive Jenkins has the gift of the gab in a big way. Cannon is said by everyone to be the ablest of the lot. W. said you could talk business with Scanlon but he does not control his executive, so you have no assurance that any deal with him will be implemented. Jack Jones ignores his executive and takes his orders from his shop-stewards.

Monday, November 24th, 1969

Ray Gunter to lunch – what a charming man he is! He finds in his Welsh valleys disapproval of the so-called liberal legislation. He had begged Gardiner to allow abortion reform to get forgotten before the Bill legalizing homosexuality was brought in, but Gardiner would not listen. Law and order is becoming increasingly a source of un-easiness among his friends in the party, and many trades unionists (and more wives) are fed up with constant wild-cat strikes. He said this Government can do nothing about wage claims, nor can Wilson in a new government, if he wins the election. He confirmed that

Wilson decided to fight the seamen's strike to a finish but found it too expensive and gave up. The fight to a finish was made in the teeth of Ray's advice, who was at the time Minister of Labour. Ray thinks a new Tory government would have to call the trades union movement to order at once. Whatever they decide to do must be finished within the first eighteen months. He said the Tories had an excellent report in 1964 for coping with the trades unions but took fright and ran away from it. I gather it was never published.

On a personal note he said that when he had left the Government, he met Mary Wilson in the Scilly Isles. In the course of conversation she laid her hand on his arm and said she knew nothing of the disagreement between him and Harold but that he must remember that Harold was a very lonely man. He said in the House of Commons and in Cabinet Wilson is immensely clever, playing off one group against another: look what he has done to the left wing – uses them to get into power and when he has got in, pursues a policy that is anathema to them and yet keeps their support. Constant changes of ministers, which Ray called 'stirring the pot', is a deliberate policy to prevent any minister acquiring any separate reputation. Ray said his removal from the Ministry of Labour was because he was becoming too popular with the trades unions. He complained that ministers can never see Harold alone; a civil servant or Marcia Williams is always summoned. If by chance the P.M. is alone he agrees with everything his visitor says. This is a quick way of getting rid of him and means nothing. When Ray complained to other ministers both Roy Jenkins and Dick Crossman said they had the same experience. Ray says the reason is that Wilson is terrified of any confrontation with a minister on policy.

I said Lady Bolton was startled when sitting next to Peart (now Leader of the House) at dinner to listen to a long tirade against Wilson. She had never met Peart before. Ray said his hostility to Wilson is notorious.

Wednesday, November 26th, 1969

Dinner last night with the Plowdens; present Reay Geddes, —— [a senior civil servant] and a Tory ex-M.P. whose name I did not catch. During dinner I had a long conversation with Lady Plowden – an excellent woman, able, intelligent, forceful and cultured, of whom far greater use should have been made in public life. We talked about all manner of things. She wondered why her daughters read trashy books and magazines for their happy endings. She said that in future there would be no intelligent, educated women, they had to spend too much time on household chores and anyway a lot of the culture of the last century depended on weekend house-parties which were no longer possible. She thought the academics had cut themselves off from real life and produced paper plans quite unrelated to the practical possibilities.

When the ladies retired I had some talk with Reay and we afterwards joined in with the others at a point when Plowden said we should not get out of our present difficulties without shooting. ——, instead of saying he hoped not, pooh-poohed the whole idea. He said the country was in good shape, money was plentiful, employment was good, old age was being provided for. I remained mainly silent while the others put the position as they saw it at Dunlop and Tube Investments. They both impressed on ——, who apparently found it difficult to believe, that it is impossible for any private industry to stand up to the trades unions. It can only be done by the Government – who incidentally are both the largest and the weakest of the employers. Geddes pointed out that Rootes had tried standing up to the unions and but for the support of Chrysler would now be bankrupt. It is always hard with these top civil servants to infer whether they are putting forward the Government point of view, whistling in the dark to keep their spirits up – or saying what they really think.

Friday, December 5th, 1969

Drinks yesterday evening with Ted Heath in the Albany. Of general impressions the following were the most obvious. (1) Ted has been slimming. He looks a smaller and a nicer man. Any idea that he could master the dangerous situation ahead of us seemed to me out of the question. (2) Reggie Maudling, friendly as ever, has given up. (3) Willie Whitelaw was as friendly as ever, but Ruth did not recognize him. He has, she says, undergone a transformation and is now a leader. (4) Amery was there. How does anyone attach any importance to this unattractive little man ?

299

Ted is off to Australia to take part in some Australian sailing races. Meanwhile as Leader of the Opposition he hardly registers. It was left to Enoch to denounce the teachers' strike in appropriate terms. I think Ted should be here providing leadership, not playing about in Australia.

I had some talk with Frank Kearton who seemed to me, as usual, a very woolly-minded man. He says the squeeze is taking great effect, and that Courtaulds have difficulty in getting their bills paid even by their biggest customers. So sticky is the situation that he is spending a disproportionate amount of time collecting debts.

His point of view, which was generally favourable to the Government, was in direct contrast with that of Kenneth Keith, who was alarmed over the wage increases, which are large and widespread. He had recently had some talk with Wilson at dinner and said it is quite impossible to have any real discussion with him. His conversation is a long monologue of self-justification, aimed apparently more at bolstering up his own self-esteem than at convincing the man he is talking to.

Willie Whitelaw and Reggie Maudling think Wilson is contemplating a spring election, using the improvement in our balance of payments and the Common Market as the election-winning themes. The Conservative Party is committed to the Common Market, so Wilson would capture a measure of support if he said he would only enter if the move meant no increase in the price of food. I cannot myself see that a cautiously anti-Market stand would win an election. However, that is the thinking among leading Conservatives now.

I said I thought Wilson would not call an election unless he *knew* he would win. A certain year in 10 Downing St is better than a doubtful five years and I could not see how he could be sure of winning. The Wellingborough by-election today shows a 10 per cent swing to the Conservatives, which would mean a Conservative majority of a hundred and fifty in an election. If he had any foresight Wilson would play for a defeat, leaving the Conservatives to incur the odium for all the measures that will have to be taken to straighten out the situation left behind by Labour. However, that would not be Wilson's way.

Later, dinner with the Weinstocks, whom we like, in part to meet

Annenberg, the new American Ambassador. He is often represented as little better than a buffoon. This is quite unfair. He is an able publisher who has made a great success of *Seventeen* and of *T.V. Guide*, and has recently sold the *Philadelphia Enquirer* to Jack Knight for £23 million. I should imagine he knows nothing of foreign affairs and very little indeed about this country, but he intends to try conscientiously to be a worthy representative of the U.S.A. in these parts and should have some success. He is no David Bruce, but then he is a totally different kind of person with success in quite other fields.

Saturday, December 6th, 1969

A further point from my talk with Kenneth Keith yesterday. He said he did not know where the Government got their figures for invisible earnings. They could only be guessed at, so he did not take the alleged dramatic improvement very seriously.

Wednesday, December 10th, 1969

Had a few words with Mike before going on to a big drinks party with Joe Hyman. Mike was present when a C.B.I. deputation met Barbara Castle about her impending White Paper. This exerts a good deal of pressure against price increases but none against wage increases. Mike said it was very noticeable that while Barbara expounded her case, none of her officials backed her in any way. This is most unusual and indicated to Mike a distaste for her policy and a dislike for her personality.

At Joe Hyman's were all and sundry: no particular news. Charles Clore was there. Rees-Mogg looked thinner, and more worried; Lee Howard, the *Mirror* editor, looked thinner and less worried. He thought the *Sun* would continue to do badly. It is currently selling about 1,200,000. The *Mirror* is not noticeably affected and the *Sketch* has only a small loss. He knew nothing about the *Mirror* colour supplement, alleged by Murdoch to be losing £80,000 a week.

Friday, December 12th, 1969

The announcement that Dick Beeching is to be the new chairman of Redland Ltd was made this week. I said to Reay Geddes that this seemed rather small fry, but Geddes said he found Dick a marvellous analyst but doubted his constructive ability, and thought perhaps I.C.I. were right to reject him as their chairman. This sounds to me like Reay speaking for the establishment, as he was indifferent to the ejection of Joe Hyman as chairman of Viyella two days ago. Whatever faults Joe may have – and I can well believe he is hard to work with– he has drive and enthusiasm, two rare virtues in the British world of today.

Monday, December 15th, 1969

—— [a senior civil servant] to lunch. I asked him why the Government is persisting with the meaningless remnants of their trades union legislation. He said the best comment on this was Wilson's, who said that Barbara was like a mother with a dead baby – she wouldn't believe it was dead!

On recent Government changes, —— said the final outcome was quite different from the original plan – for instance until the last moment Peter Shore was to go, but Wilson could not summon up the courage actually to sack him. Barbara was offered Tony Crosland's job but refused it.

He said he thought Roy Jenkins was doing well. He has kept expenditure under control by threatening increases of taxation if any additional expenditure is incurred. He has good relations with Wilson who doesn't bother about the Treasury details but backs Roy.

I asked —— why Marsh had gone. He said it was due to 'insufficient reverence' towards Wilson. Marsh was regarded as a serious loss by his departmental chiefs. His successor, Mulley, —— described as a mere party hack.

Wednesday, December 17th, 1969

There has been a great debate on capital punishment – now abolished 'for ever'.* In the teeth of a public opinion 85 per cent in favour of the death penalty and a rising tide of violent crime, the decision seems

* Capital punishment had been suspended in 1965 for an experimental period of five years. The motion to make the abolition permanent was carried on December 16th in a free vote in the House of Commons by 343 to 185. In the House of Lords on December 17th–18th an amendment to continue the temporary suspension till 1973 was defeated by 220 votes to 174.

absurd. Like so many of these so-called liberal reforms it will doubtless be reversed in due course.

A call on Leslie O'Brien this afternoon. I had not seen him for some months. He was extremely friendly and answered all my questions. He did not comment on the changes in the Court, but this was the picture he presented. On our balance of payments, the situation is better than he hoped for a year ago. The improvement is mainly due to a 15 per cent improvement of world trade in which we have held our share. This was likely to fall off to a 10 per cent improvement or less in 1970. Though we are inflating so are other countries and our competitive position is therefore still strong. In the longer term the Germans will not allow their currency to depreciate as much as ours. I said the dire consequences internally of serious inflation would not be modified by the thought that other countries were in similar plight. He said a Labour Government did not seem concerned by the effect of inflation in altering the relevant affluence of different classes. I said they should, as it was the ruin of the middle classes by inflation that had brought in Hitler.

O'Brien is worried by wage inflation. Wilson assured him that to make wage agreements enforceable, contracts would not work – and gave as part of the reason the concessions his Government had recently given to men put out of work by strikes!

He had had a recent talk with the new Governor of the Bank of France who seemed mildly optimistic. Both O'Brien and Carli (at the Italian Central Bank) are unhappy about the political outlook in Italy. A coup of some sort is becoming increasingly likely.

There has been a large and continuing outflow of reserves from Germany. It has gone much further than was expected and is due to a desire to enjoy the high rates available in the Eurodollar market. This high rate again is due to the American banks trying to counteract the squeeze at home by borrowing Eurodollars at these high rates.

The gilt-edged market had been giving no trouble for some months though he wondered what would happen when the tax-gatherer got busy next month. He said Jenkins would be under great pressure to loosen the purse-strings in an election year and might be compelled to do so. This would add to the inflationary effects of wage increases and start imports on their way upwards. Recently imports

303

have kept fairly steady: investment is too low but not so low as seemed likely a few months ago; prices have not risen much and he thought the recent increase in wages would not work through the economy into prices before the end of 1970. Other opinions that have reached me are that this will happen by June.

1970

Saturday, January 3rd, 1970

Dinner last night with Sigmund Warburg. I have a great affection and respect for him, though I find his views on people hard to follow. He thinks the West is going downhill in every way and that in about twenty years' time the world will be taken over by the Chinese and Japanese working together. This opinion seemed to be based on his impressions of the United States rather than the United Kingdom, and he obviously thought more favourably of contemporary Germany than the U.K. However, he would put us ahead of both the Italians and the French, whose societies he described as 'very sick'.

He thought there would be an election in September which Labour would lose. He thought Heath would be a worse P.M. than Wilson and that after an interval – round about 1972–3 – there would be a coalition under Wilson. He thought Powell resembled the German party that in the 'thirties was to the right of the Nazis. In any case he thought Powell's outlook very German, very intellectual, and quite unpractical. He thought Denis Healey might emerge; spoke highly of Barbara Castle and thought Wilson was 'learning'. I see no signs whatever of the latter. He said Wilson was so much better informed than Heath – and this may well be so.

We went on to talk of Joe Hyman, who sounds even more of a bull in a china shop than I thought. After the original deal between I.C.I. and Viyella he offered to join the I.C.I. board and straighten out its management! He made the same offer to Sigmund and to Jacob Rothschild! Ruth said surely he is like a young puppy, full of ill-organized, ill-considered energy. Sigmund would have none of this.

He had just returned from Israel, where he had been four times in 1969. He thought the present state of undeclared war would continue. He said that if the Arabs would recognize the State of Israel, the Israelis would make great territorial sacrifices. They apparently attach immense importance to this recognition.

Sigmund made the rather surprising comment that while Israeli agriculture, science and defence were first-class, their business organizations were 'sloppy' beyond words.

Thursday, January 15th, 1970

Just leaving for Lagos after four days in Accra. It seems I had not been in Ghana for seven years and much had happened in the meantime. Then, the Akosombo dam was under construction; Tema port was receiving its first ship; Nkrumah was in power. Now the dam is complete with its four generators and two are to be added; the aluminium smelter is working to full capacity; Tema is a booming industrial town; Busia is the newly elected Prime Minister; Nkrumah is in exile in Guinea, all hope of return to Ghana gone; his Egyptian wife has divorced him and lives with her children in Cairo.

I think the main impression Ghana gives after so long is of great prosperity. The country's debts may be huge but the economy is booming. One of the first acts of the newly elected Busia Government was to order the expulsion of all immigrants within fourteen days. It was then revealed to ministers that the gold mines, the cocoa crop, and much else, depended on foreign labour, so the regulation has been modified; but will Ghanaians undertake the heavy manual labour they have hitherto been glad to leave to foreigners – mostly from Upper Volta and Mali?

The only man of importance I met on this visit was Bawa Yakubu, the Chief of Police, a very tough northerner. He was a member of the National Liberation Council which ruled the country before the recent elections. It sounds as if the rule of the N.L.C. was more competent and less corrupt than that of the politicians is likely to be. Yakubu is apparently incorruptible and determined that his police should be the same. At home he is a prince of the Dagomba, much given to his people's traditional dances.

Friday, January 16th, 1970

I began the day by calling on Colonel Johnson, the military governor of Lagos. He is a tall powerful man of only thirty-two, though he looks more. General Gowon made an excellent statement last night – the most magnanimous of any victor in any civil war I ever read about. There are to be no reprisals and all federal employees are to be invited back to their old jobs. There had been a current of feeling that Gowon had been too conciliatory and if the war had not ended this year he might have been removed; but with total surrender, he is supreme.

But to return to Colonel Johnson – a man of integrity and force of character who completely dwarfs anyone we have in public life. He was indignant that the B.B.C. had broadcast four times a silly statement by Ojukwu that he would return, while omitting General Gowon's pronouncement. The latter was issued late but was important; the former was mere verbiage, since one man can implement his views, the other cannot.

Yesterday we lunched with Dr Biobaku and his wife. He is Vice-Chancellor of Lagos University and showed us around some of the buildings. I had met him before and judge him to be one of the most intelligent men I have ever met. I met him first when he was Secretary of the Cabinet and then when he was Registrar of Ibadan University. And of course he is just the man for his present job, intelligent, able, charming and devout. I didn't realize till today that his integrity depends on the fact that he is a devout Moslem. His wife is intelligent and charming with a spiritual quality which he may not possess. I did not know she was a Moslem and only heard she was a Hajja* after we left the house. The idea that the white man is in any way superior to the black man is dispelled by meeting men like Biobaku and Johnson who are head and shoulders bigger, better, abler men than their opposite numbers in the U.K.

Saturday, January 17th, 1970

Last night we had a buffet supper with Dr Elias, the Attorney-General, and a number of Africans, lawyers, judges and civil servants. He looks rather stupid but talks well and must be fairly indispensable as he has been Attorney-General in a succession of regimes over a number of years. There has been only a short intermission when he refused to serve with General Ironsi.

Here they believe that Ojukwu and his Ibos intended to take over the whole of Nigeria. When this was seen to be impossible Ojukwu would have settled for the sovereign independence of the Eastern

* Someone who has made the pilgrimage to Mecca.

309

Region. But when it became clear that the non-Ibos in the East would not accept this, there was really nothing left to fight for, as Ibo-land by itself is not a viable entity. Ojukwu's publicity put out by Markpress from Geneva undoubtedly helped to prolong the war to no one's advantage. Elias told me the Ibo negotiators said that Ojukwu had received £2 million from the French a few days before he fled and that he had this money in his possession when he left. They also speak of thirty tons of luggage and a white Mercedes car, though it is not clear how all this could have been got out with nineteen people in a Super-Constellation.

Thursday, January 22nd, 1970

In Benin – after a long drive from Ibadan (about 250 miles). I had expected the road to be blocked with military and relief traffic to Asaba. But this proved not to be the case. We saw one bullet-riddled lorry cab by the roadside and not another sign of war except for the bridges. One had been destroyed by an Ibo before secession (who afterwards accidentally blew himself up in the Federal Palace Hotel at Lagos) and two others had been blown by the Federal troops in their initial withdrawal.

Saturday, January 24th, 1970

Back in Lagos after an early start from Benin. General Gowon had brought forward my appointment with him from Monday, so we left at six so as to be certainly in time for Gowon at noon. We eventually saw him at 12.15 and he kept us for an hour. He could not have been more friendly. He ended by bringing us his two-month-old son Ibrahim to see. Gowon is evidently an entirely honest and religious man. He sincerely believes in a policy of reconciliation and is desperately hurt to find that the false and tendentious statements by Ojukwu have consistently better coverage in the world's press than his own sincere and truthful ones. I have myself found this discrepancy hard to understand – how much more difficult for him. At home politicians continue to belly-ache about the relief arrangements here. Doubtless they are not perfect, but the Nigerians quite rightly are quite determined to manage their own affairs in their own way. The thing that has surprised people about developments in the East is that practically all the top brass, military and other, in Biafra have turned up alive and well. If there was any heavy fighting it did not affect the higher-ups. This has surprised everyone from Gowon down. The people here claim that the suffering among the refugees is mostly on the part of the non-Ibos. The Ibos look all right and in some cases have emerged with their cars and sped to Lagos.

The future of the Biafran officers has not been decided but they will not be shot, though on the other hand they will mostly not be reinstated. Ojukwu has turned up in the Ivory Coast where he is to be allowed to stay provided he ceases all political activity. One wonders whether the Ivory Coast Government really means to enforce this condition.

Yesterday we went to Agbor where many of the people are western Ibos, though they prefer to call themselves something else. The Obi, a pleasant young man, gave us a figure of Christ with a sheep – rather good wood-carving for a small town in the bush. He afterwards gave us a song and dance of a rather more vigorous kind than is usual in Nigeria. There was no sign of war or even mild tension. The only thing I commented on was the very poor state of the rubber plantations. I was told that the tappers and estate workers were Ibos and had fled so that no work had been done on most of the plantations for two years or more. One of the villages was in the throes of its annual female circumcision ceremony. This is normally carried out on girls of fifteen or so, but the three little mites we saw coloured bright orange all over with camwood and with feather headdresses were about five and under. Perhaps they only played a part in the ceremony.

Monday, January 26th, 1970

Lunch today at the Metropolitan Club. One of the Africans present had been Zik's secretary when he was Governor-General. His wife is an Ibo and a cousin of Ojukwu. He told us that Ojukwu had received $20,000 'spending money' on his way to the Addis Ababa conference in December. This was given to him in the Ivory Coast but was supposedly from France. Gowon on Saturday said that Ojukwu's first plan was to add to the Eastern Region the belt of fertile land south of the Benue and north of the Eastern Region boundary, but

then later he had designs on the Middle West south of the Niger –
later perhaps on the whole region south of the Niger. The Nigerian
army at the outbreak of hostilities was only 8,000 and Ojukwu
attached little importance to these. Most of the young officers were
Ibos and he thought he could quickly build a more effective fighting
force. He seems to have suffered from poor information and wild
over-confidence.

Sunday, February 1st, 1970

Lunch with Norman Collins etc. at Radlett Place. Patrick Gordon
Walker is an old friend of his and has surprised Norman by his
attitude of extreme hostility to Wilson. [Nigel] Fisher said he over-
heard Patrick talking to Wilson in the House. Patrick asked who
would be to Wilson the most dangerous leader for the Tories. Wilson
'almost spat out the words' – Iain Macleod; but, he said, fortunately
for Labour the Tories would never have the sense to choose him.
This is, of course, Wilson once again thinking of politics purely in
Parliamentary terms.

Wednesday, February 4th, 1970

Alf Robens to lunch – very friendly and in great form. He said there
are atomic stations producing power at a higher cost than coal-fired
stations and the coal orders thus lost to the N.C.B. amount to 14
million tons. He says the enthusiasm for atomic power at the ministry
is not due to a cold-blooded estimate of its ability to provide cheap
power but because it gave their people an immense lift to tell the
world at power conferences that we produced more power from
atomic stations than the whole of the rest of the world put together.
This illustrates the real objection to nationalization. If a mistake is
made it is made over the whole field.

Monday, February 9th, 1970

Lunch with Kenneth Robinson, my first talk with him for a long time.
He is a very nice man and most friendly. He paid a new compliment
to Michael Stewart. He said he and Enoch Powell were the only two
speakers in the House whose speeches were always grammatical.
Everyone else has to have his grammar tidied up for *Hansard*.

I commented on the fact that when a minister is out, he is treated far more cavalierly than the executive of any business. He asked had I heard the story of Churchill and Horace Wilson? I had not. Apparently when Churchill took office in 1940, Horace Wilson (Chamberlain's *éminence grise*) had a room or flat on top of No. 10. Churchill told one of his aides to arrange about him relinquishing this accommodation. Wilson said he would be out in a fortnight. Churchill said, 'Tell that evil man that if he is not out by Friday I will make him Governor of the Falkland Islands.'

Saturday, February 21st, 1970

Last night in Birmingham, giving a political speech to the local Monday Club. They were professional people, the chairman a very able young barrister of twenty-seven, one of the women a doctor, another a solicitor. The woman who sat on one side of me at dinner told me she busied herself collecting money for the Conservative Party and it was made clear to her that the businessmen of Birmingham looked to Powell more than to Heath. One man said she could have a cheque for £5 for the Conservatives but £1,000 if it was for Enoch. She said the racial feeling in Birmingham is very ugly. She had a small accident because she was driving while painting her nails! The car she ran into was driven by a coloured man and immediately about twenty people collected including a policeman and accused the coloured man of causing the accident. She had some difficulty in convincing them that she was entirely to blame.

Friday, February 27th, 1970

Lunch today with Denis Hamilton. He said he had twice been pressed to take Bob Fraser's job at the I.T.A. I expressed astonishment that he should be offered a job so clearly inferior to his present one. He gave no reason why they thought he would consider the job. Denis had lunch with Wilson three weeks ago. Wilson expressed some gloom over the wage inflation but said that we were in good company in this. It is not likely to cause us balance-of-payments trouble this year. He did not seem to bother about the rise in prices later this year nor about next year. Denis also had lunch with Reggie Maudling within the last week. He said the Tories are determined to press

313

ahead with their trades union legislation immediately on taking office – unless they only scramble in with a very small majority. As Denis said, their idea of making trades union agreements enforceable contracts might have been introduced some years ago and would be respected now if this system had been in operation for a number of years, but he did not think it would be possible to introduce such a radical change now. Denis assumes that Wilson will hang on to the end – April next year.

Both at dinner last night and at lunch today when I ran into Norman Collins as well as lunching with Denis, the big job is the plight of I.P.C. What deep trouble they fell into – and how soon!

Tuesday, March 3rd, 1970

Rupert Murdoch to lunch. He claims that the *Sun* will be doing $1\frac{1}{2}$ million this week, taking 80,000 from the *Sketch* and 300,000 from the *Mirror*. If this is roughly true it is a considerable triumph. He says the *Mirror* is down to $4\frac{3}{4}$ million and that the *Daily Express* is doing very badly, though the *Sunday Express* is 'going from strength to strength' (his words).

He said that last summer he was at Chequers on Sunday for dinner. Other guests were Michael Berry and Max Aitken and perhaps he mentioned another. For five hours, from seven till midnight, Wilson held forth on the necessity of pushing through the trades union legislation even if it meant losing half his Cabinet. He said the crunch would come on Tuesday and then they would see who was master. The crunch did indeed come on Tuesday and Wilson it was who gave way.

Wages in Fleet St seem to be in more of a muddle than usual. Owing to 'productivity deals' the whole structure is completely haywire. Murdoch said some reel hands on the *Telegraph* get £71 for a nineteen hour week.

Wednesday, March 4th, 1970

Lunch today for Robin Gill. Such a nice man and so able. He came and dined with us some weeks ago to talk about a proposed takeover of I.P.C. in conjunction with Rothschild's and Lazard's. That came to nothing because of the Reed bid. He has now been offered the chairmanship of Staveley, the managing directorship of Debenham's, and also of Tesco at £60,000 a year! However, he does not want to be anyone's nominee but his own man. So he has formed with friends the 1970 Trust and so far has tried to impose his management on British Thermostat and Piccadilly Securities. In both cases he was overtaken by a bid before he had built up a large enough holding. However, he will have made a very handsome profit on both deals.

He is a non-executive director of Reed's and is in Don Ryder's confidence. He said the first approach was from Frank Rogers who came to see Ryder to say that I.P.C. was faced with imminent collapse unless Ryder and Reed's intervened. Ryder said he could do nothing unless invited by Cudlipp and the I.P.C. board. It was thought difficult to get any decision out of Cudlipp; however, he did come back some days later with Rogers and asked to be taken over. Terms were agreed and then were unanimously accepted by the I.P.C. board. Warburg's naturally were to work for Reed's and Kleinwort, Benson were brought in for I.P.C. They had to do something for their fee and hence the revised terms which, to my mind, were somewhat worse.

Gill is having a very interesting time and is reluctant to think of the wider political outlook, but the state of anarchy in industry has obviously not escaped his notice. He thinks like most people, that the election will be in a year's time and that the Tories will win, but everything from then on is entirely unforeseeable to him.

Saturday, March 7th, 1970

Lunch for Maudling yesterday. Intelligent and charming as usual but he has signed off. If events are to be turbulent in the period when his party is in office he will seek an embassy or the F.O.! He thought if the Tories get in with a sufficient majority, they may well tackle the unions seriously, but as usual with these Tories there was no sense of crisis or urgency.

Thursday, March 12th, 1970

William Whitelaw for lunch. He had no specific news but his points were as follows. (1) Wilson's entourage is really deplorable. Last night there was a lobby party to say goodbye to the P.A.* lobby man, who is retiring. The P.M. was there with Marcia Williams, Kaufman, Trevor Lloyd-Hughes, and two other even more junior members of the 10 Downing St staff. He apparently cannot carry on without their incessant flattery. (2) Whitelaw thinks if Wilson had an election this year he would win or lose by a small margin – say twenty-five seats. Next year he would have a much larger majority against him. (3) Whitelaw says Wilson is not interested in Government or in administration. He likes to have all sorts of trivial matters referred to him but is not interested in finding the answers. Labour representatives on unimportant international delegations have to be chosen or approved by the P.M. It is usually impossible to get an answer until the last moment. (4) Wilson's present plan is to run the election campaign on the basis of rip-roaring abuse of the Tories. Whitelaw thinks this may rally the faithful but will certainly not bring in any doubters. It will also still further discredit the politicians.

Friday, March 20th, 1970

Lunch with Robens at the Coal Board – in good form and most friendly. He has recently been offered the chairmanship of Cammell Laird. He is likely to stay at the Coal Board if he is invited. The money may be better elsewhere but the prestige is not so good. I thought he might do well to go at the end of a successful ten years rather than face the difficulties of the near future. He didn't seem to have looked ahead as far as this.

He is confident that the election will be in the autumn. Cabinet ministers expect it, though Tony Benn told him he expects Labour to lose. The argument is that Wilson may well lose in the autumn but would be head of a pretty large Parliamentary Party and this would be a good launching-pad for a return to office. If he stays on until April, Labour is likely to fare much worse. This is all on the assumption that Wilson has prospects of office in the future. If (as I believe) he has none, it might be well, from his point of view, for him to hang on to the bitter end.

Ted Heath sent for Alf a few days ago and they had a long talk about the Tory Party's plans for curbing the trades unions. Alf

* Press Association.

pointed out that employers will not sue their workmen or their employees' trades unions. The best course would be to allow 'out-relief' as a loan, to rebate any income tax due over the succeeding twelve months, and declare that an unofficial or illegal striker automatically loses his right to redundancy pay. Personally I cannot see that this would work under the very difficult times ahead of us. It would be too slow, though these and other similar measures might be appropriate in the final settlement. Alf thought that in the immediate future we should see an extension of the welfare state and soaring taxes. If the Tories do win the election and fail to cope with the ensuing crises, there will be an authoritarian regime of the Right. Enoch Powell, he thought, might play a part.

His opinion of the Bank of England falls steadily. Sidney Greene of the railwaymen's union is the new trades union member of the Court. He has no idea what it is all about. Alf thinks the Bank is now a branch of the Treasury and should cease to pretend to be anything else. Some of its activities are unnecessary and the non-executive directors play no useful part of any kind.

Wednesday, April 8th, 1970

Lunch yesterday for Jo Grimond. He seemed to me to have ceased kicking against the pricks. He thinks we are encountering a growing degree of anarchy; does not think Heath is capable of coping with the situation he will inherit; doubts if any government can curb the trades unions. Like others, he cannot envisage anything *really* unpleasant happening to us, but is quite sure there is no government in sight which would be tough enough to crush a general strike. In fact he was gloomy but assumed we should muddle through somehow.

Saturday, April 11th, 1970

Lunch for Dick Beeching yesterday. He said, 'I feel as if I was living in a vacuum: there is nothing even to kick against.' He had no particular news. He took a more favourable view than I do of the Tory plans for trades union legislation. He thought the General Secretaries are as keen to regain control of their members as the employers are to regain control of their labour. This would mean a lot of abuse from the trades union leaders but little action. I said I did not think the

317

shop-stewards would surrender their power without a struggle. Beeching agreed with this, thought the Government should be ready for a general strike but doubted if it would come to that. His main theme was the way politicians continue to mouth the old ideology while disregarding the fact that events have falsified all predictions. We continue to hear political speeches suggesting that easier treatment of criminals and delinquents of all kinds will reduce the attraction or compulsion of crime. But all the evidence is the other way. That if we treat workmen as responsible citizens they will behave responsibly. But we know they don't and that fiddles of all kinds proliferate. When will the theory and the practice be brought together?

Tuesday, April 21st, 1970

Lunch with John Stevens at his request. He had seen Kennedy, Burns and others in Washington fairly recently and was told there that there is no way of halting inflation. In days gone by strikes were broken by strong-arm methods. Can the new rash of strikes, in the end, be halted in the present day and age by such methods?

Stevens said that Harry Pilkington has taken the strikes that have closed fourteen of his seventeen factories very hard. He had no idea that his chaps would behave like other people's chaps. He is one of the nicest men I have ever met, but simple and naive. Just the man to be figurehead of a paternalistic family enterprise, but lost in the world of modern trades unionism.

Friday, April 24th, 1970

The polls published recently show improving prospects for Labour. Of three that reported in the last week, two showed Labour in the lead and one showed a diminished Conservative lead. There is still talk of a possible (but not probable) June election. It is likely to depend on the results of the borough elections on May 7th.*

Gordon Richardson for lunch. Such an intelligent, attractive man. Both he and I are reading *Present at the Creation* by Dean Acheson,

* The voting showed a marked swing to Labour, which had a net gain of 443 seats on borough councils, compared with a loss of 592 in 1967. (The swing was not large enough to change the control of any major city or borough.) In the Scottish burgh council elections on May 5th the Labour Party had a net gain of 57 seats.

who comes out of the book marvellously well. He is reconciled to seeing Eden occasionally now, so Richardson says, because they are two of the few survivors from the post-war diplomatic scene. Richardson has evidently had long talks with Acheson who, he said, had nothing but contempt for Eden and only saw him for old time's sake. Acheson's hero is Truman whom he rates as a great President. In the Truman–Acheson days the United States had a foreign policy, which has not been true in most of the ensuing years. Acheson told Richardson that Truman – with no experience and from the start – insisted on hearing both sides together before any major decision. He would not allow himself to be lobbied by one side. Before major decisions he also insisted that the problem should be argued out on paper before a crucial meeting, so making certain everyone had stood up and been counted.

Saturday, April 25th, 1970

Lunch with the Hymans at Ewhurst. He talks a lot and is at times hard to follow, but he talked more sense than at other times and was in excellent form. After being ousted from Viyella he has been busy fixing up the takeover by I.C.I. of Viyella. Now he sees himself in the not-very-near future as chairman of I.C.I. or in some government post. I don't myself see him in any post other than one of his own creation. He has gifts of enthusiasm, of intuition and of warmth that are so rare these days that they must surely be put to some use.

He thinks Wilson will see the shape of things to come – and have a June election. He will expect to win it, but will lose, though not by very many. He thinks we shall run into crisis in the autumn – low liquidity and consequently investment, high imports, higher unemployment, and a deterioration in our balance of payments. He thinks Wilson a nice man at bottom and a patriot but so weak and so uninterested in government as to be (in his words) a master of the spoken word and the undone deed. He thinks these last years have been disastrous for the country, partly from the lack of leadership provided by Wilson and his friends, but even more from the inability of Heath and his Tories to look like a viable alternative. He knows Keith Joseph well and says he is intelligent and able but would never (like Wilson) do anything unpopular. He knows Goodman and Harold Lever well. He thinks Lever did an excellent job as Financial Secretary to the Treasury, that his value was probably enhanced by the fact that he and Jenkins cannot bear one another.

He thinks Beeching a good executive but no chairman. Beeching's announcement that he would become chairman of A.E.I.* if Weinstock's bid failed was made because he understood from Paul Chambers that he would have the votes of the I.C.I. Pension Fund. It was also believed that this move by the I.C.I. Pension Fund would be followed by the other Institutions. In the outcome, the matter rested not with the I.C.I. board but with one of their number who was Trustee for the Fund. On the merits of the case he decided in favour of the Weinstock bid; his lead was indeed followed, thus leaving Beeching high and dry.

Wednesday, April 29th, 1970

In the evening yesterday, dinner with the Norman Collinses. Among the guests Ted Heath, Rebecca West and Bob Renwick. Ruth sat next to Heath and had some talk with him: I had none. He has not made a convincing impression on either Renwick or Collins, who both play a part in the Tory organization, collecting money.

Thursday, April 30th, 1970

Called on Leslie O'Brien today, the first time for some months. He is a very nice, very friendly man, very well disposed to the Labour Government which gave him his job. He had little actual news but seemed much less buoyant than when I saw him last.

He is obviously worried by the wage explosion and wants the election over as soon as possible so that this problem can be tackled. (He did not indicate any means by which this could be done.) He returned to the theme dear to all officials these days: (1) the wage explosion is not our fault as it is happening elsewhere, and (2) as it is happening elsewhere it will only have a limited effect on our balance of payments. Internal stresses and strains are ignored.

Leslie clearly thought the election would be in October and described Wilson as a man who would fight hard in the last ditch. In

* Associated Electrical Industries.

view of the craven way he ran away from trades union legislation last summer, this seemed a strangely partisan statement.

Things in Italy and France are looking better, but the outlook in the United States is alarming. Leslie said important Americans were talking of the dangerous possibilities of a revolution.

Friday, May 1st, 1970

Lunch for Ray Gunter. What a nice and honest man he is! He said that Wilson is keen to have a June election but their organization in the constituencies is not nearly as advanced as is the Tory one and that for this reason alone it must be October not June.

Yesterday the *Evening News* published a poll showing that Labour would lose half its present quota of seventy-eight London seats, and that alone would mean defeat. The Labour strategists would be keeping an eye on the borough elections next Friday not so much for the results, which they expect to leave the situation much where it is, but for the percentage of voters who actually vote. Wilson thinks on the one hand that his organization won't be ready for a June election. On the other hand, by October, prices will really be on the move. Gunter is afraid of an election that leaves the two parties more or less level, but thinks that if the election is postponed to April Wilson is out in a landslide. He thinks Wilson will lose anyway.

He was very critical of Ted Heath and said he was still getting nowhere: that he should not go into details about trades union legislation. His proposals only served to antagonize and unite trades unionists who had been divided. He did not think Wilson could do anything about the wage explosion even if he did win an election. I asked him what he thought should be done: he said there would have to be a wages tribunal which would adjudicate on all wage claims. I said that surely that would lead to a general strike or its equivalent. He said he did not think so.

We talked of the Permissive Society, which he said is a matter not of sex, but of the abandonment of all kinds of rules formulated by society for its own protection. This could not be corrected by politicians: it would need someone more like Wesley (Gunter is a Methodist).

I said Douglas Houghton had expressed unhappiness over the

very slack performance by M.P.s of their duties in the House. He said that until recently they were so sure they would lose their seats that they were not interested. Now they are so busy discussing their prospects in the bars and tea-rooms that they are still not interested.

Tuesday, May 5th, 1970

Lunch at the Belgian Embassy. I had a short chat with the Ambassador. He thinks the French are doing well and that the weak government in Italy does not matter as Italians look to the Pope not to the prime minister for leadership. When I expressed doubts about the present Pope's capacity to fill that role, he said the Pope's weakness is in the world at large and that in Italy he is as strong as ever. This seems to me very doubtful.

Meanwhile the U.S. is in deep trouble. Nixon's new offensive seems to be beating the air and the death of four students (two of them girls) in a campus riot at Kent State University in Ohio is likely to cause widespread trouble.*

Wednesday, May 6th, 1970

Mike to lunch; he had a crumb of information. He had recently had lunch with the Commercial Counsellor at the Russian Embassy, who told him that the wage explosion was by no means confined to this country – or to the West. In Russia productivity was rising by $3\frac{1}{2}$ per cent while wages were up by $7\frac{1}{2}$ per cent and they have no idea how to cope with the problem.

Thursday, May 7th, 1970

Frank Byers to lunch. He is an energetic, nice little man, but has if anything diminished since his days as Liberal M.P. for North Dorset.

---

* In April United States and South Vietnam forces launched a combined offensive against Communist bases in Cambodia. Although President Nixon asserted that the troops would be withdrawn from Cambodia as soon as the Communist forces were driven out and the military supplies destroyed, the adventure aroused widespread misgivings.

On May 4th four students (including two girls) were shot dead by National Guardsmen in the course of campus riots against United States involvement in Vietnam and Cambodia at Kent State University, Ohio. Fifteen others were injured. The riot at Kent State University was the worst of many such incidents that followed United States intervention in Cambodia.

His main theme was that the Conservative front bench was so weak that he feared a Conservative Cabinet would be even less effective than the Labour one.

Later at a reception at the Japanese Embassy, the second man, the Minister Plenipotentiary, seemed mainly worried by the slump on the Tokyo Stock Exchange. Marcus Lipton (M.P. for Brixton) was cock-a-hoop confident that Labour is now in for five years. Smirnovsky (the Russian Ambassador) very perturbed by American behaviour in Vietnam.

Monday, May 11th, 1970

Lunch for Dick Marsh. He had a bad setback when he was dismissed from office but now seems to have recovered. He is thinking of giving up politics – 'The people are such a grubby lot at the top' – and hopes to be chairman of the Electricity Council. In the meantime he has a couple of small directorships.

He had some talk this last week with O'Neill (former Ulster premier). O'Neill said the Stormont Government was all over the place; that Paisley was a much cleverer man than was generally reported; and finally that he thought civil war in Northern Ireland now inevitable. It remained to be seen whether the British would intervene or leave the Irish to fight it out. O'Neill said both sides are well supplied with weapons.

In spite of the opinion polls Marsh thought the situation in the marginal constituencies not favourable to Labour and that therefore the election would be in October.

Marsh said that Stewart's speech in the Cambodian debate* was unbelievably bad – bad from the point of view of the Left, Centre, or Right, of the party. It was so bad that when Stewart sat down Mellish (the Chief Whip) called Michael Foot out of the chamber to assure him that Stewart's speech did not represent Government policy. This manœuvre, shameful in itself, was quite unsuccessful and the anti-Government feeling was unexpectedly high.

Marsh spoke about the Anguilla episode, which Wilson in Cabinet spoke of in terms suitable for the D-Day landing on the Normandy beaches. Wilson came over all dramatic when discoursing on the

* The debate in the House of Commons on U.S. intervention in Cambodia.

invasion programme, speaking of the 'First Wave', which was only a few London bobbies.

Marsh was very vocal on the immense vanity of Wilson: his belief that in the end the world's problems will have to be referred to him to clear up. He apparently wants to be P.M. longer than any recent P.M. and then talks of retiring to an academic life and writing the definitive book on the British Government. This would mean retiring after two years if he wins the election. Anyway, Mary Wilson hates the life and is anxious for Wilson to get out of politics.

He said that when he was dismissed, Wilson gave three different versions of his plans for the Minister of Transport to Crosland, Marsh and Mulley, all within two hours – apparently unaware that within one further hour the three would have compared notes. Crosland was told he would be supremo; Mulley was told he would be in full charge of the ministry, though without a seat in the Cabinet. On the following Monday Crosland sent for the Permanent Under-Secretary, but Mulley forbade him to go! Now Crosland sits with a secretary, a telephone, four volumes of the Maud Report* and nothing to do.

We spoke about the trades union legislation abandoned in the summer. Marsh said there had never been a chance of getting it through the House. Wilson thought he could treat it as a matter of personal confidence in himself and get away with it. But this had never been a runner. I said there were those who said he would have got his Bill if he had told the P.L.P. that it was the Bill or dissolution. Marsh said it would have been an empty threat which no one would have taken seriously. One of Wilson's problems is that no one believes a word he says. This is weakness, apparently, not Machiavellism.

Marsh was harshly critical of Heath: the Conservatives have had everything in their favour for three years but have been quite unable to become an effective opposition. Marsh was secretary of the Labour Party in Heath's constituency and has been in touch with him for

* The Report of the Royal Commission on Local Government under the chairmanship of Lord Redcliffe-Maud. It had been published on June 11th, 1969, and the Government had accepted its recommendations in principle. Generally, these were for very large changes in the structure of local government in Britain, in the course of which some 120 county and borough councils and more than 1,000 district councils would disappear.

fifteen years. He says he has no friends; that he (Marsh) is on closer terms with all the other members of the Tory front bench than with Ted. He is impossible to know and the team he has built up is most unconvincing.

I asked who would succeed if Wilson fell under a bus this afternoon. He said probably Jim Callaghan, but he is too obviously ambitious and also distrusted so it might fall to Roy Jenkins.

Tuesday, May 12th, 1970

Lunch for Barbara Ward. Her Tory friends say they hope Labour will win as the outlook is so threatening they want Wilson to have to answer for the consequences of his own blunders. She thinks the world today is not unlike that of the 1840s – widespread disturbances, many of them for no very obvious reason. She is appalled by her students at Columbia University having no knowledge of history at all, and attributes their tendency to shout down people they disagree with to an inability to express themselves. She also said that it has now been discovered that if you haven't learnt to talk properly by the age of five, it is afterwards too late to do so and inadequate powers of speech remain with you for life.

We spoke about the Pope, as she belongs to an international committee of laity appointed by the Vatican. She says Pope Paul was all right in the traditional Vatican setting, but that in the new atmosphere created by Pope John he is lost. In this connection she said his insistence on celibacy for the clergy only makes sense in the case of lifelong dedication to the poor and helpless. Celibacy for priests and bishops leading comfortable middle-class lives is meaningless.

She thinks a spiritual revival is due fairly soon and that the first sign of it is the unrest among the young everywhere. They feel the world of science and technology is out of control and want no part of it. In fact in a few years you might have an anti-science movement.

Thursday, May 14th, 1970

Last evening at the annual Plowden party at Bridgewater House. I spoke to various tycoons and others, and am once more struck by the contrast to the politicians provided by the business leaders, who are all very pessimistic. They reflect anything from gloom to despair, while politicians of all persuasions are optimistic – not optimistic about anything in particular, but optimistic. Drogheda said the N.P.A. was going to appoint Goodman as chairman. This must mean that Robens declined. I cannot help feeling Goodman will repent if he actually does take up the job.

Lunch today with Ted Heath. We had lunch in his flat, the only other guest being Cowdrey, the Kent cricketer. People say Ted is cold, unfriendly, unapproachable, and all that kind of thing. But he was very easy to talk to, warm, friendly and forthcoming. I think it would be fair to say that he is no politician and certainly no Leader of the Opposition. He is essentially an able civil servant, but the Tories have no one better. He was naturally depressed as the polls, for no very clear reason, have taken a sudden turn to Labour and it is now generally assumed by the commentators and by Ted that the election will be in mid-June and will be announced on Sunday or Monday. The sudden change of sentiment seems due to (1) the wage explosion, which has taken place with no equivalent price explosion, (2) the inability of the Tories to present themselves as a more attractive alternative government, and (3) Ted's plans for trades union reform, which were unnecessarily detailed and have antagonized a large number of trades unionists who were not against reform in principle. The polls at the moment suggest a Labour majority of thirty or eighty.

The conversation at lunch did not get down to nuts and bolts, but Ted did give one or two pieces of news. Wilson is demanding £225,000 from the *Sunday Times* for his memoirs; Crossman has accepted £30,000. Alec Home saw Nixon on Monday and Nixon seemed quite cheerful and thought events in Indo-China might well operate to his advantage. He hoped to accelerate the withdrawal of troops from Vietnam and so win back popular support by November and the elections. I said this would all depend on the Vietnamization programme and the Washington newspaper people regarded this as a dismal failure. Ted then said you need pay no attention to this as the Washington commentators were uniformly hostile to Nixon. That Ted and Alec should speak so warmly of Nixon seems to me extraordinary. He gives a pathetic performance on T.V. and has a miserable record.

326

In the course of conversation Ted said foreigners thought us mad to put up with such a prime minister as Wilson: Willi Brandt had virtually said so to Ted when he was in Bonn a few days ago.

Events in Indo-China and the Middle East, inflation, student dissent and race riots all suggest to me a degree of world instability which is not going to just melt away. In such an unstable world we are the most vulnerable of all the major powers and are worse led at all levels and in all areas than we have been for centuries. That we can get out of this without a major crisis seems to me incredible. The continued weakness of the world's stock exchanges here, in the U.S. and in Japan shows that others indeed share this view, but politicians all speak as if this were a routine election of the late Victorian era and that defeat of one's own party is the worst we have to fear. A further period of no government with the machinery of law and order in Wilson's hands is to me frightening.

Unknown to the vast majority of educated people, an incoming administration by convention does not see the correspondence of its predecessor in office. I said to Ted that when he is in office I hope he will abrogate it. Ted gave no definite reply but I got the impression then and at other points in our conversation that he understands playing the game by the rules, whether or no they are now appropriate. I think you can safely say there will be no bold initiatives or new horizons in a Heath administration.

Wednesday, May 20th, 1970

So it is to be June 18th.* The latest opinion polls put Labour by 2 per cent in the lead, which would mean a majority of around fifty. The opinion polls have changed dramatically in a matter of a very few weeks. However, the electorate is in a very volatile mood and much can happen before mid-June. On television Wilson lacks all authority but looks genial and confident; Heath looks a nice man but is just not convincing – it is hard to say why.

On Monday we went to Southall to talk to representatives of the big Indian – mostly Sikh – community there. I asked the local

* On May 18th Mr Wilson recommended a dissolution of Parliament to the Queen, and the announcement that the Queen had agreed was made that evening; a General Election became due on June 18th. Parliament was dissolved on May 29th.

community relations official why there was this congregation of Indians at Southall. He said there was formerly a rubber factory there which found it difficult to get labour as the works were so hot. The manager had been an officer in the Indian Army and thought of importing Sikhs to do the work, as they are more familiar with heat. The rubber factory has closed down but it was from this nucleus that the present Indian community was formed.

The Indian Workers' Association now has nine thousand members, mostly Sikhs but also including some Bengalis (these are Hindus from East Pakistan), Gujaratis and Pakistanis. Of the coloured population of Southall, more than 10 per cent are West Indian. I asked why there were no Tamils and was told that many of the northern Indians came in the wake of highly educated relatives (doctors and so on). The southern Indians are a far more depressed group and if they emigrate they go to Malaysia or Ceylon.

We were told two other items of interest. (1) The headmaster of one of the Ealing schools told the officials that educational standards had risen as the result of the arrival of Indian boys at his school. They were intelligent and ambitious and had made a great difference to the Sixth Form. (2) Illegal immigration is proceeding on a considerable scale and is not just small parties crossing the Channel.

Tuesday, June 2nd, 1970

Lunch for Denis Hamilton. Denis is a cheerful soul and I have never seen him so near despair: too worried by the Fleet St scene to bother about the nation's affairs. He said he had come from a meeting of the N.P.A. where they are confronted with a demand for a 25 per cent increase from SOGAT.* In addition the price of newsprint is going up by £6 a ton on January 1st. The *Express* group are losing money on the daily and evening papers and only making it on the Sunday. Denis was startled by Michael Berry a few days ago who said he was so short of cash he could not afford a strike that lasted more than fourteen days. He could increase the price of his papers – or close the Sunday, but that would not solve his liquidity problem.

* Society of Graphical and Allied Trades.

Lord Poole told Denis that when he managed the *Financial Times* it made a profit of £950,000 on a turnover of £3 million. This year it would make a profit of £600,000 on a turnover of just under £8 million. Denis showed me some average wages. The *Financial Times* stereotypers *average* £92 per week and stereotyping is only semi-skilled. Bush Africans in Lagos learnt to be good newspaper stereotypers in ten weeks. Denis said *The Times* is losing £1½ million per annum; The *Guardian* £1¼ million. He had got Eric Roll (a director of *The Times*) to approach Richard Scott in Washington. Scott is the *Guardian*'s Washington correspondent but also chairman of the Board of Trustees that control the paper. When asked if there was a possibility of a deal between *The Times* and the *Guardian*, Scott said he regarded his main duty as keeping the *Guardian* independent. The obvious plan – put forward by me in the past – is for the *Guardian* to return to Manchester, leaving the South to *The Times*, while the *Guardian* shares the same news service and looks after the North. Though rejected by Richard Scott, Denis is now to tackle Laurence Scott, the chairman of the company. I don't suppose he will have any success particularly as the *Guardian* people have been talking of entirely deserting Manchester for London!

I asked why Arnold Goodman had accepted the chairmanship of the N.P.A., a bed of nails if ever there was one. Denis said he is always on the look-out for a power base and sees one at the N.P.A.

Wednesday, June 10th, 1970

An urgent call to lunch from Norman Collins last Thursday ended with lunch at Claridge's on Friday with him and Bob Renwick. The purpose of the meeting was to try and do something about the election, which seems to be going steadily in favour of Labour. The Conservatives are making some effort at criticism: the Prime Minister is not seriously trying to do anything. He feels things are coming his way so why pretend to any serious discussion of problems? Foreign affairs have hardly been mentioned. Collins's plan was that some time this week a group of three should issue a pronunciamento urging the disastrous consequences of a further five years of Labour. The group to consist of self, flanked by Cromer and Shawcross. I doubted whether anything would be achieved and anyway thought the group – if the others would consent to take part – should be Cromer flanked by Shawcross and me. My own private argument for doing anything of the kind is that when disaster strikes I can say I issued warnings earlier when perhaps something could still have been done.

Last night we went to an election meeting in Twickenham. Jessel, the new member, has just been elected to the G.L.C. He seemed a nice young man and intelligent; his wife had more to her than he had. But this is the fourth new member for a safe Conservative seat that I have met. Nice chaps all but with no colour, no political gift, no force of character. Surely something better could have been found!

Thursday, June 11th, 1970

We gave a dinner-party at Claridge's last night. I had a long talk with Arnold Goodman with whom I had had previously no serious conversation. I had wondered why he accepted the chairmanship of the N.P.A. He now wonders the same thing! I urged on Goodman, as I did a few days ago on Murdoch, the vital importance of closing down one of the newspapers – at least the *Sketch*. It seems doubtful if Esmond [Rothermere] can be induced to make up his mind to do this. In conversation with Ruth, Goodman held forth on the folly of Wilson's approval of demonstrations. Wilson said they are legal, which apparently they are not, and his recommendation that they must be allowed can only lead to disorder.

Robens said he would not be seeking a further extension of his term as chairman of the Coal Board. Within his experience the swing to Labour is entirely due to the wage explosion. Eve Robens thought Wilson had let wages up in order to win the election. I don't think this is true. Wilson did make a feeble effort last summer to do something about it.

The opinion poll this morning shows a further swing to Labour. If verified next week this would mean a Labour majority of a hundred.

Another lunch set up by Norman Collins took place at Brown's Hotel, Bob Renwick in the chair. Others present: Crowther, Shawcross, Paul Chambers, George Cole, McFadzean (of Shell) and Joe

Lockwood of E.M.I.* Collins had drawn up a rather verbose paper with Shawcross's help. Crowther, Cole and Lockwood said they couldn't sign anything anyway as they held official positions. I thought the discussion went quite well, but the gist that emerged was that: (1) it was too late to affect the election; (2) all a pronunciamento could achieve would be an alibi for us when things went wrong (they thought the second objective not worth achieving); and (3) any statement of the kind would effectively prevent any signatory having any subsequent effect on policy and surely if you cannot affect votes, you want to affect policy. Shawcross said he was going to make a personal statement anyway.

Paul Chambers and McFadzean were very clear in stating what was wrong and how to put it right. But with the newspaper strike it might only be possible to put it over in the provincial mornings.† I felt all along I was being pushed into something by Collins and my tepid enthusiasm seeped away during the discussion. I left early, committed to nothing. The most interesting aspect of the lunch to me was the way they all assumed that we are heading for the rocks – and soon. They thought we should be in trouble with the balance of payments next year. They all thought nothing of the Labour Government but had no respect for Heath and his men either.

McFadzean buys ships and equipment for Shell. He said a 60,000-ton bulk carrier takes eight months to build in Denmark and an uncertain fifteen months here. In Denmark you can have a fixed-price contract for delivery in 1973. In this country there are now no fixed-price contracts. In Denmark the shipbuilders want nothing else as this is the only means of keeping wages in bounds. He said the grant of a £20 million loan to Upper Clyde Shipbuilders was a disaster. When they knew the money was there the men put in demands for more wages and that is where most of the money went. Harland and Wolff men wanted parity and that wrecked their finances and compelled the Government to give *them* a loan. Whereupon Cammell Laird's men also demanded more money and now they too have been bailed out with a Government loan.

* Electrical and Musical Industries Ltd.
† The strike by SOGAT in support of their wage-claim (see p. 328) began on Tuesday, June 9th, and lasted until the following weekend.

331

Two incidental remarks that were interesting: Wilson had forbidden the Lord Chancellor or the Attorney-General to attend a dinner given by Shawcross.

Crowther, chairman of the Royal Commission on the British Constitution, said that he could see now no future for democracy nor could he see what would take its place!

Saturday, June 13th, 1970

To Malcolm Muggeridge at Salehurst yesterday. He was in whacking form after doing a series for the B.B.C., 'In the Steps of St Paul'. I offered the opinion that we are entering a new Dark Age with power in the hands of the stupid, the lazy and the ignorant. Malcolm argued that we are already in this Dark Age with at least a period of chaos in front of not only this country but the other advanced industrial countries of the West. He said the local odd-job contractor told him he is often asked for someone to do some small repair job: 'But don't send anyone under fifty.' The reason is that the younger men are lazy, unreliable and ill-trained.

Malcolm had recently met Paisley in Belfast, and Enoch Powell. These are the only real politicians on the horizon, but Enoch is so unpractical in so much of his policy and Paisley is of purely Irish importance. Malcolm said the future is often foreseeable but the timing is not. Even when the position seems hopeless, human beings will cling to existing institutions rather than give way to anarchy. In this country one would suppose any revolution would be from the Right, but what is the political loyalty of the Army and how strong are the subversive forces behind Mr Wilson and the trades unions?

The newspaper strike is over, with an interim payment of £5 million which the newspapers cannot afford – and no newspaper is to shut down. This can only be a patched-up peace and when the crash does eventually come, the effect on Fleet St will be all that much worse, the survivors that many fewer.

The main election news is that the latest opinion poll shows Labour with a 12½ per cent lead, equivalent to a majority of 150. This represents an extraordinary swing of 25 per cent since February. A feeble Opposition and bulging pay-packets may well be the reasons but the transformation of the political scene is unprecedented and disastrous. Enoch Powell is to make a major speech this afternoon in Birmingham. It is assumed that this is a bid for the Tory leadership after the Labour win on the opinion polls on Thursday.

Tuesday, June 16th, 1970

Lunch with Don Ryder at Reed's. I saw him last four and a half months ago. We talked about the newspaper strike which he claimed to have settled with Lord Goodman's help. I said I thought it a pity that no newspaper was closing down. The settlement is an expensive one and is bound to make some newspapers wildly unprofitable. Apparently Roy Thomson talks of closing *The Times*, but Esmond [Rothermere] has shown no willingness to close the *Sketch* or the *Mail*. Don's argument was that if the strike had not been ended when it was, it would have dragged on for weeks; the *Sketch* and *The Times* would have closed and the final settlement would have been more expensive. Now the unions have agreed to work out a new wages structure in the coming twelve months. I have heard this story before and wonder what the result will be (if any).

On the subject of Fleet Street generally, he said that Gordon Brunton, who will take over the Thomson organization when Thomson moves on, is taking more and more part at *The Times*; Don thought the prospect for *The Times* is bleak. Cudlipp looks a different man and concerns himself with editing the *Mirror*.

During the strike negotiations Don had had some talk with Wilson, who assumed he had won the election and was considering his victory speech.

I.P.C., like other concerns, is short of cash and will be selling off its freeholds and, later perhaps, its trade investments. If things go wrong in America there is nothing we can effectively do here. With inflated wages and other costs, the need for increased working capital is felt by everyone and the capital is not obtainable. A price freeze by the new Government would make matters worse. I said the people at the Bank of England expect trouble next spring, but Don did not think it would now be deferred beyond October.

Saturday, June 20th, 1970

On Thursday evening we went to the *Daily Telegraph* party expecting a Labour majority of somewhere between 30 and 150, depending on which public opinion poll carried most conviction. However, the first four results – Guildford, Cheltenham, Salford and Wolverhampton – showed that a Tory victory was almost certain. And so it was. The final result is a Tory majority of about 40.* The polls' forecasts seem to have been falsified by the 'don't knows' and the low poll. The latter is presumably due to the very low respect in which both parties are held by the public. The victory puts Heath in a very strong position as Wilson chose to fight the election on a Wilson v. Heath basis. In the course of the campaign Heath was seen to be at serious odds with Enoch Powell. However annoying this may have been to him, it does not seem to have done the Tory vote any harm. The main casualties of the election were George Brown, Jennie Lee and the Liberal Party. The latter had been cut from thirteen to six. Bernadette Devlin rather unexpectedly kept her seat in mid-Ulster and Paisley is in for North Antrim. These two should enliven any Irish debates at Westminster though I imagine Paisley will use his Westminster seat as a platform for addressing Ulster. I cannot imagine him being a regular attendant in the House of Commons.

Heath is the hero of the hour, but how long will he so remain? He seems to misjudge the importance of Powell and the swing to the Right he represents. Heath does not seem to realize the head-on collision with the trades union movement that lies ahead. And Powell will make it difficult to join the Common Market. As Prime Minister Wilson was pathetic, but as Leader of the Opposition he was formidable and may be so again, though now he is handicapped by his performance in office. I hope Heath will be a success and I have no idea what will happen if he fails.

* The final results of the General Election were: Conservatives, 330; Labour, 287; Liberals, 6; Speaker, 1; Others, 6. The percentages of the total votes cast gained by each party (with 1966 percentages in brackets) were as follows: Conservative, 46·4 (41·9); Labour, 43·0 (47·9); Liberal, 7·4 (8·5).

BIOGRAPHICAL NOTES
for front-benchers and those mentioned frequently in the text

ACHESON, Dean. U.S. Sec. of State 1949–53 under President Truman.
AITKEN, Sir Max. Son of Lord Beaverbrook. Chairman and principal proprietor *Express* group of newspaper since 1964.
ALLEN, Maurice. Fellow of Balliol College, Oxford 1931–48, where he taught economics to Edward Heath, Harold Wilson and other senior politicians. Executive director Bank of England 1964–70.
AMERY, Julian. Con. M.P. for Preston North 1950–66, for Brighton (Pavilion) since 1969. Son of Rt. Hon. Leopold Amery, son-in-law of Harold Macmillan. Min. of Aviation 1962–4, for Housing and Construction since 1970.
ANNENBERG, Walter. Newspaper and magazine publisher. U.S. Ambassador in London since 1969.

BALL, George. Lawyer and journalist. Formerly Assistant Sec. at the U.S. State Department in Washington.
BALOGH, Thomas (Lord Balogh). Born Budapest 1908. Sometime Fellow of Balliol College, Oxford. Reader in Economics at Oxford since 1960. Economic Adviser to the Cabinet 1964–7, to the Prime Minister 1968.
BARBER, Anthony. Con. M.P. for Doncaster 1951–64, for Altrincham since 1965. Min. of Health 1963–4, Chancellor of the Duchy of Lancaster 1970, Chancellor of the Exchequer since 1970.
BEECHING, Richard (Lord Beeching). Chairman Redland Ltd since 1970. Director I.C.I. 1957–61 and 1965–8. Chairman British Railways 1963–5.
BENN, Anthony Wedgwood. Lab. M.P. for Bristol 1950–60 and since 1963. Renounced title of Viscount Stansgate 1963. Postmaster-General 1964–66, Min. of Technology 1966–70.
BERRY, Michael (Lord Hartwell). Second son of Lord Camrose. Editor-in-chief of *Daily Telegraph* and *Sunday Telegraph*.
BIRK, Ellis. Solicitor. For many years a director of companies in the *Daily Mirror* group.
BLANKENHORN, Herbert. West German diplomat. Ambassador to NATO 1955–8, to France 1958–63, to Italy 1963–5, to London 1965–70.
BOLTON, Sir George. Chairman and president Bank of London and South America since 1957. Director Bank of England 1948–68, executive director 1948–57.
BOTTOMLEY, Arthur George. Lab. M.P. for Chatham 1945–59, for Middlesborough since 1962. Sec. of State for Commonwealth Affairs 1964–6, Min. for Overseas Development 1966–7.
BOWDEN, Herbert William (Lord Aylestone). Chairman I.T.A. since 1967. Lab. M.P. for Leicester 1945–67. Lord President of the Council and Leader of the House of Commons 1964–6, Sec. of State for Commonwealth Affairs 1966–7.

335

BOYLE, Sir Edward (Lord Boyle of Handsworth). Pro-Chancellor Sussex University since 1965, Vice-Chancellor Leeds University since 1970. Con. M.P. for Birmingham (Handsworth) 1950–70. Min. of Education 1962–4.

BRANDT, Willi. Chancellor of Federal German Republic since 1969. Mayor of West Berlin 1957–66, Vice-Chancellor and Foreign Min. 1966–9.

BROWN, George (Lord George-Brown). Lab. M.P. for Belper 1945–70. Deputy Leader of the Labour Party 1960–70. Min. of Works 1951, Sec. of State for Economic Affairs 1964–6, for Foreign Affairs 1966–8.

BRUCE, David. U.S. Ambassador in London 1961–9. Ambassador in Paris 1949–52, Ambassador in Bonn 1957–9.

BUNDY, McGeorge. President the Ford Foundation, U.S.A. Brought by President Kennedy into government from Harvard University; Special Assistant to the President for National Security Affairs 1961–6.

BUTLER, R. A. (Lord Butler of Saffron Walden). Master of Trinity College, Cambridge, since 1965. Con. M.P. for Saffron Walden 1929–65. Brilliant academic career. Min. of Education 1941–5, Chancellor of the Exchequer 1951–3, Home Sec. 1957–62, Sec. of State for Foreign Affairs 1963–4.

CALLAGHAN, James. Lab. M.P. for South Cardiff since 1945. Assistant Sec. Inland Revenue Staff Federation 1936–47. Chancellor of the Exchequer 1964–7, Home Sec. 1967–70, Labour Party Treasurer since 1967.

CARRINGTON, Peter (6th Baron Carrington). Sec. of State for Defence since 1970. High Commissioner for the U.K. in Australia 1956–9, First Lord of the Admiralty 1959–63, Min. without Portfolio 1963–4. Chairman Australia & New Zealand Bank 1967–70. Former director of important companies.

CASTLE, Barbara. Lab. M.P. for Blackburn since 1945. Housing correspondent and Forces adviser Daily Mirror 1944–5. Chairman of the Labour Party 1958–9. Min. of Overseas Development 1964–5, of Transport 1965–8, Sec. of State for Employment and Productivity 1968–70.

CHALFONT, Lord (Arthur Gwynne Jones). Regular soldier 1940–61. Defence Correspondent The Times 1961–64. Min. of State at the Foreign Office 1964–70.

CHAMBERS, Sir Paul. Chairman I.C.I. 1960–68. Chairman Royal Insurance group since 1968. Former civil servant here and in India. Expert on tax problems.

COLLINS, Norman. Deputy chairman A.T.V. Played a leading part in the establishment of commercial television. At different times worked with News Chronicle, Victor Gollancz Ltd (publishers) and the B.B.C. Is best known for his books, notably London Belongs to Me.

COUSINS, Frank. General Sec. Transport and General Workers' Union 1956–69; was seconded to Labour Government 1964–6. Lab. M.P. for Nuneaton 1965–6.

CROMER, Rowley (3rd Earl of Cromer). U.K. Ambassador in Washington since 1971. Managing director Baring Bros 1957–61. Head of Treasury Delegation and Economic Min. in Washington 1959–61. Governor Bank of England 1961–6. Chairman and managing director Baring Bros 1967–70.

CROSLAND, Anthony. Lab. M.P. for South Gloucester 1950–55, and for Grimsby since 1959. Lecturer in Economics Trinity College, Oxford, 1947–50. Sec. of State for Education and Science 1965–7, President of the Board of Trade 1967–9, Sec. of State for Local Government 1969–70.

CROSSMAN, Richard. Lab. M.P. for Coventry East since 1945. Brilliant academic record; Fellow and Tutor of New College, Oxford, 1930–37. Assistant editor *New Statesman* 1938–55, editor 1970–72. Min. of Housing and Local Government 1964–6, Leader of the House and Lord President of the Council 1966–8, Sec. of State for Social Services 1968–70.

CROWTHER, Geoffrey (Lord Crowther). Died 1972. As editor of *The Economist* 1938–56, he brought that publication to a position of great influence and authority. Subsequently became chairman of Trust Houses Forte and a director of several large companies.

CUDLIPP, Hugh. Chairman of I.P.C. since 1968. Journalist and editor. First edited national newspaper at the age of 24. The outstanding popular newspaper editor of his day.

DEAN, Sir Patrick. Diplomat. U.K. Ambassador in Washington 1965–9.

DE COURCEL, Baron Geoffroy. French Ambassador in London 1962–72. Joined Free French forces 1940. Chef du Cabinet to General de Gaulle in London 1940–41. Civil servant and diplomat.

DOUGLAS-HOME, Sir Alec (14th Earl of Home). Inherited title in 1951, disclaimed it in 1963. Con. M.P. for Lanark 1931–51, for Kinross since 1963. Sec. of State for Commonwealth Relations 1955–60, for Foreign Affairs 1960–63, Prime Minister 1963–4, Sec. of State for Foreign Affairs since 1970.

DROGHEDA, 11th Earl (Garrett Moore). Chairman *Financial Times* since 1971. Managing director 1945–70. Chairman Royal Opera House, Covent Garden. Chairman Newspaper Publishers' Association 1968–70.

DU CANN, Edward. Con. M.P. for Taunton since 1956. Founder of Unicorn group of unit trusts. Now chairman of Keyser Ullman, merchant bankers. Chairman Conservative Party Organization 1965–7.

ECCLES, David (Viscount Eccles). Con. M.P. for Chippenham 1943–62. Chairman Trustees of British Museum 1968–70. Min. of Works 1951–4, of Education 1954–7, President of the Board of Trade 1957–9, Min. of Education 1959–62, Paymaster-General since 1970.

EDEN, Anthony (Earl of Avon). Con. M.P. for Warwick 1923–57. Sec. of State for Foreign Affairs 1935–8, for Dominion Affairs 1939–40, for War 1940, for Foreign Affairs 1940–45, Sec. of State for Foreign Affairs and Deputy Prime Minister 1951–5, Prime Minister 1955–7.

FEATHER, Victor. General Sec. T.U.C. since 1969. Co-op employee 1923–37. Joined T.U.C. staff 1937. Assistant General Sec. 1960–69.

FOWLER, Henry. Under-Sec. of the U.S. Treasury 1961–4, Sec. of the U.S. Treasury 1965–8.

FRANCK, Louis. Director of Samuel Montagu, merchant bankers, now retired.

FRASER, Hugh. Con. M.P. for Staffordshire (Stone) since 1955. Sec. of State for Air 1962–4. Merchant banker.

FREEMAN, John. Chairman and chief executive London Weekend Television since 1971. Lab. M.P. for Watford 1945–55. Editor *New Statesman* 1961–5. U.K. High Commissioner in India 1965–8. U.K. Ambassador in Washington 1969–71.

337

FULBRIGHT, William. U.S. Senator (Democrat) for Arkansas since 1945. Elected to Congress 1942. Chairman Senate Committee on Foreign Relations since 1959.

GARDINER, Gerald (Lord Gardiner). Barrister; K.C. 1948. Lord Chancellor 1964–70.

GEDDES, Sir Reay. Leading industrialist.

GOODMAN, Arnold (Lord Goodman). Solicitor. Chairman Arts Council of Great Britain 1965–72. Chairman *Observer* newspaper since 1967.

GORDON WALKER, Patrick. Lab. M.P. for Smethwick 1945–64, for Leyton since 1966. History tutor Christ Church, Oxford, 1931–40. Sec. of State for Commonwealth Relations 1950–51, for Foreign Affairs 1964–5, for Education and Science 1967–8.

GORE-BOOTH, Sir Paul Henry (Lord Gore-Booth). Diplomat. U.K. Ambassador to Burma 1953–6. U.K. High Commissioner in India 1960–65. Permanent Under-Sec. of State Foreign Office 1965–9.

GOWON, General. Supreme Commander Nigerian Army and head of Nigerian Government. Trained at Sandhurst. Took over government of Nigeria at the outbreak of civil war.

GRAHAM, K. (Mrs Philip Graham). Daughter of former proprietor *Washington Post*. Widow of Philip Graham, in his turn proprietor of the same paper. Now herself publisher of *Washington Post* and *Newsweek*.

GREENWOOD, Anthony (Lord Greenwood of Rossendale). Lab. M.P. for Radcliffe 1946–50, for Rossendale 1950–70. Sec. of State for Colonial Affairs 1964–5, Min. for Overseas Development 1965–6, of Housing and Local Government 1966–70.

GRIFFITHS, James. Lab. M.P. for Llanelly 1936–70. Min. of National Insurance 1945–50. Sec. of State for the Colonies 1950–51, for Wales 1964–6.

GRIMOND, Jo. Lib. M.P. for Orkney and Shetland since 1950. Leader of the Liberal Party 1956–67. Rector of Aberdeen University since 1969.

GUNTER, Ray. Lab. M.P. for South-Eastern Essex 1945–50, for Doncaster 1950–51, for Southwark 1959–72. Min. of Labour 1964–8, of Power 1968. Member National Executive of the Labour Party since 1955. President of Transport Salaried Staff Association 1956–64.

HAMILTON, Denis. Journalist. Editor-in-chief Times Newspapers Ltd since 1967. Editor *Sunday Times* 1961–7.

HEALEY, Denis. Lab. M.P. for Leeds since 1952. Sec. of State for Defence 1964–70.

HEATH, Edward. Con. M.P. for Bexley since 1950. Administrative civil service 1946–7. Government Chief Whip 1955–9, Min. of Labour 1959–60, Lord Privy Seal attached to Foreign Office 1960–63, Sec. of State for Trade and Industry 1963–4. Prime Minister since 1970.

HOGG, Quintin (Lord Hailsham). Lord Chancellor since 1970. In 1950 succeeded his father as Viscount Hailsham but disclaimed peerage in 1963. Fresh peerage conferred in 1970. Con. M.P. for Oxford City 1938–50, for St Marylebone 1963–70. First Lord of the Admiralty 1956–7, Min. of Education 1957, Lord President of the Council 1957–9 and 1960–64, Sec. of State for Education and Science 1964. Brilliant academic record.

338

HOUGHTON, Douglas. Lab. M.P. for Sowerby since 1949. Chairman Parliamentary Labour Party since 1967. Sec. Inland Revenue Staff Federation 1922–60. Chancellor of the Duchy of Lancaster 1964–6, Min. without Portfolio 1966–7.

HUGHES, Cledwyn. Lab. M.P. for Anglesey since 1951. Solicitor. Sec. of State for Wales 1966–8, Min. of Agriculture 1968–70.

HUMPHREY, Hubert. U.S. Senator Democrat from Minnesota 1949–64 and since 1970. Vice-President U.S. 1965–9.

HYMAN, Joe. Chairman Viyella International 1962–9, John Crowther group since 1971. Rich textile magnate.

JAY, Douglas. Lab. M.P. for Battersea since 1946. Brilliant academic record. Journalist on staff of *The Times*, *The Economist* and *Daily Herald* 1929–41. Civil servant during World War II. President of the Board of Trade 1964–7.

JENKINS, Roy. Lab. M.P. for Southwark 1948–50, for Birmingham (Stechford) since 1950. Son of Arthur Jenkins, M.P. from South Wales. Excellent academic record. Author of several important biographies. Min. of Aviation 1964–5, Home Sec. 1965–7, Chancellor of the Exchequer 1967–70.

JOHNSON, Lyndon Baines. U.S. President 1963–9. Congressman 1937–48. Senator (Democrat) from Texas 1949–61, Vice-President 1961–3.

JONES, Aubrey. Con. M.P. for Birmingham (Hall Green) 1950–65. Min. of Fuel and Power 1955–7, of Supply 1957–9. Chairman National Board of Prices and Incomes 1965–70. Now an industrialist and a director of several large companies.

JONES, Sir Elwyn. Lab. M.P. for West Ham since 1945. Eminent lawyer. Attorney-General 1964–70.

JOSEPH, Sir Keith. Con. M.P. for Leeds since 1956. Sec. of State at the Department of Health and Social Security since 1970. Min. of Housing and Local Government 1962–4.

KEARTON, Frank (Lord Kearton). Chairman Courtaulds Ltd since 1964. Joined I.C.I. after leaving Oxford 1933. Worked in Atomic Energy Projects 1940–45. Joined Courtaulds 1946 in charge of Chemical Engineering.

KEITH, Sir Kenneth. Chairman of Hill, Samuel & Co., merchant bankers. Chartered accountant. Also director of several important companies.

KENNEDY, David M. American banker. President Continental Illinois Bank 1956–8 and later. Appointed to Cabinet by President Nixon 1968. Sec. of the Treasury 1969–70. Ambassador at large since 1970.

KENNEDY, Edward. U.S. Senator (Democrat) from Massachusetts. Sole surviving son of Joseph Kennedy, sometime American Ambassador in London, and brother of John F. Kennedy, American President assassinated in 1963.

KIESINGER, K. G. Member of the Bundestag 1949–58 and since 1969. Chancellor Federal Republic of Germany 1966–9. Min.-President Baden-Würthemberg 1958–66.

KING, Michael. Eldest son of Cecil King. Now Public Relations Officer at the C.B.I. From Reuters he became Foreign Editor of the *Daily Mirror*.

KISSINGER, Henry Alfred. Assistant to U.S. President for National Security Affairs since 1968. Held various teaching posts mostly at Harvard University from 1950.

339

LEE, Frederick. Lab. M.P. Lancashire (Newton) since 1945. Member National Committee of Amalgamated Engineering Union 1944–5. Min. of Power 1964–6, Sec. of State for the Colonies 1966–7, Chancellor of the Duchy of Lancaster 1967–9.

LEE, Jennie (Baroness Lee of Asheridge). Lab. M.P. for North Lanark 1929–31, for Cannock 1945–70. Widow of Aneurin Bevan, prominent Labour minister and personality. Min. of State Department of Education and Science 1967–70 in charge of the Government's contribution to the arts.

LEVER, Harold. Lab. M.P. for Manchester (Cheetham) since 1954. Barrister. Financial Sec. to the Treasury 1967–9, Paymaster-General 1969–70.

LLOYD-HUGHES, Sir Trevor. Journalist. On staff of *Liverpool Post* from 1949, *Liverpool Echo* from 1950, *Liverpool Daily Post* from 1951. Press Sec. to the Prime Minister 1964–9, Information Adviser to the Government 1969–70. Now a consultant in public and international affairs.

LONGFORD, Frank (Francis Pakenham, 7th Earl of Longford). Lecturer in Politics Oxford University 1934–46 and 1952–64. Chairman National Bank Ltd 1955–63. Chancellor of the Duchy of Lancaster 1947–8, Min. of Civil Aviation 1948–51, First Lord of the Admiralty 1951. Lord Privy Seal 1964–5, Sec. of State for the Colonies 1965–6.

MACLEOD, Iain. Died 1970. Con. M.P. for Enfield 1950–70. Min. of Health 1952, of Labour 1955, Sec. of State for the Colonies 1959, Chancellor of the Duchy of Lancaster, Leader of the House of Commons and Chairman of the Conservative Party 1961–3, Chancellor of the Exchequer 1970.

MACMILLAN, Harold. Con. M.P. for Stockton-on-Tees 1924–9 and 1931–45, for Bromley 1945–64. Chairman of Macmillan's, the publishers. Min. of Housing and Local Government 1951–4, of Defence 1954–5, Sec. of State for Foreign Affairs 1955, Chancellor of the Exchequer 1955–7, Prime Minister 1957–63.

MCNAMARA, Robert. President International Bank for Reconstruction and Development. Joined Ford Motor Co. of the U.S. 1946 and rose to be President of that company 1960–61. U.S. Sec. of Defence 1961–8.

MARSH, Richard. Chairman British Railways Board since 1971. Lab. M.P. for Greenwich 1959–71. Health services officer National Union of Public Employees 1951–9. Min. of Power 1966–8, of Transport 1968–9.

MAUDLING, Reginald. Con. M.P. for Barnet since 1950. Min. of Supply 1955–7, Paymaster-General 1957–9, President of the Board of Trade 1959–61, Sec. of State for the Colonies 1961–2, Chancellor of the Exchequer 1962–4, Home Sec. 1970–72.

MAYHEW, Christopher. Lab. M.P. for South Norfolk 1945–50, for Woolwich East since 1951. Parliamentary Under-Sec. for Foreign Affairs 1946–50, Min. of Defence (R.N.) 1964–6.

MELLISH, Robert. Lab. M.P. for Bermondsey since 1946. Opposition Chief Whip since 1970. Official, Transport and General Workers' Union. Min. of Public Buildings and Works 1967–9, Government Chief Whip 1969–70.

MONNET, Jean. European political figure. Member British Supply Council, Washington, 1940–43. General Commissioner Plan for Modernization and Equipment of France 1946. President European Iron and Steel Community

1952–5. Chairman Action Committee for the United States of Europe since 1956.

MOSLEY, Sir Oswald (6th Baronet). Con. M.P. for Harrow 1918–24, Lab. M.P. for Smethwick 1926–31. Chancellor of the Duchy of Lancaster 1929–30. Founder of the British Union of Fascists.

MUGGERIDGE, Malcolm. Journalist and author. On staff of *Manchester Guardian* 1930–33, Calcutta *Statesman* 1934–5, *Evening Standard* 1935–6, *Daily Telegraph* 1946–52. Editor of *Punch* 1953–7.

MULLEY, Frederick William. Lab. M.P. for Sheffield since 1950. Obtained B.Sc. (Econ.), Chartered Secretaryship while a prisoner of war. Won scholarship to Oxford and 1st Class Honours in P.P.E. Min. for the Army 1964–5, of Aviation 1965–7, Min. of State at the Foreign Office 1967–9, Min. of Transport 1969–70.

MURDOCH, Rupert. Australian newspaper proprietor. Managing director News Ltd of Adelaide; principal proprietor Sydney *Daily Mirror*; founder of *The Australian* newspaper; chairman News International, publishers of the *Sun* and *News of the World* in London.

NIXON, Richard. U.S. President since 1969. Congressman 1947–50. Senator (Republican) from California 1950–53. U.S. Vice-President 1953–61. Lawyer by profession.

O'BRIEN, Sir Leslie. Governor of the Bank of England since 1966. Entered Bank of England 1927; deputy governor 1964–6.

PARSONS, Sir Maurice. Entered Bank of England 1928. Executive director 1957. Deputy governor 1966–70. While at the Bank a member of various international monetary and financial bodies.

PEART, Frederick. Lab. M.P. for Workington since 1945. Min. of Agriculture 1964–8, Lord Privy Seal 1968, Lord President of the Council 1968–70.

PLOWDEN, Edwin (Lord Plowden). Chairman Tube Investments Ltd since 1963. Director of several important companies. For many years a civil servant; chairman Atomic Energy Authority 1954–9. Married to Bridget Plowden, educationalist, who gave her name to the Plowden Report on primary education.

POMPIDOU, Georges. President of France since 1969. Began his career as a schoolmaster with brilliant academic record. In de Gaulle's Cabinet 1944–6. Subsequently director-general of Rothschild's Bank. Director-general of de Gaulle's Cabinet 1958–9, Prime Minister of France 1962–8.

POOLE, Oliver (Lord Poole). Director, S. Pearson & Sons; chairman Lazard Bros. & Co. Con. M.P. for Oswestry 1945–50. Chairman Conservative Party Organization 1955–7, deputy chairman, joint chairman and vice-chairman 1957–64.

POWELL, Enoch. Con. M.P. for Wolverhampton since 1950. Fellow of Trinity College, Cambridge, 1934–8; Professor of Greek, Sydney University, N.S.W., 1937–9. Min. of Health 1960–63. Author of numerous scholarly and political books and pamphlets.

PRENTICE, Reginald. Lab. M.P. for East Ham since 1957. Official of Transport and General Workers' Union. Min. of Public Building and Works 1966–7, of Overseas Development 1967–9.

341

REES-MOGG, William. Journalist. Editor *The Times* since 1967. On staff of *Financial Times* 1952–60, *Sunday Times* 1960–67.

RENWICK, Robert (Lord Renwick). Stockbroker. Chairman Institute of Directors; chairman A.T.V.; director of several important companies.

RIPPON, Geoffrey. Chancellor of the Duchy of Lancaster attached to the Foreign Office since 1970. Con. M.P. for Norwich 1955–64, for Hexham since 1966. Called to the Bar 1948. Mayor of Surbiton 1951–2. Member of L.C.C. 1952–61. Min. of Public Building and Works 1962–4.

ROBENS, Alfred (Lord Robens). Chairman Vickers Ltd since 1971. Director Bank of England since 1966. Official Union of Distributive and Allied Workers 1935–45. Lab. M.P. for Northumberland divisions 1945–60. Min. of Labour 1951. Chairman National Coal Board 1961–71.

ROBINSON, Kenneth. Lab. M.P. for St Pancras 1949–70. Min. of Health 1964–8, for Planning and Land 1968–9. Director British Steel Corporation since 1970, in charge of Social Policy.

ROLL, Sir Eric. Director of S. G. Warburg & Co. and of Bank of England. Professor of Economics Hull University 1935–46. Civil servant holding important posts 1946–66. Head of U.K. Treasury Delegation and Economic Minister, Washington, 1963–4, Permanent Under-Sec. Department of Economic Affairs 1964–6.

ROSS, William. Lab. M.P. for Kilmarnock since 1946. Sec. of State for Scotland 1964–70.

ROTHERMERE, Lord (Esmond Harmsworth). Newspaper proprietor and publisher. Chairman *Daily Mail* and General Trust. Chairman Associated Newspapers 1932–71. Unionist M.P. for Thanet 1919–29. Chairman, Newspaper Proprietors' Association 1934–61.

RUSK, Dean. U.S. Sec. of State 1961–9. President Rockefeller Foundation 1952–61. Official in U.S. State Department 1947–51.

SANDYS, Duncan. Con. M.P. for Norwood 1935–45, for Streatham since 1950. Min. of Works 1944–5, of Supply 1951–4, of Housing and Local Government 1954–7, of Defence 1957–9, of Aviation 1959–60, Sec. of State for Commonwealth Relations 1960–64. Very active in European movement since 1947.

SHAWCROSS, Hartley (Lord Shawcross). Chairman Thames Television since 1969. Called to the Bar 1925, retired 1958. Lab. M.P. for St Helens 1945–58. Attorney-General 1945–51, President of the Board of Trade 1951. Has held many official posts and is now a director of many important companies.

SHORE, Peter. Lab. M.P. for Stepney since 1964. Political economist. Head of Labour Party Research Department 1959–64. Sec. of State for Economic Affairs 1967–9, Min. without Portfolio 1969–70.

SHORT, Edward. Lab. M.P. for Newcastle upon Tyne since 1951. Headmaster, Secondary School, Blyth, 1947. Postmaster-General 1966–8, Sec. of State for Education 1968–70, Deputy Leader of the Parliamentary Labour Party 1972.

SILKIN, John. Lab. M.P. for Deptford since 1963. Government Chief Whip 1966–9, Min. of Public Building and Works 1969–70.

SMITH, Ian. Prime Minister of Rhodesia 1964–5 and Leader of Rhodesia Front regime since 1965. Served in the R.A.F. 1941–5. Min. of Treasury 1962, of External Affairs 1964, of Defence 1964–5.

SOAMES, Sir Christopher. Ambassador to France since 1968. Con. M.P. for Bedford 1950–66. Sec. of State for War 1958–60, Min. of Agriculture 1960–64.

SOSKICE, Frank (Lord Stow Hill). Barrister. Lab. M.P. for Birkenhead 1945–50, for Sheffield (Neepsand) 1950–55, for Newport, Monmouthshire, 1956–66. Solicitor-General 1945–51, Attorney-General 1951, Home Sec. 1964–5, Lord Privy Seal 1965–6.

STEVENS, Sir John. Managing director Morgan Grenfell (merchant bank) since 1967. Executive director Bank of England 1957–64, non-executive since 1968. Head of Treasury Delegation and Economic Minister, Washington, 1965–7. A director of many important companies.

STEWART, Michael. Lab. M.P. for Fulham since 1945. Sec. of State for Education 1964–5, for Foreign Affairs 1965–6, for Economic Affairs 1966–7, for Foreign and Commonwealth Affairs 1968–70.

STONEHOUSE, John. Lab. M.P. for Wednesbury since 1957. Director London Co-operative Society 1956–62, President 1962–4. Postmaster-General and Min. for Posts and Telecommunications 1968–70.

STRAUSS, Franz Josef. Member of the West German Bundestag since 1949. President Christian Social Union since 1961. Min. for Defence 1956–62, of Finance 1966–9.

THATCHER, Margaret. Con. M.P. for Finchley since 1959. Sec. of State for Education since 1970. Research chemist 1947–51; called to the Bar 1953.

THOMAS, George. Lab. M.P. for West Cardiff since 1950. Sec. of State for Wales 1968–70. Schoolmaster by profession.

THOMSON, George. Lab. M.P. for Dundee since 1952. Editor *Forward* 1948–53. Chancellor of the Duchy of Lancaster 1966–7, Sec. of State for Commonwealth Affairs 1967–8, Min. without Portfolio 1968–9, Chancellor of the Duchy of Lancaster 1969–70.

THOMSON, Roy (Lord Thomson of Fleet). Newspaper proprietor. Controls *The Times, Sunday Times* and a group of provincial newspapers; has extensive newspaper interests in Canada and the U.S. Has also a big interest in package holidays, North Sea Oil and other ventures outside publishing.

WALDEN, Brian. Lab. M.P. for Birmingham (All Saints) since 1964. Member National Union of General and Municipal Workers. University lecturer.

WALKER, Peter. Con. M.P. for Worcester since 1961. Sec. of State for the Environment since 1970. Chairman Rose, Thomson, Young & Co. (Lloyd's brokers) 1956–70; Deputy chairman Slater Walker Securities 1964–70.

WALSTON, Harry (Lord Walston). Research Fellow in Bacteriology, Harvard University, 1934–5. Director of Agriculture British zone of Germany 1946–7. Crown Estate Commissioner since 1967. Parliamentary Under-Sec. of State at the Foreign Office 1964–7. Prominent Labour Peer.

WARBURG, Sir Sigmund. President and founder of S. G. Warburg & Co., merchant bankers. Born and educated in Germany. Partner in banking firm of M. M. Warburg & Co. of Hamburg 1930–38.

WARD, Barbara (Lady Jackson). Schweitzer Professor of International Economic Development, Columbia University (New York), since 1968. University extension lecturer 1936–9. Assistant editor *Economist* from 1939. Visiting

343

Scholar Harvard University 1957–68. Governor B.B.C. 1946–50. Member Pontifical Commission for Justice and Peace from 1967.

WEINSTOCK, Sir Arnold. Managing director General Electric Co. since 1963. Junior administrative officer Admiralty 1944–7. Engaged in finance and property dealing 1947–54. In Radio and Allied Industries 1954–63.

WHITELAW, William. Con. M.P. for Cumberland since 1955. Chief Opposition Whip 1964–70. Lord President of the Council and Leader of the House of Commons 1970–72, Sec. of State for Northern Ireland 1972. Farmer and landowner.

WILLIAMS, Shirley. Lab. M.P. for Hitchin since 1964. General Sec. Fabian Society 1960–64. Held various junior ministerial posts in the Labour Government 1964–70.

WILSON, Harold. Lab. M.P. for Huyton since 1945. University lecturer on economics 1937–45. Sec. for Overseas Trade 1947, President of the Board of Trade 1947–51. Leader of the Labour Party since 1963. Prime Minister 1964–70.

WOODCOCK, George. Cotton weaver 1916–27. 1st Class Honours in Philosophy and Political Economy at Oxford 1933. Civil servant 1934–6. Assistant General Sec. T.U.C. 1947–60, General Sec. 1960–69. Chairman Commission on Industrial Relations 1969–71.

INDEX

345

Brown, George (Lord George-Brown), 19, 33, 36, 39, 55–7, 61, 62, 69, 78, 120, 134–5, 144, 148, 149, 159, 162, 205, 214, 283; Prices and Incomes policy, 32, 36, 56, 58, 72, 122, 195; dislike and criticism of Wilson, 38–9, 56, 117, 170, 186, 276; and Common Market, 56, 57, 65, 67, 94, 95, 97–8, 122, 131; at D.E.A., 63, 65; urges devaluation, 79–80, 84; apparent aim to oust Wilson, 80, 117; as Foreign Secretary, 83–4, 85, 96–8, 100–102, 107, 129, 131, 133, 187; on Rhodesia, 97; on Cabinet changes, 97, 101; and de Gaulle, 101; press attacks on, 126, 130; and Middle East, 134–5; coolness to King, 150, 151; abuses press, 153, 154; seeks City post, 170, 191, 202; resigns, 184, 187, 202; decision not to rejoin Government, 275–6; defeat in 1970, 334

Brown, Sophie (Lady George-Brown), 100–101, 129

Brown, Wilfred (Baron Brown), 144

Bruce, David, 33–4, 65, 131–2, 162, 171, 186, 222–3, 277, 279

Brunton, Gordon, 333

Bundy, McGeorge, 40, 92, 134

Bundy, William, 88–9

Burns, Dr Arthur F., 247, 281, 318

Busia, Dr Kofi, 308

Butler, Lord, 48, 85, 124, 191, 267

Byers, Lord, 322

Caccia, Sir Harold, 41

Callaghan, James, 28, 29, 57, 61, 85, 95, 108, 136, 148, 150, 154, 159, 190, 205, 212, 257, 275; as Chancellor of Exchequer, 28, 53, 56, 60, 62, 63, 67, 69, 76, 79–80, 82–3, 97, 99, 107, 109, 130, 137, 156–7, 158; and Common Market, 57, 58, 62, 63, 143; and devaluation, 82, 83, 134, 156–7, 158, 159, 173; as possible successor to Wilson, 99, 101, 117, 160, 203, 224, 239, 242, 244, 256, 261, 271, 325; hint at resignation, 133, 134; talk with King, 143–5; as Home Secretary, 161

Cannon, Leslie, 202, 211, 240, 272, 297

Caradon, Lord, 41–2, 249

Carmichael, Neil, 289

Carrington, Peter (Lord Carrington), 233, 291

Castle, Barbara, 31, 38, 63, 73, 84, 95, 115, 182, 193, 195, 201, 210, 255, 289, 307;

Secretary for Employment and Productivity, 188, 196, 263, 287, 301; defeat of trades union legislation, 263, 302

Ceauşescu, Nicolae, 127

Central Electricity Generating Board (C.E.G.B.), 269, 287

Central Intelligence Agency (C.I.A.), 86–8, 92, 134

Chaban-Delmas, Jacques, 281

Chalfont, Lord, 143, 152–3, 154, 249

Chambers, Sir Paul, 159, 173, 320, 330, 331

Champion, Ralph, 86

Chesterfield, Arthur, 26

Chiang Kai-shek, 87, 276

Chichester-Clark, Major James, 238n, 273

Christiansen, Arthur, 82, 83

Churchill, Sir Winston, 124, 182, 313

Clifford, Clark M., 262

Clore, Charles, 260, 301

Cole, George, 330, 331

Collins, Norman, 147, 172, 174, 254, 312, 314, 320, 329, 330–31

Commonwealth Relations Office, 84, 120, 140

Confederation of British Industry (C.B.I.), 82, 108, 159

Conservative Party Conferences: (1967) 160; (1968) 213; (1969) 292

Cooper, John (Baron Cooper), 202

Cousins, Frank, 27, 36, 38, 56, 61, 63, 73, 75, 77–8, 186, 201

Couve de Murville, Maurice, 77, 82, 112, 113

Cowdrey, Colin, 226, 326

Cowles, Mike, 282–3

Cowles, Virginia, 42

Crawley, Aidan, 42

Cromer, Lord, 25, 75, 82, 126–7, 146, 154, 174, 329–30; and financial crisis, 28, 60, 126, 158, 160, 161, 175; speculation over future as Governor of Bank, 46, 47, 48, 54, 56, 67; resignation, 68

Crosfield, Paul, 211

Crosland, Anthony, 33, 61, 99–100, 136–7, 182, 197, 257, 324; and Lib-Lab pact idea, 34; possible successor to Wilson, 84, 100, 132, 152; as Secretary for Education, 132, 136; at Board of Trade, 140, 141; 'overlord' of Local Government, Housing and Transport, 286, 289

Crossman, Douglas, 292

346

Crossman, Richard, 38, 39, 59, 61, 94–5, 117, 130, 132–3, 171, 195, 197, 211, 224, 241, 257, 298, 326; Lord President and Leader of House, 84; as possible successor to Wilson, 194; Secretary for Social Services, 214, 220, 257, 287, 293
Crowther, Sir Geoffrey, 21, 22, 26, 202, 330, 331, 332
Cudlipp, Hugh, 20, 29, 36, 57, 61, 62, 63, 70, 71, 79, 81, 95, 130, 141, 146, 152, 156–7, 161, 171, 173–4, 187, 192, 195, 196, 267, 315, 333; meeting with Wilson over Rhodesia, 43–5; Moscow visit, 118–19, 125, 126; Wilson's talk to (May 1967), 123–6; talk with Mountbatten, 138–9; dismisses King from I.P.C., 197–8; succeeds him, 198, 199

Daily Express, 26, 37, 77, 126, 141, 153, 192, 246, 314; and D-Notice affair, 128–9, 133
Daily Mail, 26, 32, 241, 333
Daily Mirror, 33, 43, 61, 77, 81, 94, 114, 115, 123, 147, 150, 152, 154, 209, 221, 255, 314; in 1966 election, 65, 66; 'Enough is Enough' article, 192–3, 198; losses, 295, 301
Daily Sketch, 301, 314, 330
Daily Telegraph, 148, 238, 246, 314, 333
Daly, Lawrence, 286
Davidson, Basil, 215
Day, Robin, 187, 286
Dayan, General Moshe, 180
De Courcel, Baron Geoffroy, 25, 142–3, 199, 219, 272
De Gaulle, General Charles, 17, 26, 54, 67, 92, 110–11, 129, 131, 177–8, 186, 247, 275; and Common Market, 24, 55, 101, 105, 110, 111, 114, 123, 159, 242–3; and Ben Barka affair, 54–5; Wilson's 'mistimed' meeting with (June 1967), 129, 130; and May 1968 riots, 195–6, 199; and 'Soames affair', 242–3, 251–2; and April 1969 referendum, 251, 253, 254; resignation, 255; and Algeria, 272
Dean, Sir Patrick, 39, 40, 41, 91
Debré, Michel, 178
Deedes, William, 238
Defence, Ministry of: Healey at, 22–3, 31, 78, 100, 116, 129, 131, 174, 203, 239, 261
Defferre, Gaston, 177–8
Devlin, Lord, 27

Devlin, Bernadette, 238n, 334
Diamond, John (Baron Diamond), 224
Director, The, 173
Donnelly, Desmond, 188
Douglas-Home, Sir Alec, 17, 21, 130, 133, 240, 263, 287, 326; resignation, 23–4, 29; as leader, 26, 116, 132, 207, 254; and Rhodesia, 97, 99
Drogheda, Earl of, 182, 326
Du Cann, Edward, 29
Dubček, Alexander, 207
Duncan, Sir Val, 271–2
Dupont, C., 44, 46

Eban, Abba, 134
Eccles, David (Viscount Eccles), 175–6, 191, 206, 217
Economic Affairs, Department of (D.E.A.), 63, 196, 286, 289; Brown at, 65, 84, 85, 101; Stewart at, 83, 86, 152; Shore at, 141; Wilson takes main responsibility for, 141, 152
Economist, The, 46, 130, 202
Eden, Sir Anthony (Lord Avon), 45, 73, 124, 125, 233, 319
Education, Ministry of, 99, 132, 136, 140, 141
Elias, Dr, 309
Elworthy, Marshal of the R.A.F. Sir Charles, 203
Erhard, Dr Ludwig, 52, 54
Evening News, 321
Evening Standard, 162, 192
Evensen, Alfred, 200

Faisal, King of Saudi Arabia, 18, 223, 234, 235–6, 240
Feather, Vic, 201–2, 255–6, 263
Financial Times, 26, 182, 198, 222, 225, 241, 329
Fisher, Nigel, 312
Fletcher, Eric, 173
Foot, Michael, 270, 323
Forbes, Sir Archibald, 172
Foreign Office: Stewart at, 19, 23, 86; Brown at, 83–4, 85, 93–8, 100–102, 107, 129, 131, 133, 187
Fowler, Henry H., 39, 88, 220, 280
Franck, Louis, 81, 94, 148, 194, 258
Fraser, Hugh, 19, 205, 256, 263
Freeland, General Sir Ian, 273, 275
Freeman, John, 125, 246, 247, 280, 288
Fulbright, Senator William, 41, 276

347

possible leader, 192, 204, 256, 264, 267, 268, 274, 313, 333; King's talks with (July and Sept. 1969), 268–70, 274–5; on floating the pound, 268, 272, 274; in 1970 election, 333, 334
Prentice, Reginald, 19, 141, 285
Present at the Creation (Acheson), 277, 318
Prices and Incomes Board, 75, 122, 210, 240, 245, 267
Prichard, Montague, 53
Pungan, Vasile, 127

Quaroni, Pietro, 110

Radcliffe, Lord, 128, 175
Railton, Dame Ruth (Mrs Cecil King), 18, 42, 75, 80, 96, 115, 133, 150, 151, 154, 179, 192, 213, 221, 227, 253–4, 260, 295, 299, 307
Rayne, Sir Max, 21n, 22
Redcliffe-Maud, Lord, 59n, 324n
Rees-Mogg, William, 137, 193, 225, 257, 301
Reeve, Humphrey, 257
Renwick, Robert, 26, 29, 254, 320, 329, 330
Richardson, Gordon, 210, 318–19
Richardson, Sir William, 126
Rippon, Geoffrey, 132, 206, 241, 257, 291–2
Riyad, Mahmud, 237
Robens, Lord, 63, 64, 81, 99, 129, 144, 249, 259, 270, 286–8, 316–17, 326; at Coal Board, 36, 70, 155, 194, 269, 312, 316, 330; at Bank of England, 82, 86, 151, 155, 156, 194, 222, 271, 317; and Aberfan Report, 137–8; offer to resign from Coal Board, 137n, 138; favours National Government, 159–60, 213, 270, a possible P.M. in businessmen's government, 173, 241, 287
Roberts, Sir Frank, 111n, 126
Robinson, Kenneth, 100, 211, 312–13
Rockefeller, David, 223
Rockefeller, Nelson, 223, 258, 283
Rogers, Frank, 197, 315
Rogers, William P., 223, 247, 261
Roll, Sir Eric, 56, 75, 206, 209, 245, 329
Ross, William, 188
Rothermere, Lord (Esmond Harmsworth), 32, 201, 224, 225, 330, 333
Rothschild, Guy de, 256
Rueff, Jacques, 252

Rusk, Dean, 40, 101
Ryder, Don, 197, 315, 333

Sainsbury, Baron, 144
Salisbury, Lord, 124
Sandys, Duncan, 116, 211
Scanlon, Hugh, 186, 201, 240, 297
Schmelling, Max, 93
Schon, Sir Frank, 53
Scott, Laurence, 291, 329
Scott, Richard, 329
Scott, Senator (Pennsylvania), 89, 90, 277, 278
Seamen, National Union of, 69
Shawcross, Lord, 21, 173, 213, 275–6, 329, 330, 332
Shinwell, Emanuel (Baron Shinwell), 128, 187
Shipping, Chamber of, 204
Shore, Peter, 109, 141, 182, 188, 263, 302
Short, Edward, 59, 85, 196
Sieff, Israel (Baron Sieff), 159
Silkin, John, 59
Smirnovsky, Mikhail N., 323
Smith, David, 172, 217
Smith, Ian, 18, 37, 96, 216; declares independence, 42, 43, 45–6; Wilson's attitude to, 45–6, 47–8, 53, 56, 66–7, 76; *Tiger* talks, 96–7, 98–9, 102
Soames, Sir Christopher, 145, 146, 242–4, 251–2, 257
Socialist Commentary, 147
Society of Graphical and Allied Trades (SOGAT), 328, 331n
Soldatov, Aleksandr A., 20, 119, 125, 126
Solomons, Nathan, 278
Soskice, Sir Frank, 19, 27, 36, 38, 58
Springer, Axel, 93
Stephens, Peter, 54, 176
Stevens, Sir John, 48, 67, 78, 107, 209, 222, 247–8, 318
Stevenson, Adlai, 21
Stewart, Sir Michael, 92
Stewart, Michael, 19, 29, 30, 61, 73, 82, 97, 122, 197, 216, 246, 312, 323; as Foreign Secretary, 23, 39, 63, 86, 102; at D.E.A., 83, 84, 86, 102, 105, 152; First Secretary, 141; as possible successor to Wilson, 190, 193, 196, 256
Stokes, Sir Donald (Lord Stokes), 238, 239
Stokes, Richard, 31
Stonehouse, John, 250, 294

351